Pedagogical Leadership in Early Childhood Education

Also Available from Bloomsbury

Issues and Challenges of Immigration in Early Childhood in the USA,
Wilma Robles-Melendez and Wayne Driscoll
Postdevelopmental Approaches to Childhood Art, Mona Sakr and Jayne Osgood
Children's Transitions in Everyday Life and Institutions, edited by
Mariane Hedegaard and Marilyn Fleer
Ethics and Research with Young Children: New Perspectives, edited by
Christopher M. Schulte
Feminist Research for 21st-century Childhoods, edited by B. Denise Hodgins
Feminists Researching Gendered Childhoods: Generative Entanglements, edited
by Jayne Osgood and Kerry H. Robinson
Friedrich Froebel: A Critical Introduction to Key Themes and Debates, by
Tina Bruce
Give Children the Vote: On Democratizing Democracy, by John Wall
Post-Qualitative Research and Innovative Methodologies, edited by
Matthew K. E. Thomas and Robin Bellingham
*Promoting Children's Rights in European Schools: Intercultural Dialogue and
Facilitative Pedagogy*, by Claudio Baraldi, Erica Joslyn, Federico Farini,
Chiara Ballestri, Luisa Conti, Vittorio Iervese and Angela Scollan
*Qualitative Studies of Exploration in Childhood Education: Cultures of Play
and Learning in Transition*, edited by Marilyn Fleer, Mariane Hedegaard,
Elin Eriksen Ødegaard and Hanne Værum Sørensen
Research Methods for Early Childhood Education, by Rosie Flewitt and
Lynn Ang
Rethinking Philosophy for Children: Agamben and Education as Pure Means, by
Tyson E. Lewis and Igor Jasinski
Supporting Difficult Transitions: Children, Young People and their Carers, edited
by Mariane Hedegaard and Anne Edwards
*The Bloomsbury Handbook of Culture and Identity from Early Childhood
to Early Adulthood: Perceptions and Implications*, edited by Ruth Wills,
Marian de Souza, Jennifer Mata-McMahon, Mukhlis Abu Bakar and Cornelia Roux

Pedagogical Leadership in Early Childhood Education

Conversations From Across the World

Edited by Mona Sakr and June O'Sullivan

BLOOMSBURY ACADEMIC
LONDON • NEW YORK • OXFORD • NEW DELHI • SYDNEY

BLOOMSBURY ACADEMIC
Bloomsbury Publishing Plc
50 Bedford Square, London, WC1B 3DP, UK
1385 Broadway, New York, NY 10018, USA
29 Earlsfort Terrace, Dublin 2, Ireland

BLOOMSBURY, BLOOMSBURY ACADEMIC and the Diana logo are trademarks of Bloomsbury Publishing Plc

First published in Great Britain 2022
This paperback edition published 2024

Copyright © Mona Sakr and June O'Sullivan and Contributors, 2022

Mona Sakr and June O'Sullivan and Contributors have asserted their right under the Copyright, Designs and Patents Act, 1988, to be identified as Author of this work.

Cover design: Charlotte James
Cover image © Isabelle Johnson/London Early Years Foundation

All rights reserved. No part of this publication may be reproduced or transmitted in any form or by any means, electronic or mechanical, including photocopying, recording, or any information storage or retrieval system, without prior permission in writing from the publishers.

Bloomsbury Publishing Plc does not have any control over, or responsibility for, any third-party websites referred to or in this book. All internet addresses given in this book were correct at the time of going to press. The author and publisher regret any inconvenience caused if addresses have changed or sites have ceased to exist, but can accept no responsibility for any such changes.

A catalog record for this book is available from the Library of Congress.

ISBN: HB: 978-1-3502-5048-2
PB: 978-1-3502-5089-5
ePDF: 978-1-3502-5049-9
eBook: 978-1-3502-5050-5

Typeset by Deanta Global Publishing Services, Chennai, India

To find out more about our authors and books visit www.bloomsbury.com and sign up for our newsletters.

Contents

List of Illustrations   vii
List of Contributors   viii

Introduction   *June O'Sullivan and Mona Sakr*   1

1. 'Intellectually Alive Early Childhood Education': A Conversation about Pedagogical Leadership with Julian Grenier   *Julian Grenier*   11

2. Pedagogic Cultures in Early Childhood: Framing Children's Experiences   *Lorna Arnott*   21

3. The Pedagogical Leader at London Early Years Foundation: Defining and Developing the Role   *June O'Sullivan*   35

4. Trauma-responsive Pedagogical Leadership in ECE: What It Is and Why It Matters   *Julie Nicholson*   51

5. Pedagogical Leadership in Practice with Babies   *Mandy Cuttler*   65

6. Plan-Do-Review: What Can We Learn from Change Management Theories about Pedagogical Leadership?   *Helen Perkins*   79

7. Pedagogical Leadership: Comparing Approaches and Practices in England, Greece and Sweden   *Ioanna Palaiologou, Eleftheria Argyropoulou, Maria Styf, Catarina Arvidsson, Amanda Ince and Trevor Male*   93

8. Pedagogical Leadership among Directors and Deputies in Early Childhood Settings in Australia, Finland and Norway: A Summary of a Small-scale Study   *Leena Halttunen, Margaret Sims, Marit Bøe, Karin Hognestad, Johanna Heikka, Manjula Waniganayake and Fay Hadley*   105

9. An Organisational Approach to Supporting Pedagogical Leadership: Reporting on a Case Study with London Early Years Foundation   *Mona Sakr*   119

10 'If You're Going to Build a House Where Everyone Develops and Learns, You Can't Have Hoarders': A Conversation about Pedagogical Leadership with Nichole Leigh Mosty
    Nichole Leigh Mosty — 133

11 Fostering Pedagogical Leadership through Action Research: A Practical Perspective *Mandy Cuttler and Nick Corlett with Mona Sakr* — 141

12 Interpretations of Pedagogical Leadership among Community-based Early Childhood Education Leaders in Azerbaijan *Ulviyya Mikailova and Gwendolyn Burchell* — 155

13 Pedagogical Leadership in Italian Early Childhood Education Settings: Managing Conflicts While Facilitating Participative Decision-making *Federico Farini* — 167

14 Advancing Pedagogical Leadership at National Level: Looking for a Policy Window *Sara Bonetti and Mona Sakr* — 181

Conclusion: Sustaining the Vision of Pedagogical Leadership
June O'Sullivan and Mona Sakr — 195

Index — 199

Illustrations

Figures

3.1	LEYF pedagogy	38
3.2	LEYF leadership model	38
11.1	The spectrum of action research and pedagogical leadership	146

Tables

7.1	Overview of the Methods and Participants	98

Contributors

Amanda Ince is Associate Professor at UCL Institute of Education, University College London, UK, working on MA Primary Education and MA Early Years Education programmes. Her research interests are in professional learning and supporting practitioners through facilitated action research.

Catarina Arvidsson is Senior Lecturer at the Department of Education at Mid Sweden University, Sweden. She is Programme Leader for the Preschool Teacher Education at the university and have long experience from working in preschool, both as teacher and as leader.

Eleftheria Argyropoulou is Associate Professor in the Department of Preschool Education, at the School of Education, University of Crete, Greece. Her expertise are in organization, management and leadership in education. Her research interests include new forms of school leadership with an emphasis on ethical leadership.

Federico Farini is Associate Professor of Sociology at the University of Northampton, UK. Federico has published books, chapters, articles and edited books in Italian, English, Croatian and Slovenian languages around themes such as inclusive education, intercultural communication, young people's social participation and methodology of social research. Federico's current interests mainly revolve around inequality in the access to education as well as participatory research methods and public sociology.

Gwendolyn Burchell (MBE) is a UK national who lives and works in Azerbaijan since 1998, when she established UAFA, a local NGO which focuses on building new early childhood development services for children excluded by poverty, disability and location. Gwen's academic background includes MSc in Social Policy & Planning and BSc in Management Science. Gwen is a strong proponent of evidence-based policy planning, with all UAFA programs being built upon research related to early child development, disability, poverty, deinstitutionalization and alternative family care. Her extensive field and academic experience is now in high demand internationally, having developed a number of tools to support the training and development of frontline personnel working with children with disabilities and their families. All research and tools can be downloaded from www.uafa.az and the Better Care Network.

Helen Perkins is Senior Lecturer in Childhood and Family Studies at the University of Wolverhampton, UK. She began her early years career working in nursery and reception. Following thirteen years as head of school for early childhood education in a college of further and higher education Helen joined the University of Wolverhampton as a senior lecturer working on undergraduate and postgraduate courses. Helen's doctoral research predominately focuses on agendas and policies in the early years with a focus on the workforce and their qualifications. Helen served as an expert panel member for the Nutbrown Review of Early Years qualifications and is a member of the Executive for the Early Childhood Studies Degree Network focusing on workforce issues and professionalism. Helen has co-edited a book recently with Routledge, *Using Innovative-Methods in Early-Years Research-Beyond the Conventional* (Brown & Perkins 2019) and has published peer reviewed Journal articles.

Ioanna Palaiologou (CPsychol AFBPsS) is a chartered psychologist with the British Psychological Society with a specialism in child development and learning theories. Since December 2021 she works for the School of Education (Psychology in Education) at University of Bristol, UK. Her research interests focuses on ethics, child development, the role of digital technologies, leadership and implications on pedagogy.

Julian Grenier is Headteacher of Sheringham Nursery School and Children's Centre in Newham, East London, UK, and co-founder of the East London Partnership Teaching School Alliance. He is a well-known author and blogger on ECE, and is lead advisor on the 2020 revision of Development Matters, which offers curriculum guidance to ECE professionals in the English system.

Julie Nicholson is Professor of Practice in the School of Education at Mills College, United States, and co-director of the Center for Equity in Early Childhood Education.

June O'Sullivan (MBE) has developed and leads the award-winning London Early Years Foundation (LEYF), the largest early childcare social enterprise in the UK. LEYF has designed a model of ECE which provides accessible, affordable and high quality ECE to children from disadvantaged backgrounds. She has written extensively on the issues of child poverty, pedagogy and social enterprise; advises governments, academics and business; and is a sought-after speaker and media commentator.

Lorna Arnott is Senior Lecturer and director of Early Years in the School of Education, University of Strathclyde, UK. Lorna's main area of interest is in children's early play experiences, particularly in relation to technologies, social and creative play. She also has a keen interest in research methodologies, with a specialist focus on consulting with children and methods derived from pedagogy. Lorna is the convener for the Digital Childhoods, STEM and Multimodality Special Interest Group as part of the European Early Childhood Educational Research Association, and is the deputy editor for the *International Journal of Early Years Education* and assistant editor for the *Journal of Early Childhood Research*.

Mandy Cuttler is Head of Pedagogy at London Early Years Foundation (LEYF), UK where she leads the delivery of the unique LEYF Pedagogy, the action research programme and the pioneering LEYF Degree. Mandy has worked in education for fifteen years in a variety of roles including in outdoor education settings, Montessori schools and community nurseries. She holds a master's degree in Early Years Education and has explored the experiences of babies in early years settings for her dissertation research.

Maria Styf is Senior Lecturer at the Department of Education at Mid Sweden University, Sweden. She is the research leader for the research group Education Leadership and School Development at the university. She has been working at the department for twenty-two years and also has former experience as a preschool teacher.

Mona Sakr is Senior Lecturer in Education and Early Childhood at Middlesex University, UK. As a researcher in Early Years (EY) provision, she has published extensively on creative, digital and playful pedagogies. Mona's current research is an exploration of pedagogical, organisational and community leadership in EY and how leadership can be more effectively developed through innovative practice-based and digitally mediated professional development.

Nichole Leigh Mosty over twenty years working in Early Childhood Education, there isn't a role Nichole hasn't taken on from care giver through to Director and even taking on a role as policy maker as the first woman of foreign origin elected to serve as MP in Icelandic Parliament. The past three years Nichole has spent working as a Early Childhood Education consultant working with curriculum development, leadership counselling, classroom management, and teacher training to name a few of the fun things she has the honour of helping out with in the field. Nichole has a passion for inclusive education and sustainable social development and social leadership in ECE.

Nick Corlett is Senior Nursery Manager and Sustainability Lead at the London Early Years Foundation (LEYF), UK. He is passionate about the role of early childhood education in sustainability and recently published, with June O'Sullivan, the book *50 Fantastic Ideas for Sustainability* with Bloomsbury.

Sara Bonetti's research focuses on early years education and particularly on elements of structural quality of provision. Currently she is the PI of a project funded by the Nuffield Foundation focused on the early childhood workforce and the CO-PI of a study on the employment trajectory and working conditions of early childhood staff qualified at degree level. She also leads on a project on the early years workforce stability in England commissioned by the Social Mobility Commission, which will be published in the coming months.

Trevor Male is Associate Professor in the UCL Centre for Educational Leadership, UCL Institute of Education, University College London, UK, where he is programme leader for the MBA in Educational Leadership (International). His research interest has been in the field of education and the development of educational leaders. His current research interests are in the field of early childhood education, multi-academy trusts and pedagogical leadership.

Ulviyya Mikailova is an international consultant from Azerbaijan, with valuable experience as an Early Childhood and Inclusive Education Training, TOT and Policy Expert with diversified ECE & SNE training design, delivery project experience, curriculum development and policy analysis in Azerbaijan, Uzbekistan, Tajikistan and Kyrgyzstan. She also has extensive experience in early childhood development (ECD), special needs education (SNE), child friendly schooling (CFS) and other education research project. She is a Fulbright scholar (Teachers College, Columbia University, 2006) and has taught university course: Introduction to Gender and Gender and Politics (Baku State University), Monitoring and Evaluation in Education (Azerbaijan State Economic University) and Evaluation of Educational Projects (Baku State University). She currently teaches several courses within Leadership and Management in Education Master Program at ADA University (Azerbaijan), and Social Research Methods (Moscow High School of Social and Economic Sciences at the Academy of State Governance and National Economics under the Administration of RF President).

Leena Halttunen is working as Head of Department of Education, University of Jyväskylä, Finland. Her research focuses on leadership and especially on deputy directors in Early Childhood Education and on organizational culture. She is also involved in leadership in-service training for ECE staff.

Marit Bøe is Associate Professor at University of South-Eastern Norway, Norway and her teaching responsibilities concern further leadership education programs at master level. She has published in the areas of early childhood leadership at director level and teacher leader level (e.g. pedagogical leadership, leadership training and professional development and leadership within a practice perspective).

Fay Hadley is Director of Initial Teacher Education and Associate Professor of Early Childhood at the School of Education, Macquarie University, Australia. Her research interests examine leadership in ECE. This includes investigating mentoring, professional learning and career pathways for early childhood teachers. Fay is especially interested in the socio-political environment and how this affects teachers' work.

Johanna Heikka works as University Lecturer at University of Eastern Finland, Finland. Her current teaching focuses mainly on organizational and leadership issues in education. Her research interests focus on leadership, quality and pedagogical development in early childhood education.

Karin Hognestad is Head of Center for Early Childhood Education Research, Development and Innovation at University of South-Eastern Norway, Norway. Her research interests are leadership in ECE and in ECE teacher education. Her research includes both teacher leadership and leadership at director level. Karin focuses on leadership as social practice and use qualitative shadowing in her research.

Margaret Sims is Professor of Early Childhood at the University of New England, Australia and Honorary Professor at Macquarie University, Australia.

Her research explores professionalism and the impact of neoliberalism in the early childhood sector. Her research encompasses multiple nations and leads her to speculate on the creation of hybrid spaces.

Manjula Waniganayake is Professor of Early Childhood Education, Macquarie University, Australia and holds a *Honoris Causa in Education* from the University of Tampere, Finland. Manjula opened the dialogue on the application of distributed leadership paradigm within ECE settings, and this work continues through collaborations with Scandinavian researchers.

Introduction

June O'Sullivan and Mona Sakr

Welcome

This book emerged from conversations with colleagues from across the world and is intended to contribute to our understanding of pedagogical leadership in early childhood education (ECE). In this book, colleagues from academic, policy and practice organisations discuss pedagogical leadership, how it is defined and delivered in a range of international contexts. This chapter highlights gaps and weaknesses in the existing literature on pedagogical leadership and explains how the contributors to this book respond to these, and in doing so how they advance the field.

The Words We Use

Words matter and we want to be explicit about the words and phrases we are using throughout this book. We recognise that terminology in this field is contested and complex and that each term has its own rich history and associations. However, we are also aware that constant shifts in language can make it difficult to follow the thread of a book, particularly when there are many contributors from across the world. We have therefore opted for consistency with regards to the following phrases.

Early Childhood Education

Throughout the book we refer to our sector as ECE. When we use this term we are referring to a broad range of services including day nurseries/long day-care, childminders/home educators, family day care, playgroups, play centres, preschool kindergartens and nurseries within schools. We are aware that others will use alternative terms to refer to these services, such as 'childcare', 'early years', 'early learning and care' or 'early childhood education and care (ECEC)'. While we understand why these alternatives are in use, particularly the latter, we use the term 'ECE' for its simplicity and on the basic understanding that education includes care and so the two terms need not be separated. Since we believe that effective education (at all ages and stages, though perhaps particularly so for the youngest children) will depend on interpersonal care, we are happy to use the term 'ECE'.

ECE Professionals

When referring to individuals working in ECE, we generally use the term 'ECE professional'. We are conscious that adults working in ECE are sometimes described as 'practitioners', 'educators', 'pedagogues' and 'teachers' but for consistency we have chosen the term 'ECE professional'. We truly believe that working with our youngest children is a valuable profession and those who enter it are worthy of being recognised as professionals no matter where they are on their training and qualification journey.

Pedagogical Leadership in ECE

Pedagogical leadership comprises the leadership knowledge, skills and behaviours that advance pedagogical thought and practice in the context of ECE. Pedagogy can be thought about as the values and practices through which learning and teaching operates. Even when pedagogy is not made explicit, it frames the day-to-day work of ECE: it is the 'silent partner' (Stephen, 2010) of ECE professionals and what they do. When we make pedagogy explicit, we are in a position to shape it – as a statement and as an enactment – according to our values and vision of ECE. Pedagogical leadership is the work of making pedagogy explicit and of extending pedagogical thought and practice, both within oneself and with others. In the literature, pedagogical leadership has traditionally been detached from positional leadership. That is, pedagogical leadership practices are not embedded in formal hierarchies; it is not only the manager of a setting, for example, who can be a pedagogical leader (McDowall Clark, 2012; O'Sullivan, 2015).

Pedagogical leadership matters because its advancement improves outcomes for children. A working paper prepared by Anne Douglass (2019) for OECD offers a review of studies that demonstrate a convincing link between the development of pedagogical leadership and measures of process quality in ECE. The paper presents pedagogical leadership as a bundle of practices relating to:

- Relationship building;
- Professional development among teams;
- Support for collaborative working environments;
- Community, family and cross-sector partnerships.

Looking across five studies focused on the impact of these practices (Sebastien et al., 2016; Arbour et al., 2016, Whalen et al., 2016, Cheung et al., 2019; Dennis & O'Connor, 2012), Douglass concludes that the development of pedagogical leadership leads to 'greater knowledge and skills to develop staff leadership, a positive workplace climate, and an organisational culture of learning and improvement' (p. 21). These factors then facilitate improvements in children's learning, as measured by children's outcomes (e.g. in communication abilities at a particular age) and by measures of process quality (e.g. the CLASS tool, which focuses on the quality of teacher-learner interactions).

Such studies suggest that pedagogical leadership matters a great deal and is a key lever for improving ECE. There are, however, various gaps in our understanding of pedagogical leadership and how it can be developed in diverse contexts around the world. The following section highlights the principles, lines of inquiry and themes that run through the book.

Principles, Lines of Inquiry and Themes in the Book

The book is founded on a common understanding among the contributors that there have been too few personal and public conversations about pedagogical leadership in ECE. We are committed to generating new ideas and reflections on pedagogical leadership and to do this through conversations about research and experiences. Pedagogical leadership needs a bigger and deeper discussion. Given its importance, there is too little research and dialogue about all types of leadership in ECE and this includes pedagogical leadership. The book is first and foremost a contribution to the task of addressing the importance of pedagogical leadership and increasing our conversations on this important topic.

During our conversations with the contributors we have been introduced to new ideas and new perspectives on pedagogical leadership. Conversations – more than formal academic discussions – have the power to change our mindset about the world and shift our practices and this book is shaped around those conversations. We have tried to ensure that the chapters are in conversation with each other, for example not only by highlighting points of connection between the chapters but also by including two conversations as chapters. The book opens on a conversation with Julian Grenier and later includes a conversation with Nichole Leigh Mosty, both of whom bring their own interpretations of pedagogical leadership alive within their own contexts, experience and understanding.

We have divided (imperfectly) the book into two halves. While Part A is more concerned with interpretations of pedagogical leadership, Part B observes more closely the practices of pedagogical leadership and its development. However, throughout the book, there is a recognition that pedagogical leadership is not a singular construct (Male & Palaiologou, 2015; Heikka & Waniganayake, 2011) but is both contextually layered and multifaceted. All of the chapters in this book address the relevance of context and explore the impact of the particular context on the translation and demonstration of pedagogical leadership. The chapters examine different levels of context. Halttunen et al., Palaiologou et al., and Mikailova and Burchell examine pedagogical leadership in particular national contexts. Bonetti and Sakr look more specifically at pedagogical leadership in the national policy context of England. Cuttler explores pedagogical leadership in the Baby Room. Farini explores pedagogical leadership in the context of pedagogical planning dialogues. Finally, Nicholson explores the need for trauma-responsive pedagogical leadership.

In the book, we have used the work of London Early Years Foundation (LEYF) to better understand pedagogical leadership within the context of a specific ECE organisation. We do not present LEYF as a 'perfect' context for pedagogical leadership but rather as a relatively large ECE organisation that makes an explicit commitment to fostering pedagogical leadership. O'Sullivan presents a vision for the role of 'pedagogical leader' in the work of LEYF, while the practices and processes within the organisation are the focus both in Chapter 11, where Cuttler and Corlett look closely at action research, and Chapter 9, where Sakr considers how pedagogical leadership can be developed as part of professionals' everyday working conditions. These chapters give an insight into the relationship between pedagogical leadership and organisational culture and how this manifests through concrete day-to-day experiences. We hope that this closer look at LEYF is relevant in its insights to many ECE organisations around the world and how they think about pedagogical leadership in the context of what they do.

There appears to be a lack of clarity in the literature regarding who is responsible for pedagogical leadership. In this book we question whether there is an assumption that pedagogical leadership fits within the idea of the distributed leadership model or a more adaptive approach. Perkins examines this further, positioning pedagogical leadership within broader theories of change management. Palaiologou et al. offer further exploration of who, within ECE organisations, has the opportunity to show pedagogical leadership and how pedagogical leadership practices are distributed among teams. Halttunen et al. consider the work of centre directors and centre deputies in three countries (Australia, Finland and Norway) in relation to pedagogical leadership. O'Sullivan explores the role of the 'pedagogical leader' as a distinct position within an organisation, while in the conversation with Leigh Mosty, we explore attempts to bring everyone in an organisation, regardless of level or position, into the work of pedagogical leadership on an everyday basis.

We are concerned that some of the literature on pedagogical leadership seems to rest on the foundation that pedagogy is something settled. Our understanding of pedagogical leadership of course depends on our understanding of pedagogy and the enactment of pedagogical leadership depends on the pedagogical approach. We cannot talk about one without the other since there is no 'pure pedagogy' from which pedagogical leadership emerges. Pedagogies are dynamic, multiple, multi-layered and complex, and so we give space in this book to understanding pedagogical leadership in relation to a range of pedagogies. In Arnott's chapter, and also O'Sullivan's chapter, an understanding of pedagogical leadership is inextricably intertwined with a vision of what pedagogies are and how they come to exist. In this, we reject and move past equating pedagogical leadership purely with 'instructional leadership'. The term 'instructional leadership' suggests that leaders simply need to show/teach others how to instruct better, but pedagogy is far more interesting and complex than 'instruction'. The two are not equivalent. And so we are interested in a vision of pedagogical leadership that creates space for envisioning and re-envisioning pedagogies in ECE.

Chapter Overview

Part A (Chapters 1–7) presents thinking about pedagogical leadership from around the world. The chapters present ideas about what pedagogical leadership is and why it matters.

Chapter 1 is a conversation about pedagogical leadership with Julian Grenier. Grenier presents a vision of pedagogical leadership as the key to elevating ECE from the offer of physical care to young children (important as this is) to something that is 'intellectually alive' and has the power to transform children's life opportunities.

In Chapter 2, Lorna Arnott explores the nature of pedagogy and how our understanding of pedagogy shapes our conceptualisation of pedagogical leadership. Using ideas from sociocultural theorists including Bernstein, Rogoff and Corsaro, she examines pedagogical leadership which is framed within a dynamic, contextual and co-constructed pedagogy.

Chapter 3 explores the role of 'pedagogical leader' in the LEYF. June O'Sullivan considers how the role fits within the organisation's pedagogical approach and then examines the systems and processes that are used in LEYF to foster pedagogical leadership. In this, she highlights the importance of coaching, pedagogical conversations and action research for the advancement of pedagogical leadership in practice.

In Chapter 4, Julie Nicholson argues that pedagogical leadership must adapt depending on the changing social circumstances of the children and families served by ECE services. She highlights the increasing need for trauma-responsiveness approaches in ECE and presents an emerging vision of trauma-responsive pedagogical leadership, illustrated through conversations with centre leaders in California.

Chapter 5 is an exploration of pedagogical leadership with babies. Mandy Cuttler addresses the urgent need for more understanding on this topic. The majority of literature on pedagogical leadership is designed around the work of professionals with children aged two and over. This chapter therefore considers why pedagogical leadership with babies matters and what it looks like.

In Chapter 6, Helen Perkins examines how emerging theories of pedagogical leadership can benefit from change management concepts within the business sector. She uses case studies from her undergraduate ECE students to examine the strengths and weaknesses of applying change management theories to the task of advancing pedagogical leadership in ECE settings.

Chapter 7 is a comparison of approaches and practices of pedagogical leadership in England, Greece and Sweden. Ioanna Palaiologou and international colleagues explore interpretations of pedagogical leadership among ECE setting leaders in the three national contexts. They highlight how the particular expectations of pedagogical leadership outlined (or not) in national ECE policy impacts professionals' understanding of what pedagogical leadership is and how it can be fostered.

Part B (Chapters 8–14) takes a practical look at the work of pedagogical leadership and who does the work of pedagogical leadership, how it is enacted in practice and the ways in which it can be developed 'on the ground'.

Chapter 8 presents a study of pedagogical leadership among directors and deputies in ECE settings in Australia, Finland and Norway. Leena Halttunen and international colleagues examine how pedagogical leadership relates to the roles of the centre director and their deputy. They consider how pedagogical leadership practices are divided between this duo and how national context influences who understands pedagogical leadership to be part of their role.

In Chapter 9, Sakr considers how pedagogical leadership can be developed as part of professionals' everyday working conditions as a result of the processes and practices within organisations. It presents the case study of LEYF, where the development of pedagogical leadership is embedded in the organisation's systems and processes. It considers how LEYF fosters pedagogical leadership and examines the applicability of this approach in other settings, particularly those that are smaller in size.

Chapter 10 is a conversation with Nichole Leigh Mosty, former director of Ösp playschool in Reykjavik, Iceland, now Icelandic politician with a focus on cultural integration. Leigh Mosty describes her experiences of pedagogical leadership in various settings and the overarching values and principles that have guided her in developing pedagogical leadership at all levels. In essence, her vision of pedagogical leadership is one of constant communication and collaboration. She concludes, 'if you're going to build a house where everyone develops and learns, you can't have hoarders.'

In Chapter 11, Mandy Cuttler and Nick Corlett explore how they foster pedagogical leadership through the application of action research. Cuttler is the pedagogy manager for LEYF, and Corlett is a LEYF senior nursery manager as well as the lead for Green Leyf, the organisation's sustainability initiative. In this chapter, they share their thoughts about how action research can strengthen pedagogical leadership.

Chapter 12 examines pedagogical leadership practices as enacted by community-based ECE leaders in rural Azerbaijan. Ulviyya Mikailova and Gwen Burchell discuss how pedagogical leadership is interpreted and enacted by these centre leaders. It presents pedagogical leadership as a modus operandi that emerges through everyday practices and through centre leaders having to figure things out as they go.

In Chapter 13, Federico Farini takes a close look at the interactions that unfold during pedagogical planning meetings in a Reggio Emilia settings in Italy. He unpicks how pedagogical leadership is used to manage conflicts emerging during the meetings. Even though settings may state that they are founded on democratic participation, we need to pay close attention to the micro-interactions in pedagogical planning to see whether the pedagogical leadership upholds these principles.

In Chapter 14, Sara Bonetti and Mona Sakr explore how a national policy context can shape the concept and delivery of pedagogical leadership. They use Kingdon's policy streams approach to consider whether there is a 'policy window' for pedagogical leadership opening up in England, and if so, what would be needed to promote pedagogical leadership.

References

Arbour, M. et al. (2016). *Improving Quality and Child Outcomes in Early Childhood Education by Redefining the Role Afforded to Teacher in Professional Development: A Continuous Quality Improvement Learning Collaborative among Public Preschools in Chile*. Evanston, IL: Society for Research in Educational Effectiveness.

Cheung, A. C. K., Keung, C. P. C., Kwan, P. Y. K., & Cheung, L. Y. S. (2019). Teachers' perceptions of the effect of selected leadership practices on pre-primary children's learning in Hong Kong. *Early Child Development and Care*, 189(14), 2265–2283, http://dx.doi.org/10.1080/03004430.2018.1448394.

Dennis, S., & O'Connor, E. (2012). Reexamining quality in early childhood education: Exploring the relationship between the organizational climate and the classroom. *Journal of Research in Childhood Education*, 27(1), 74–92, https://doi.org/10.1080/02568543.2012.739589.

Douglass, A. L. (2019). *Leadership for Quality Early Childhood Education and Care*. OECD Education Working Paper No. 211. Accessed 2 March 2021 online: http://www.oecd.org/officialdocuments/publicdisplaydocumentpdf/?cote=EDU/WKP%282019%2919&docLanguage=En

Heikka, J., & Waniganayake, M. (2011). Pedagogical leadership from a distributed perspective within the context of early childhood education. *International Journal of Leadership in Education*, 14(4), 499–512.

MacDowall Clark, R. (2012). 'I've never thought of myself as a leader but…': The early years professional and catalytic leadership. *European Early Childhood Education Research Journal*, 20(3), 391–401.

Male, T., & Palaiologou, I. (2015). Pedagogical leadership in the 21st century: Evidence from the field. *Educational Management Administration & Leadership*, 43(2), 214–231.

O'Sullivan, J. (2015). *Successful Leadership in the Early Years*. 2nd Edition. London: Bloomsbury.

Sebastian, J., Allensworth, E., & Huang, H. (2016). The role of teacher leadership in how principals influence classroom instruction and student learning. *American Journal of Education*, 123(1), 69–108.

Stephen, C. (2010). Pedagogy: The silent partner in early years learning. *Early Years*, *30*(1), 15–28.

Whalen, S. et al. (2016). A development evaluation study of a professional development initiative to strengthen organizational conditions in early education settings. *Journal of Applied Research on Children: Informing Policy for Children at Risk*, *7*(2), 9.

1

'Intellectually Alive Early Childhood Education'

A Conversation about Pedagogical Leadership with Julian Grenier

Julian Grenier

What does pedagogical leadership mean to you?

When I first started working in early years, a huge amount of the focus on leadership in early years was really management. It was rotas, staff sickness and absences, budgets, just keeping everything on the road day in, day out, all of which of course remain really important. There was comparatively less focus on the idea that the head of an early years setting would be a pedagogical leader. I remember working with a brilliant head of centre who has shaped everything I've done since working with her, but if we had staff professional development about children's learning, she wouldn't attend that. She would use that as time to catch up on lots of the work that needed to be done. She saw it as valuable for the staff working in the rooms, but she didn't really see her own role as a pedagogical leader.

With the Effective Pre-School, Primary and Secondary Education project (EPPSE) report (1997), we have realised more and more that while it's essential to offer a well-run, caring, responsive, warm, lovely place for children to come to, those things are not enough. If we are going to make a difference for children, we've got to think about them as learners. That is quite a big paradigm shift for people in the early years, particularly when you're thinking about babies and toddlers. We have to think about children as learners and understand our responsibilities towards them as active and curious intellectual minds, as well as bodies that need keeping dry and warm with nappies that need changing.

What does pedagogical leadership mean to me? It means that all of the time, if I'm thinking about running a child-centred organisation, I'm not just thinking about ratios and physical care and children being safe and well, important though all of those things are. I'm also considering whether this is an awe-inspiring, exciting, irresistible space for a baby or toddler or young child to come and learn and make friends and have new experiences. Is that happening as far as humanly possible every day here so that we are giving all of our children the best start to learning and life?

When I first went into the profession, children in East London were doing really badly in the school system in this country. The disadvantage they faced as a result of a poor experience of schooling was staggering. We recognised that unless we did more in the early years to support children as learners and communicators and creators, they were going to start compulsory schooling with very little chance of keeping up with children around the country. So investment in places like Newham and Tower Hamlets and Islington, where I've been working in the early years, had to be about children as learners and about their life chances, not just about childcare, otherwise we wouldn't do enough for the children.

In any group of children there are always many children who are much cleverer than us. We have to be really humble about the fact that that's the case, and do everything we can to recognise and celebrate all of the many intelligences and creativities that children have. When I first started working in inner London, the prevalent view was that the children already had a hard enough life, so our role was to keep them as happy as possible in their early years education and schooling. That was the extent of the ambition and it's patronising. I think pedagogical leadership is about being much humbler than that and about respecting and valuing the children that we work with as intellectuals and thinkers who can do brilliantly in their lives, and not see them as children to feel a little bit sorry for, or to think that if we give them a few happy and warm hours in the day that's enough. Because it certainly isn't.

So is pedagogical leadership a hat that you wear as a leader, or is it something that is intertwined through everything you're doing?
I think the New Zealand Te Whariki image of the interwoven mat in early years absolutely holds true. There isn't a way of splitting up your leadership role and thinking 'this is the pedagogical leadership bit'. It all comes together in our decisions. How we decide to spend our budget or work our ratios is pedagogical leadership. In my opinion it's not good childcare unless learning is going on, and therefore you can't split those things up either. So that weaving metaphor is really powerful.

What has inspired your thinking on pedagogical leadership?
In the 1990s I worked in a centre in north London that was part of the EPPSE project. One of the personal experiences I had there was one of the EPPSE researchers talking to me about my approach to what we were doing with the children. They asked me 'why do you do it that way?' and I have to admit I was completely floored by that question. I did it that way because that was the way it was being done there. I saw my role as keeping things as they had been and I was very influenced by history and tradition and what I'd seen and heard and very uninfluenced by the idea of critical reflection. Having those questions asked of me and my practice was a seminal moment for me.

Following on from that research, I was invited to join a group that Iram Siraj was running at that time at the Institute of Education. There, I met Bernadette Duffy among other people and that was so important for me because I'd never been part of those sorts of discussions before where we really thought about why we were doing things and what the evidence might suggest was effective and not effective. They were constantly modelling curiosity and questioning and asking 'what is it that you're noticing that makes you so confident to say that?' or 'why do you think that?' or 'what have you seen elsewhere?'

I was extremely fortunate to develop links with Pen Green and Margy Whalley there. Margy created a climate where people were fearlessly asking questions about what we were doing and whether it was right for the children and for the communities we were working with. The whole idea of asset-based community development as I would think about it now was also really powerful for my development. I think she disrupted a certain view of professionalism which I might have had, which was that your job as an early years teacher or leader was to read up on the best evidence and do the best you could. I still strongly believe this is essential, but Margy would say, 'remember that it's not your community and they're not your children; what does the community want for these children, how can you mobilise the community?'

Is pedagogical leadership something you can see and feel when you walk into an ECE setting?
I think the honest answer to that is 'yes' but I would also say that it's vital to be sceptical about those gut feelings. Sometimes we go into a setting and we have certain things we're looking for and of course that really structures what we see and hear and we don't necessarily realise the full approach that that setting is taking.

Research for my doctorate in education involved meeting regularly with groups of early years educators from a range of settings in disadvantaged areas and having semi-structured conversations about the children they work with. It was incredibly illuminating how thoughtful and creative a lot of those practitioners were. I realised that it's very easy to underestimate the work people are doing with children and jump to conclusions. We have to work very hard to guard against that. We often have to work really hard to understand the qualities of the setting we go into.

At the same time though, I do listen out for those conversations between educators and parents at the end of the day. Are there only details about the physical life of the child (how they ate, slept and used the potty) or is there a conversation about the intellectual life of the child? That is something I look out for. And sometimes you'll see settings putting a strong emphasis on developmental journals that are essentially an assembly of photographs with happy looking children, rather like a gorgeous family scrapbook, often lovely and very valued by the children and families, but nothing about learning. Or nothing about the struggles children have when they learn or how they persevered and overcame things. That would worry me too.

So I guess I have a mental checklist of signs of what seems to be an intellectually alive early years setting, but I'm also really aware that I have to try and control for the bias that I might bring to that.

How do you think about pedagogical leadership in the English ECE sector as a whole? What do you think about where we're at currently and where we need to go?
If you go back to the term 'climate', let's think about the climate from the point of view of being an early years educator in a setting where (a) maybe your pay is little more, or no more, than someone who does something like replenishing the shelves in a supermarket, (b) probably the support and level of dialogue and critical thinking that you had in your initial training was quite limited, (c) probably you're not accessing much professional development because your setting is living somewhat hand to mouth and (d) probably you're working really long hours and you go home at the end of your shift exhausted and there is little or no time to have that kind of reflective dialogue with your colleagues about what the children are doing and what it means for their learning.

So how would it be that a climate like this would foster something that was full of creativity and learning potential for the children attending? It just seems really unlikely to me that it would. Unless we have the structures to train staff really well and to support reflective dialogue among colleagues, and unless we have more graduate-level practitioners, I can't see that we're going to make the shift that we need to make.

What really worried me about graduate-level practitioners is the number we have interviewed here who despite having a degree in Early Childhood Studies still find it really difficult to talk about how children learn and what their role is in promoting that. We need to build reflection into all levels of our early childhood education (ECE) training and we haven't got there yet.

Lindsay Foster, here at Sheringham Nursery School, leads a programme called Outstanding Early Years Teaching. What's really great about this programme is that it's actually about creating a community of learners who work together for a year looking at practice in a range of different settings in East London, critically interrogating it. They have lots of online engagement between the sessions, using WhatsApp and Twitter, and share a lot of resources and insights. There's a coaching element to it around helping participants to focus on what it is they think they're seeing and what they want for the children they're working with. It's about peer learning and every year that group reminds us that there are so many practitioners out there who are brilliantly reflective and thoughtful and have great ideas. It's really magical to see them flourish but they do need that coaching support, that learning community, that opportunity to view settings outside of their own immediate circle, to actualise all of that potential that they've got.

Is it about policy then? Is it about the policy shifts and signals that enable a climate where there is the time and space for reflective practice?
Yes, but what I would say is that my experience of working in the early years suggests to me that looking for policy signals of that kind is naïve. I think the best change happens because people on the ground act with determination to do something different and better and they show that it works and percolates up until eventually the world of policy notices it.

Those effective settings that the EPPSE project identified didn't happen because of policy, it happened because those leaders on the ground – people like Bernadette Duffy, Carol Walden and Margy Whalley – made it happen and then via EPPSE it came to the attention of policy that there was a better way of doing things.

We do need policy, most definitely, and the right structures, but I just can't believe that hanging around and waiting for that to happen is the best thing, and often there's much more potential to do things than people imagine.

If I look at the context in Newham, the funding arrangement for private voluntary initiatives (PVIs) includes the requirement that there should be a certain number – I think it's three – of whole day professional development trainings for PVI staff and so that's built into the funding structure. So what we did in Manor Park is we said to our PVIs, 'well look, we can all try and do our own thing with the funding we've got but it's probably really hard for all of us, but if between 10 and 20 of us collaborated on a single project, we'd get massive economy of scale and we'd learn more from each other and we'd get more impact'. And that was really the inspiration behind the project we did in Manor Park, which was called Manor Park Talks. At that scale, you can bring in really experienced trainers, you can train in big rather than small groups and you can pay for monthly coaching for everyone. We could get the Institute of Education to work with us around the evidence base and create the iterative relationship between evidence and practice on the ground. So what's needed is that sort of collaborative work at community level to improve practice, not waiting for someone else to show us the way.

It sounds like community partnerships are absolutely central to this. Is an element of pedagogical leadership about community leadership?
Yes – and that also involves other aspects of community, so yes, other settings and childminders, but also your community more widely, and how you are working in that community development way. We are at a very early stage of doing that despite thinking that it is important.

It can be difficult to achieve. For example, one of the common challenges faced in Newham is that a lot of children will appear in a nursery setting either at three or even appear at reception class at four with really quite complicated special needs, and no one will know about the children. And then there's this enormous effort to try and understand what their needs are and to meet them and to provide as far as possible for them. This has been understood in terms of parents being 'hard to reach', with the idea that they are hiding their children away and not coming into contact with services earlier because perhaps there are feelings of shame and embarrassment or whatever. But we worked with a really gifted children's centre lead from Tower Hamlets, Sue Cox, and she turned it on its head: Is it the family that's hard to reach or the service?

If you're a family in this part of Newham, maybe your English isn't great, maybe you don't understand the English early years system, maybe you've tried to go to a stay and play session at your children's centre and you've been humiliated about your child's reaction to it. In this situation, who is hard to reach: the parent or the service? Sue argued that the service was very hard for the parents to reach, not that the parents were hard for us to reach. She did some work with parents of children of special needs about what sort of service they would find accessible and she created a service based on those findings and actually we haven't had any difficulty engaging at all with parents who have a young child with Special Educational Needs and Disability (SEND) in that service. Now, we very rarely come across two-, three- and four-year olds with complex needs who the children's centres know nothing about. So the narrative of 'hard to reach' is a narrative we need to shift.

I would add to that a couple of other narratives that we, as pedagogical leaders, need to shift. One is that children speaking English as an additional language (EAL) are somehow a vulnerable group of children rather than a magnificent cohort of cognitively brilliant children who are going to really flourish. At the same time, we also need to get rid of the flipside myth that they'll come into our setting and learn English easily because young children are just so brilliant. The truth like in all of these things is that it's somewhere in the middle, which is that they *are* brilliant but that it is also hard work to come into a setting at the age of three and not know the words that everyone else knows. Practitioners have to work hard to help you to learn English in that situation. It will come more naturally to some children than others, but it's not going to be easy.

A lot of our thinking on that was informed by one of our teachers, Tania Chowdhury, who put together a piece for a book we made which was about Bangladeshi parents and what they thought about their children as learners. It really shook up a lot of things that people thought about EAL learners.

I think the other narrative that we need to shift is that sense that we're marvellously inclusive in the early years, because we have lots of children with SEND and they have a positive experience day to day. Sara Bonetti at the Education Policy Institute (EPI) would point us towards the rather uncomfortable fact that at the end of early years foundation stage (EYFS), children with SEND are not doing well and actually the gap between them and other children is growing year on year and that reminds us as well that it's not just about having children physically in our space having a positive experience overall. It's about thinking about them as learners and maximising their learning opportunities and being really focused on what the barriers to those children's learning is and having that belief that they can access every bit of our curriculum as long as we help them to overcome those barriers.

If community collaborations are so important for advancing pedagogical leadership, what practical steps can practitioners or settings take to develop these community links?

I think we have to be clear that there is an awful lot further for us to go. But I would cite things like Tania just spending time in conversation with Bangladeshi British parents about their understanding of their child's early learning, and the fact that Tania is herself of Bangladeshi heritage and is herself an East Londoner and has succeeded wonderfully in the school system, that's really powerful for the community too. That's important, along with the focus on listening and understanding.

There is a really interesting tight rope that we often get wrong: that is, on the one hand, groups of parents like that may well want to be listened to and understood and have very specific desires for their children, but, on the other hand, they also appreciate respectful dialogues about the things that will give your child a really good start to your learning. It's that coming together of professional expertise with listening to communities and community leadership, and again where we get it wrong is where we get that seriously out of balance.

All of the parents that I've spoken to here, they – without exception – want the best for their child and they are there to help them. It's harder for some parents than others. Sometimes it's really hard for us to maintain positive dialogues when parents have such divergent views from our own, but we can always bring it back to 'we all want the best for the child' and that process of respectful dialogue and finding compromises and ways forward is really important.

When I first came to work in Newham, the mayor Robin Wales put a lot of money into a programme called Every Child a Reader in Newham (ECARN), which began in reception and it was very focused on finding the approaches to phonics that had the best evidence base and supporting schools to invest in those phonics approaches, to get the training and resources they needed. There was also another vision about what it means to be a young reader based on enjoying books, having lots of books in schools, lots of opportunities for children to share stories which also dove-tailed into programmes such as every child in Newham going to the theatre and so on. ECARN was also independently evaluated.

I was adamantly opposed to ECARN at the time. I thought it was really wrong of the mayor to mandate so clearly what sort of pedagogy for which he was prepared to provide extra funding. I was really sceptical about the phonics approach in general and whether that was at odds with what's best for young children. Many years later I re-read the ECARN independent evaluation which showed that it had a staggeringly positive impact on outcomes for children in Newham, especially for children who were identified as struggling to read during their reception year. We have a really close relationship with the secondary school up the road from us, and they told us that for the first cohort of ECARN children to make it to year seven, they had to re-write the year seven curriculum because the children were such good readers, knew so much more and could study things so much more independently.

I really had to eat humble pie over ECARN which I'm happy to do in public. I guess what it taught me is that there are times when community leaders – and we have to be careful with this – can go out on a bit of a limb and say the best evidence is telling us that we should do this, so even though a lot of people are opposed to it, we're going to evaluate the idea independently to make sure we're not getting it wrong, and we're going to hold a line here, no matter how controversial. So I retrospectively admire that approach even though at the time I was against it.

That comes back to something I said right at the beginning, which is that when our thinking is over-informed by tradition and the traditional values around early years that we pick up on along the way in our careers, we can get some things really wrong. I feel that I got that wrong because all my instincts suggested that this approach to learning in reception was an anathema and I wasn't prepared to be open-minded and look at the evidence and consider what this programme was trying to do.

There's a really big class dimension around pedagogical leadership. I have to own the fact of my own middle-class upbringing, private education and every advantage in life, and that's important for me to bear in mind all of the time. First of all to make sure that I don't assume that other people have had a similar hand up in life but also try and remember that is what everyone should get. We must not romanticise aspects of the early years tradition because those very laissez-faire approaches to giving children in disadvantaged circumstances just a nice environment (but nothing more), what Mary Jane Drummond at Cambridge University calls 'the benevolent approach', doesn't rock the class system. It keeps working-class and Black and Minority Ethnic (BAME) children in 'their place' in schools where achievement doesn't happen. I do my best to keep my consciousness as highly raised as it can possibly be so that children in places like Newham have all the opportunities that children in private schools get. And that shakes some of the more romantic traditions in ECE for me.

2

Pedagogic Cultures in Early Childhood
Framing Children's Experiences
Lorna Arnott

Introduction

This chapter explores the ways in which adults' decision-making through pedagogical leadership and children's interpretation of the physical and social environment frames children's playful experiences in early childhood. Elsewhere, I introduce these concepts with the specific focus on children's negotiation tactics (Arnott, 2018) and creative play (Arnott & Duncan, 2019) and I argue that these elements of experience are nestled in a pedagogic culture which children and practitioners inhabit in early childhood education. This chapter consolidates my interpretation of practitioners' and children's responsive planning and learning experiences as embedded in a pedagogic culture.

In a typically sociocultural fashion, I recognise that my interpretation is not developed in a vacuum but rather is born from key influential perspectives which have shaped my view of the world. I have previously drawn on the principle of human ecology which seeks to understand the interplay between humans and their social and physical environment (Arnott, 2016). This chapter extends my theorising by progressing the application of ecologies into practice, through children's and practitioners' interpretation of pedagogy and to explore how this insight can transform leadership in early childhood education.

To achieve this, I consider two threads of discussion – structure and dynamic cultures – which knit nicely together to articulate my overarching consideration of pedagogic cultures. I describe three key works which are inseparable in my thinking and shape my perception of the environment within which children are learning. The first is Bernstein's pedagogic discourse (1975, 1990), where we see the more structural nature of the playroom feeding into leadership planning and pedagogy. Indeed, I have been intrigued by his interpretation of the structural nature of visible and invisible pedagogies which classify and frame children's learning experiences.

The second and third do not relate directly to leadership and planning in a formal pedagogical sense but are authors who explore the cultures apparent in education and learning experiences. Barbara Rogoff is a prolific author, known for her discussion of *The Cultural Nature of Child Development* (2003) and *Apprenticeship in Thinking* (1990) and William Corsaro is a sociologist who focuses a great deal on peer cultures (1988) and interpretive reproduction (1992, 1993, 2012).

This work starts from the child and very much presents an understanding of what it means to develop, learn and socialise in unique contexts. Some of the work looks especially at minority cultures, tribal living (Rogoff, 1993) and often in informal learning contexts (Rogoff et al., 2016) but that doesn't impede us from translating this knowledge of informal learning as a cultural experience into a more formal setting. Other elements focus on peer cultures and relationships and don't relate to adult-child dynamics explicitly (Corsaro, 1988), but in a society which advocates for children engaging in leadership roles and shaping their own learning, there is much we can learn from these peer cultural experiences.

Thus, the literature is not overtly focused on leadership and pedagogical planning in formal early childhood education. Yet much of the writings of this time focused on relationships and social processes in a broad sense as part of their characterisation of culture, and that process, for me, is the very nature of pedagogy in early childhood education. It therefore has the potential to inform our understanding of leadership in formal educational settings. These works have long shaped my understanding of children's learning experiences and consequently the role of pedagogical leadership in framing children's everyday learning. Drawing on fragments of each of these theories shapes how I see early childhood leadership delivered through pedagogical planning as a cultural experience, which is dynamic, evolving and heterogeneous. This chapter will argue that because of the cultural nature of experience, pedagogies planned for in practice cannot be replicated or modelled but rather are inherently context specific. Thus, for example, play may be ubiquitous in early childhood education, but it is also unique because of the culture within which it manifests.

Pedagogy and Framing of Children's Experiences

To develop an interpretation of the cultural entity inherent in early childhood leadership planning and experience, requires first to understand the place of pedagogy in early childhood practice more generally. The notion of pedagogy in education is not new across the world, particularly in European contexts (Murphy, 2008). The challenge, however, is that pedagogy, like play, is intangible and abstract and is thus variously defined. Definitions range from encompassing phrases like, 'the act and discourse of teaching' (Alexander, 2004, p. 8) to what Murray (2015) describes as the literal translation of 'leading the child' based on the Greek origins of the word. The complex notions of idiosyncratic differences in pedagogy are also accounted for as the process is described as an 'adventure', involving lived processes with 'unique interactive aspects' (Tochon and Munby, 1993, p. 207).

In some cases, more defined pedagogies have emerged, often bound in philosophies of particular scholars who have advanced the work – a Montessorian or Froebelian pedagogy, for example. These approaches frame the ways that children's daily lives in education unfold. A degree of adult control, decision-making and planning results in varied and unique experiences for each child depending upon the philosophical assumptions that the staff and children adhere to: assumptions that cannot be learned but rather are embodied over time and space, but which are also bound by societal understandings of high-quality education.

In this case, Bernstein's pedagogic discourse provides a useful point of reference to understand the structure inherent in pedagogical planning. In particular, Bernstein's work, which focuses on the conceptualisation of classification and framing and the visible and invisible pedagogy (1975, 1990, 2000) is really helpful to understand the dynamics of pedagogy. Much like generic definitions of pedagogy, Brooker (2002, p. 178) describes the pedagogic discourse as 'the entire process of bringing about learning in a setting'. This is codified by Bernstein as involving pedagogic practices that are the underlying rules which shape the social construction of pedagogic discourse. The approach governs both how children behave and how children learn (Bernstein, 2000). Through his conceptualisation of the regulative (social order) and instructional (how children learn) discourses, Bernstein considers how framing of the environment determines who maintains control in the setting. For example, when framing is strong, the teachers have control over the transmission of knowledge, while when framing is weak the students have more apparent control. He argued that pedagogic practices can be described as either visible or invisible. The former has an explicit pedagogy while the latter is more implicit. The more explicit the transmission of knowledge the more visible the pedagogy is likely to be. With strong regulative discourse you would, therefore, expect the rules of behaviour and conduct to be explicit.

In progressive early childhood education, particularly in the West, the notion of children leading their learning (Scottish Government, 2020), child-centred practices (Georgeson et al., 2015) and responsive approaches (Wood, 2010) dominate the discussion. Thus, the pedagogic practices align more with Bernstein's invisible pedagogy. King (1979) suggests this includes implicit control where teachers are responsible for planning but children are able to manoeuvre the setting and make changes as they explore. The focus remains on affording children power to choose activities and manage social relationships rather than emphasising transmission of knowledge.

This approach applies to a particular notion of pedagogy which centres on play, which Wood (2009, p. 27) defines as:

> the ways in which early childhood professionals make provision for play and playful approaches to learning and teaching, how they design play/learning environments, and all the pedagogical decisions, techniques and strategies they use to support or enhance learning and teaching through play.

Play is often chosen as a medium through which children should learn because of key theoretical underpinnings, such as the work of Vygotsky (1930/2004) who advocated for imagination or the notion that play allows children to trial scenarios in a safe context, such as rehearsal for adult life (Bruce, 2018). Certainly, it is believed to add value to child development (Singer, 1994). Yet, casually linking play and learning can be problematic because it is not possible to say whether it is the play itself, the instructive teacher or some other social experience which has caused the learning or development to occur. This is particularly the case if you view the world from the perspective that the individual, their social world and development are inseparable (Rogoff, 1993; Sawyer, 2002).

It is for this reason that a focus on play pedagogy solely, or indeed any one pedagogy, becomes problematic and so an understanding of the various pedagog*ies* apparent in early childhood education becomes more meaningful. In this sense, pedagogies have broadened and may be better defined by their features or dominant characteristics of early childhood education. Holistic definitions in this way characterise early childhood education by 'play, wholeness, inner motivation, self-control, active child, starting where the child is' (Samuelsson and Carlsson, 2008, p. 630) rather than a pre-defined approach. They suggest the basic premise is that children learn 'by doing, by talking, by experimenting, by trying and failing or trying and succeeding or by reflection and communication as well as in play' (Samuelsson and Carlsson, 2008, p. 630). In a similar vein, Plowman et al. (2010, p. 53) suggest that pedagogy in early childhood is about 'the emphasis . . . on the whole child, play as a medium for learning, experiential learning and the crucial role of adults as supporting learning'.

This chapter builds on this broadening of perspectives, the focus on characteristics and the inherent flexibility in defining practice because 'without great flexibility neither play nor learning is possible!' (Samuelsson and Carlsson, 2008, p. 633). Such holistic notions, coupled with the understanding that context and learning are inseparable, fuel the need to better understand the cultural nature of pedagogy in early childhood practice. Although perhaps not as widely theorised as bounded approaches to pedagogies, I suggest the notions of wholeness and expansively dynamic pedagogies are important to consider and that we need to explore the characteristics of pedagogies rather than comparing and contrasting particular approaches.

A Culture of Early Childhood Education Pedagogies

The discussion of culture in early childhood education offers a route to understand and celebrate the idiosyncratic nature of pedagogies across the sector. Despite agendas to standardise provision (Jarvis & Whitebread, 2018), the nucleus that drives quality early childhood practice is the emphasis on being responsive to children's needs and interests (Wood, 2010). In this scenario, a one-size-fits-all approach to pedagogy, standardised for largely political reasons, hinders the ability of staff to lead in responsive ways. The research is abundantly clear that children's engagement and dispositions to learn are inextricably linked to their own interests and needs. We must reimagine pedagogy as a culture, inhabited by practitioners and children and that is endowed with defining characteristics, chosen by those directly involved in the context. This allows us to embrace a non-unified approach to early childhood education, which meets the needs of individual children.

Viewing playrooms and the pedagogies employed within them as a culture has been considered in the literature. For example, Shinegold et al. (1984) highlighted that 'classrooms are well established cultures, with social organisations and work-related agendas embodied in longstanding curricula' (p. 4). Similarly, Wood (2010, p. 15) argues that 'culture not only frames and pervades children's ways of learning, it also powerfully influences their identities which, in turn, are constantly created and re-created in interaction between people'. Thus, by focusing on the wider culture it is possible to see how beliefs and values shape children's experiences and the non-unified nature of pedagogy enriches children's experiences, offering diversity, linked to the values and beliefs of the cultural group (Tudge et al., 2006).

This work on culture has a real contribution to make because it moves our understanding beyond curriculum or regulatory process in formal settings. For example, Bang (2009) tells us that a sole focus on the functional, physical or programmatic environment is insufficient to understand how children's interactions and behaviours manifest. I would go further to argue that a lack of understanding beyond this area impedes our perception of learning and educational experiences, which then hinders the ability to lead.

Instead, the environment must be explored in conjunction with the social space where behaviours are restricted by temporal and spatial boundaries (Brown, Shepherd, Wituk, & Meissen, 2007, p. 402), guiding children to act within the perceived rules of social order; creating a behavioural milieu (Heft, 1988, p. 31). Analysing the way children interpret and manoeuvre the structural element of the playroom is important to understanding social interactions, not least because rules can be described as 'the cultural resources to which members orient in order to make sense of their social worlds' (Cobb-Moore, Danby, & Farrell, 2009, p. 1478). By exploring pedagogy as a cultural artefact in a social space, we can better unpick the elements of the setting that frame experience. It also allows us to recognise the dynamic and changeable nature of pedagogy as something which is a living entity growing alongside practice and continuously transforming as part of the culture.

This resembles the ideas put forward by Corsaro who argues that through interpretative reproduction, children reproduce the adult world. They do this by becoming a member of the preschool and contributing to it, rather than merely appropriating or internalising the culture already established. Corsaro (1992, p. 161) describes this process as 'children enter into a social nexus and, through interaction with others, establish social understandings'. Children's positions within the community therefore contribute to their interactions and relationships, and then ultimately their own experience.

In this conceptualisation, the culture is not static but ever changing. Corsaro's interpretation of peer cultures offers some useful thinking to better understand this process. The work argues that as children become members of the culture, they use shared knowledge to manoeuvre the context and drive forward their experiences (Corsaro & Eder, 1990). In doing so they 'exercise agency in a mediating fashion, enabling them ... [to] challenge and transform the situational contexts of action themselves' (Emirbayer & Mische, 1998, p. 994). Applying this thinking to a pedagogic culture, while assuming children's and practitioners' membership of that cultural group, shows how individuals can exercise agency and autonomy in preschool settings to offer divergent and responsive learning encounters. It also gives liberty to practitioners to continually develop their practice and build their pedagogy over time. From this perspective, pedagogy is not static. It is not bound by labels or curricula. Seeing pedagogy as cultural allows for an eclectic manifestation of learning which draws on cultural historical experiences from a range of philosophies and approaches. Through this lens, pedagogic leadership is embedded in a relational approach, where practice is never viewed statically as high or low quality but rather as a continuous journey through which practitioners and children alike strive for new adventures to spark interest and engagement with learning.

Pedagogic Culture Is Fluid and Dynamic

Building on this interpretation of culture and the invisibility of pedagogy in early childhood, it is clear to see that the framing gives rise to interpretation and individuality of experience. Inducting children into the rules and regulations of the preschool helps to create 'strong framing' which aims to guide behaviour (Bernstein, 1990), yet while the framing is created by adults, Alcock (2007, p. 281) argues that 'children re-create their own culture meaningfully by playing flexibly with the rules that surround everyday practices'.

Here we begin to see the challenges with defining pedagogy as Murphy (2008, p. 29) argues:

> there has been recognition in recent years of the unique, interactive nature of pedagogy. This interactiveness makes it difficult to capture and represent professional expertise as practiced in classrooms.

Yet a conceptualisation around culture allows for such fluidity and uniqueness in practice. Rogoff (1993, p. 6) suggests that 'culture itself is not static; it is formed from the efforts of people working together, using and adapting tools provided by predecessors and in the process creating new ones'. Thus in education, perhaps there is an understanding that pedagogy should be replicable, linked to quality indicators and should provide a sufficient guide for practitioner leadership and planning. Yet based on the understanding of Rogoff and the notion of culture as dynamic, I would argue the opposite. Pedagogies are individualised to the setting and when regarded as a culture (Rogoff, 1993) and by drawing on Corsaro's (1992) notion that children reproduce the culture alongside adults, conceptualising pedagogies as culture offers freedom to move through learning experiences, dance across concepts and mindfully engage in meaningful experiences *with* children. It provides a context where practitioners and children learn together, shifting the traditional notions of expert and novice, towards the concept of a cultural ethos with varying strengths, rather than structuring learning for children in a top-down fashion.

Vygotsky argued that traditions, practices and values inherent in any culture are passed down through generations. He suggests that not only these traditions and values shape an individual's behaviour but also that the individual continually re-moulds the cultural values and traditions. Hence, emergent work from a sociocultural perspective frequently focuses on context. Lave and Wenger's (1991) concept of 'community of practice', for example, explores the social and cultural customs and ways of operating within a community in their explorations of learning. Similarly, Rogoff's (1989, 1990) concept of guided participation focuses on the nature of tacit learning in informal learning contexts. Similarly, Edwards (2004, p. 88) explored the context of 'practice' in early childhood education, indicating that 'cultural context is incorporated into interactions and their outcomes'. Viewing pedagogy as an evolving culture which is passed down as new children and practitioners enter and contribute to the setting and which is re-moulded, perhaps on a daily basis, provides a real opportunity to 'plan for endless possibilities' (Gripton, 2017).

This understanding of pedagogy as a culturally dynamic endeavour is strengthened further as we continue to explore advances in technologies. The hyper-pace at which technologies emerge in society and in education negates the need to always view practitioners as 'educators' solely responsible for transmitting, sharing, directing and encouraging knowledge generation in proximal and distal ways. For example, we see how readily parents and practitioners embrace young children's innate capacity to tinker and learn how to use new devices, unhindered by anxiety, self-consciousness or adult-centric notions of being a luddite. Instead, these young citizens are taking a leadership role in not only learning the mechanics of the device but also in teaching the older generation how to use these devices (see Arnott et al., 2019). A dynamic shift in the pedagogic culture has become apparent, where learning together is unencumbered by intergenerationally perceived knowledge status. Power dynamics, while always present, in some cases have qualitatively shifted.

The transformation of the culture is not only shaped by the child, however. The adult's role also becomes central to the process of establishing a strong pedagogic culture which is not rigid but is alive with possibilities and idiosyncrasies to support the individual child. We know that in high-quality-early childhood education the practitioner must understand and listen to children. They must develop a relationship with children whereby they know the child's home culture and previous experiences and perspective. Drawing on this concept and not limiting our exploration to the child's role in navigating a complex social system but rather looking at the wider or holistic system as a whole, you can see that both adults and children lead the evolution of the setting and pedagogy which guides experience.

The Pedagogic Culture

Building on those underlying principles of the structure of pedagogy and the cultural exploration presented thus far, I present a conceptualisation of the pedagogic culture as a means of articulating the complexity inherent in early childhood provision. By pedagogic culture, I mean an explicit conceptualisation, recognition and application of the holistic ecological elements that frame the practice of supporting learning in early childhood. In many cases, this represents intangible, structural, social and relational characteristics which underpin children's experiences, perhaps rooted in the invisible pedagogy. It represents processes that become habit – processes that also evolve and change as children and practitioners reproduce the context; processes that underpin a cultural entity which is early childhood pedagogy. That is to say that, it is the dynamic interlinking of these holistic playroom elements that is likely to shape, and be shaped, by children's social play and by practitioner planning and leadership. Working from this lens, we must understand how the interlinking elements of a particular context shape how children experience the environment and their play in unique ways.

The notion of pedagogic culture is offered as a conduit to begin synthesising and reflecting upon the multiplicity of factors which contribute a particular way of supporting children's learning in early childhood education and to understand what leadership may look like. It draws from the very essence of play that Samuelsson and Carlsson, (2008, p. 627), drawing on Sawyer (1997), suggest is about 'improvisations where there is no manuscript, but the script is created on the spot in the interplay between children'. Just as play is not bounded and is limitless, the notion of pedagogic culture offers a valuable responsive and reflective frame to understand early childhood education. The main contribution is in the understanding that no two pedagogic cultures can ever be the same. They may mimic or resemble characteristics of another setting or another pedagogical approach (as can be seen with the overlapping pedagogies presented in the previous section) but the way that the child and staff experience their context is idiosyncratic and context specific. For play, this realisation offers interesting interpretations of what this means for practice and for framing children's learning experiences.

It is argued that play is 'transference of culture' (Jonson et al., 2005, cited in Samuelsson and Carlsson, 2008, p. 627), and I would argue that pedagogic cultures are the spaces in between play and learning, representing the evolution of that culture where play manifests. To understand this perspective, it is important to view play as something which is also dynamic. Play is not a discrete activity but rather the projection, development and cognitive/metacognitive demonstration of children's appropriation of their particular cultural context. In this sense play is more than simply the resources with which the child engages or the child's spontaneous activity. Play is unique to each context, to each child and to each practitioner, because it is the synergistic output of a specific pedagogic culture. As part of a pedagogic culture, play is the culmination of carefully considered framing. It is this conceptual understanding of early childhood education as something greater and broader than 'play-based pedagogy' that is required. We need to see children's play as an endeavour which evolves alongside society, thinking and cultures. We also need to see pedagogy as multifaceted and continually evolving and growing to demonstrate our need to always strive for better. Leadership in this lens rests on harnessing the unique and cultural qualities of play to support children to extend their explorations across time and space.

Conclusion

The theoretical considerations of pedagogy presented in this chapter suggest that pedagogical leadership must focus on the range of contexts or 'social worlds'. Thus, context is more than just the people and the things in the setting but includes historical and cultural influences on activities. It involves a relativist interpretation of multiple realities dependent upon the 'social, economic, cultural and historic nature of the group under consideration' (Tudge et al., 2009, p. 118). Activities and experiences will therefore vary, and as leaders of dynamic pedagogies, practitioners can draw on the ever changing nature of culture to justify their practice, which may look different to the norm. Understanding children's experiences as a continually evolving and vibrant evolution of individually crafted moments underpins this chapter. Newly gained knowledge, familiarity and relationships help reimagine possibilities, feeding into a newly unique pedagogic culture.

References

Alcock, S. (2007). Playing with rules around routines: Children making mealtimes meaningful and enjoyable. *Early Years*, 27(3), 281–293.

Alexander, R. (2004). Still no pedagogy? Principle, pragmatism and compliance in primary education. *Cambridge Journal of Education*, 34(1), 7–33.

Arnott, L. (2016). An ecological exploration of young children's digital play: Framing children's social experiences with technologies in early childhood, *Early Years: An International Journal*, 36(3), 271–288.

Arnott, L. (2018). Children's negotiation tactics and socio-emotional self-regulation in child-led play experiences: The influence of the preschool pedagogic culture. *Early Child Development and Care*, 188(7), 951–965.

Arnott, L., & Duncan, P. (2019). Exploring the pedagogic culture of creative play in early childhood education. *Journal of Early Childhood Research*, 17(4), 309–328.

Arnott, L., Palaiologou, I., & Gray, C. (2019). An ecological exploration of the Internet of Toys in early childhood everyday life. In G. Mascheroni & D. Holloway (Eds.), *The Internet of Toys: Practices, Affordances and the Political Economy of Children's Play* (pp. 135–157).

Bang, J. (2009). An Environmental Affordance Perspective on the Study of Development - Artefacts, Social Others and Self. In M. Fleer, M. Hedegaard, & J. Tudge. (Eds.), *Childhood studies and the impact of globalization: policies and practices at global and local levels*. Routledge.

Bernstein, B. (1975). Class and pedagogies: Visible and invisible. *Educational Studies*, 1(1), 23–41. doi:10.1080/ 0305569750010105

Bernstein, B. (1990). *The Structuring of Pedagogic Discourse*. London: Routledge.

Bernstein, B. (2000). *Pedagogy, Symbolic Control, and Identity: Theory, Research, Critique* (Revised ed.). Lanham, MD: Rowman & Littlefield.

Brooker, L. (2002). *Starting School: Young Children Learning Cultures*. London: McGraw-Hill Education.

Brown, L. D., Shepherd, M. D., Wituk, S. A., & Meissen, G. (2007). How settings change people: Applying behavior setting theory to consumer-run organizations. *Journal of Community Psychology*, 35(3), 399–416. doi: 10.1002/jcop.20155

Bruce, T. (2018). The importance of play. In Trevarthen, C., Delafield-Butt, J., & Dunlop, A.W. (Eds.), *The Child's Curriculum: Working with the Natural Values of the Young Child*. Oxford: Oxford University Press.

Cobb-Moore, C., Danby, S., & Farrell, A. (2009). Young children as rule makers. *Journal of Pragmatics*, 41(8), 1477–1492. doi: 10.1016/j.pragma.2007.04.013

Corsaro, W. A. (1988). Peer culture in the preschool. *Theory Into Practice*, 27(1), 19–24. doi: 10.1080/00405848809543326

Corsaro, W. A. (1992). Interpretive reproduction in children's peer cultures. *Social Psychology Quarterly*, 55, 160–177.

Corsaro, W. A. (1993). Interpretive reproduction in children's role play. *Childhood*, 1(2), 64–74.

Corsaro, W. A. (2012). Interpretive reproduction in children's play. *American Journal of Play*, 4(4), 488–504.

Corsaro, W. A., & Eder, D. (1990). Children's peer cultures. *Annual Review of Sociology*, 16(1), 197–220.

Edwards, A. (2004). Understanding context, understanding practice in early education. *European early childhood education research journal*, 12(1), 85–101. https://doi.org/10.1080/13502930485209331

Emirbayer, M., & Mische, A. (1998). What is agency?. *American Journal of Sociology*, 103(4), 962–1023.

Georgeson, J. Campbell-Barr, V. Bakosi, E. Nemes, M. Pálfi, S., & Sorzio, P. (2015). Can we have an international approach to child-centred early childhood practice?, *Early Child Development and Care*, 185(11–12), 1862–1879. doi: 10.1080/03004430.2015.1028388

Gripton, C. (2017). Planning for endless possibilities. In Woods (Ed.), *Child-initiated Play and Learning: Planning for Possibilities in the Early Years*, 2nd ed. London: David Fulton, 8–22.

Heft, H. (1988). Affordances of children's environments: A functional approach to environmental description. *Children's Environments Quarterly*, 5(3), 29–37.

Jarvis, P., & Whitebread, D. (2018). Wrong beginnings: Our response to a bold report. *Early Years Educator*, 19(12), 14–16.

King, R. (1979). The search for the 'invisible' pedagogy. *Sociology*, 13(3), 445–458. doi:10.1177/003803857901300305

Lave, J., & Wenger, E. (1991). *Situated Learning: Legitimate Peripheral Participation*. Cambridge: Cambridge University Press.

Murphy, P (2008). Defining pedagogy. In Murphy, P., Hall, K., & Soler, J. (Eds.), *Pedagogy and Practice: Culture and Identities*. London: Sage.

Murray, J. (2015). Early childhood pedagogies: Spaces for young children to flourish. *Early Child Development and Care*, 185(11–12), 1715–1732. doi: 10.1080/03004430.2015.1029245

Plowman, L., Stephen, C., & McPake, J., (2010). *Growing Up With Technology: Young Children Learning in a Digital World*. Routledge.

Rogoff, B., Mosier, C., Mistry, J., & Goncu, A. (1989). Toddlers' Guided Participation in Cultural Activity. *Cultural Dynamics*, 2(2), 209–237. https://doi.org/10.1177/092137408900200205

Rogoff, B. (1990). *Apprenticeship in Thinking: Cognitive Development in Social Context*. Oxford: Oxford University Press.

Rogoff, B. (1993). *Guided Participation in Cultural Activity by Toddlers and Caregivers*. Chicago, IL: University of Chicago.

Rogoff, B. (2003). *The Cultural Nature of Human Development*. Oxford: Oxford University Press.

Rogoff, B., Callanan, M., Gutiérrez, K. D., & Erickson, F. (2016). The organization of informal learning. *Review of Research in Education*, 40(1), 356–401. doi: 10.3102/0091732X16680994

Samuelsson, I. P., & Carlsson, M. A. (2008). The playing learning child: Towards a pedagogy of early childhood. *Scandinavian Journal of Educational Research*, 52(6), 623–641.

Sawyer, R. K. (1997). *Pretend Play as Improvisation: Conversation in the Preschool Classroom*. Hove: Psychology Press.

Sawyer, R. K. (2002). Unresolved tensions in sociocultural theory: Analogies with contemporary sociological debates. *Culture and Psychology*, 8(3), 283–305.

Scottish Government (2020). *Realising the Ambition: Being Me. National Practice Guidance for Early Years in Scotland*. Edinburgh: Scottish Government.

Shinegold, K., Hawkins, J., & Char, C. (1984). '*I'm the thinkist, you're the typist': The Interaction of Technology and the Social Life of Classrooms, Center for Children and Technology*, Technical report no. 27.

Singer, J. L. (1994). Imaginative play and adaptive development. In J. H. Goldstein (Ed.) *Toys, Play, and Child Development*. Cambridge: Cambridge University Press, pp. 6–26.

Tochon, F., & Munby, H. (1993). Novice and expert teachers' time epistemology: A wave function from didactics to pedagogy. *Teaching and Teacher Education*, 9(2), 205–218.

Tudge, J., Doucet, F., Odero, D., Sperb, T., Piccinini, C., & Lopes, R. (2006). A window into different cultural worlds: Young children's everyday activities in the United States, Brazil, and Kenya. *Child Development*, 77(5), 1446–1469.

Tudge, J., Freitas, L., & Doucet, F. (2009). The transition to school: Reflections from a contextualist perspective. In H. Daniels, H. Lauder, & J. Porter (Eds.), *The Routledge Companion to Education*. London: Routledge, pp. 117–13.

Vygotsky, L. (1930/2004). Imagination and creativity in early childhood. *Journal of Russian and East European Psychology*, 42(1), 7–97.

Wood, E. (2009). Developing a pedagogy of play. In Anning, A., Cullen, J., & Fleer, M. (Eds.), *Early Childhood Education: Society and Culture*. London: Sage.

Wood, E. (2010). Developing integrated pedagogical approaches to play and learning. In Broadhead, H. & Wood, E. (Eds.), *Play and Learning in the Early Years*. London: Sage.

3

The Pedagogical Leader at London Early Years Foundation

Defining and Developing the Role

June O'Sullivan

Introduction

The pedagogical leader is the champion of great practice in early years (EY) settings. Pedagogical leaders empower colleagues to strive towards practice that consistently delivers the best outcomes for children's learning and well-being in partnership with their families and the wider community. Sixteen year ago, Sylva et al. (2004) found that pedagogical leadership enables improvements in the quality of teaching, learning and children's well-being and is therefore essential to ensuring the best outcomes for children.

Research continues to support the link suggested by Waniganayake et al. (2017) between pedagogical leadership and high-quality pedagogical practice but the EY sector in England has been slow to embrace and embed the specific role of the pedagogical leader. However, the London Early Years Foundation (LEYF) was so influenced by this research that we designed a formal role to ensure pedagogical leadership became central to our continuous efforts to support quality practice across each of our thirty-nine nurseries.

This chapter will explore what pedagogical leadership looks like at LEYF, an organisation which I have led for twenty years taking it from a small local charity to the largest childcare social enterprise in the UK. I will share how we are supporting, coaching and developing staff to use the role to build and embed pedagogical confidence as well as succession planning to grow and develop pedagogical leaders across the organisation and beyond.

What Is the LEYF Pedagogy?

We began shaping the LEYF pedagogy in 2010. We started by reflecting on our purpose. Our history began in 1903 when medical and educational philanthropists were shocked by the living conditions of the urban poor. A group of doctors and childcare experts began to investigate the particular hardships experienced by the women and children in Westminster and responded by establishing a health society with a range of activities including mothers' support services, patterns for babies' clothes, cooking classes and nurseries. The services changed after the Second World War but the nurseries survived, with some staying as full day-care nurseries and others reshaped into preschools in the 1970s and workplace nurseries in the 1980s.

In 2006, LEYF began the journey to become a social enterprise so that we could support all parents – but especially those from poor and disadvantaged backgrounds – to access high-quality affordable and accessible nurseries.

> The purpose of LEYF was to demonstrate that social and commercial goals could be blended together in the pursuit of a fairer society; in this case, community nurseries using a pedagogy designed to build social capital in order to benefit all children and families but especially those most disadvantaged.
>
> (O'Sullivan, 2018, p. 324)

However, having worked out a business model, it became clear that without wrapping the business model in a social pedagogy there was a risk that the business model would not lead to quality education. Many well-meaning nurseries were established with low fees or sited in poor neighbourhoods to support disadvantaged children but without a relevant pedagogy, the educational practice was not sufficiently strong to guarantee quality or address some of the structural barriers to educational success faced by the children. It was therefore essential for LEYF to develop its own social pedagogy.

Designing the LEYF pedagogy took ten years as we developed it alongside our growing knowledge of the context in which the children were growing up. We also tested it against the increased understanding and awareness of ECE as a crucial foundation for learning and developing cognitive and non-cognitive skills important for future success (Litjens and Taguma, 2010). Neurobiological research by Knudsen (2004) highlighted the importance of a child's brain and behavioural development, the rapid pace of growth and the impact of the quality of experiences and interactions on their development (Harrison and Ungerer, 2005; Shonkoff and Philips, 2000).

The LEYF pedagogy was designed using Bronfenbrenner's (1979) five-element social-ecology model to highlight that a child's development cannot be explained by a single factor but instead must be seen in the context of a complex system of relationships in the child's immediate and wider world. Also important to the LEYF model was the work of Putnam (2000), who stated that:

> child development is powerfully shaped by social capital . . . trust, networks and norms of reciprocity within a child's family, school, peer groups and larger community have wide ranging effects on the child's opportunities and choices and, hence behaviour and development.
>
> (Putnam, 2000, p. 296)

The LEYF pedagogy is not a rigid or unchanging framework. We believe in the importance of allowing pedagogical fluidity to shape our approach as we discover more about children's development and adjust to the changing context of children's lives. Anders (2015) noted that the relative effectiveness of different pedagogical approaches in early childhood has raised substantial debate but there is no conclusive evidence to suggest that a single model leads to better educational outcomes for children. Consequently, most countries use a combination of theorists and approaches and adjust and improve the pedagogy as they learn more. We hear settings talk about being purist and holding fast to the original ideas of a particular pioneer, but my view is that if the pioneer was alive today they would be reshaping their pedagogy to accommodate the changing world in which a child is growing up, as well as new and emerging research about how children develop. For example, we cannot discount the cutting-edge brain research which is helping us understand more about children's ability to respond and adapt to the positive and negative elements of their world. Pedagogy cannot be stagnant; we must be brave and embrace what is possible and relevant.

The LEYF pedagogy interweaves seven strands, each of which has thousands of threads and when combined form a strong learning rope to support staff, children and families. Each of the seven strands is essential to deliver a great quality education for every child (Figure 3.1).

Leadership is an essential strand whether we are talking about organisational leaders, departmental, service or pedagogical leaders. Our leadership model was designed in recognition of all the elements of leadership needed to drive excellence (Figure 3.2).

At LEYF, leaders must be able to form harmonious connections, social alliances and nourish a sense of empathy and kindness. Pedagogical leaders translate this approach into the delivery of the service to children and families in

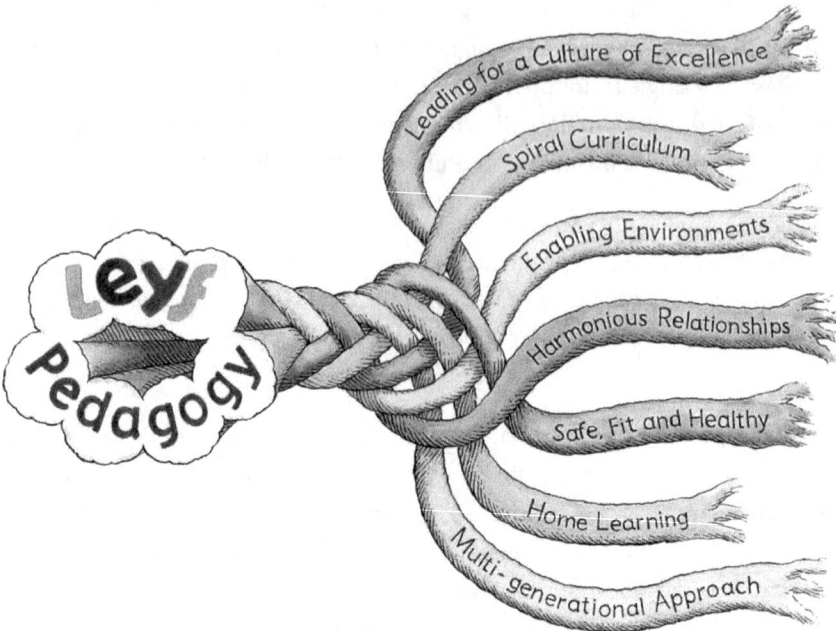

Figure 3.1 LEYF pedagogy.

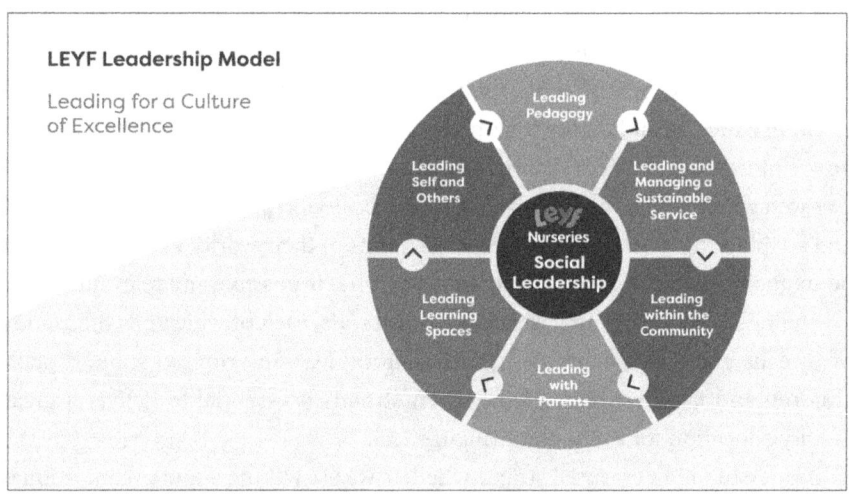

Figure 3.2 LEYF leadership model.

a way that demonstrates that they understand children's need to feel valued and loved and this is underpinned by a strong ambition for them to do well. This is particularly important at LEYF given our focus on providing for children from poor and disadvantaged backgrounds. We must build a reputation for being best in class, so everyone wants to attend.

Sutton et al. (2007) found that children learn early about their social position and the limitations it places on them from an early age. As they moved into school, Horgan (2007) found that a sense of the importance of education was strong among school pupils from both advantaged and disadvantaged backgrounds and that negative attitudes were not based on children feeling that education does not matter. Instead, the educational relationships inside and outside the classroom were significant in boosting the chances of children from disadvantaged families. This is very much why two of the seven LEYF pedagogy strands are designed to build bridges of shared understanding between home and community. Like Rogoff's (2003) developments of sociocultural theory we also consider what we can learn from the ways in which children learn at home and in their community. We believe nurseries can act as community catalysts and build a deep understanding of the child's place in their community through a multi-generational approach. Male and Palaiologou (2015) describe this as the activities and processes that are woven between contextual knowledge of the children, families and communities.

In 2015, Simpson conducted some research into the role ECE staff play in supporting parents and children experiencing poverty. The assumption was they would be helpful and have developed understanding and support. In fact, what he found was that ECE staff held a negative view about parents in poverty and attributed it to individual factors such as laziness and incompetence despite the fact that 65–70 per cent of those in poverty were working households. The consequence was a negative unconscious bias against parents, with harmful implications for how they engaged and supported these parents and slow responses to seek support for their children. In schools, it emerged that staff had lower expectations of children from poor backgrounds. Consequently, the LEYF pedagogy must be led by pedagogical leaders who understand how structural barriers and unconscious bias can impact on how we teach children. They must therefore be able to challenge views which run counter to the organisation's purpose and capacity to deliver a service that would never limit any child's horizons.

The LEYF curriculum is influenced by Bruner's (1983) concept of spiral learning and scaffolding because we need to coil the right support around the child to build individual competence and confidence by nurturing, inspiring and extending the creative and curious child. The importance of play-based learning is emphasised as well as how staff can sensitively partner the child's play and narrate their learning to introduce knowledge, build skills and support and extend their abilities by using a scaffolding approach.

How children are enabled to learn is just as important as what they learn. According to OECD (2015), the efficacy of pedagogical practice is linked to how well it facilitates play in the learning environment. Play is considered most useful to a child's development when it is meaningful and engaging (Stephen, 2010). The view suggests that unguided free play is less effective for stimulating learning, extending language and motivation than guided free play. Balance seems to be the way and not introducing formal learning too early.

LEYF staff are required to support children at a suitable pace, stretching, encouraging and celebrating as they move forward on their learning adventure. This means staff must know the child and their unique ways and understand their role in helping children make friends, find their place in the nursery and their community and value their thinking and independence.

> In high quality interactions, adults are genuinely interested in what the child is doing, adults are listening, are helping extend children's thought and knowledge and implement sustained shared thinking. In settings where such sustained shared thinking was more common, children have been observed to make greater developmental progress.
>
> (OECD, 2015, p. 5)

What we teach is critical especially as the LEYF pedagogy is designed to build on children's cultural capital by enriching and extending language and communication. At LEYF this is interpreted in many ways but central is how we give children a voice. Pedagogical leaders know this and ensure that activities such as children conducting their own planning meetings weekly, running helicopter story sessions and getting everyone confident to deliver dialogic reading are consistently and correctly delivered.

Finally, an important element of embedding any pedagogy is having a means of monitoring its delivery. At LEYF we have a self-reflective process known as the LEYF Pedagogical Development Scale (LPDS). This is a set of criteria which unpacks what each strand needs to look like to ensure it is operating well and in line with our view of good-quality provision. Quality is defined by the practice the children actually experience and what happens within a setting (Litjens and Taguma, 2010) so it is essential that there are pedagogical processes to help us reflect on this.

The LEYF Pedagogical Leader

Leadership begins with you. . . . It is unlikely that you will be able to inspire, arouse, excite and motivate others unless you can show who you are, what you stand for, and what you can and cannot do.

(Goffee and Jones, 2006)

The LEYF pedagogical leader understands children's learning and how to promote it by harnessing the extraordinary joy and enormous privilege that comes from being connected with children's learning and well-being. The ultimate purpose of the pedagogical leader is to find the fun and joy in learning in order to transform colleagues' willingness and abilities to teach. Great pedagogical leaders open new learning possibilities and build their own and colleagues' pedagogical competence through openness, trust, authenticity and compassion.

> Being a pedagogical leader means I am required to know all about the different ways the children's learning can be made more fun and more inspired by the unique and exciting experiences we provide them. As a leader I work together with my team to ensure that the children are getting enriching learning experiences whether that is through the new provocations we create to ignite their interests, the home learning we provide or the regular outings we take.
>
> (LEYF teacher)

Pedagogical leaders also need to understand how adults learn and develop in the workplace and in doing so play a significant part in supporting a culture of continuous improvement. As a champion for quality, the pedagogical leader pursues excellence in all aspects of the pedagogy and inspires others to do so also, thereby enabling the delivery of quality teaching and learning experiences for children.

> A pedagogical leader leads learning across every aspect of the nursery for staff, parents and children. I have a clear philosophical understanding of how this learning happens. My role is to empower the staff team on a daily basis to be their own pedagogical leaders by cascading my knowledge and sharing my skills. I am always aiming to be better by seeking opportunities and striving for continuous improvements to enhance the quality of the teaching and learning in my nursery.
>
> (LEYF teacher)

Professional knowledge and the ability to translate this into practice is essential for the pedagogical leader. Knowing how to transform the education and care provided to children is essential. Knowledge can be described as a collection of information, evidence, understanding and ethics garnered from a range of sources. The importance of knowledge lies not in the knowing but how it is used to shift our thinking beyond belief and opinion towards understanding. According to Boe and Hognestad (2017), pedagogical leaders need to be curious and interested in broadening their pedagogical, theoretical, contemporary research and contextual knowledge to influence and facilitate collaborative knowledge development and understanding.

For the LEYF pedagogical leader, the starting point is a grounded knowledge of the LEYF pedagogy starting with the organisational values (aspiring, nurturing, brave and fun) so that they can build their practice around those values. They need to have an understanding of how the educational theorists have shaped our seven strands and how this also is reflected in our view of the child. Pedagogical leaders need to understand the cultural and social context in which the children live to respond appropriately to their needs and build security and trust. LEYF pedagogical leaders must not only have a solid grasp of child development and how a child learns but also understand how to support children's interests, capacities, pace and dispositions of learning. They need to be able to create a physically and psychologically supportive learning environment that recognises the importance of the relationship between the child, other people, the resources and experiences.

> LEYF has given me the confidence to be a divergent thinker – I feel supported and encouraged to be creative. The LEYF approach to learning directs me to specific pedagogical theorists and influences which I am able to explore further and gain better understanding of child development and how to make a meaningful impact on the children in the nursery. LEYF has provided me with training opportunities like the degree which is just invaluable. One of the main things for me has been how LEYF has allowed me to constantly learn and evolve. An error or area of concern is seen as a learning opportunity rather than a moment to admonish or place blame.
>
> (LEYF teacher)

There is a general lack of confidence among ECE staff about what is meant by the art and science of ECE teaching. They often do not use the language of ECE teaching with confidence. It is essential that pedagogical leaders support others to articulate this language of teaching more confidently, and the first step in this is to do it themselves. Michael Oakeshott (1972) describes teaching as a variegated *activity* which includes all those teaching techniques such as coaching, hinting, suggesting, urging, coaxing, encouraging, guiding, pointing out, conversing, instructing, asking questions, discussing, experimenting, practicing, taking notes, recording, re-expressing, informing, narrating, lecturing, demonstrating, exercising, testing, examining, criticising, correcting, tutoring and drilling. These verbs are the language of educational professionals. ECE teachers need to not only feel comfortable using these terms in their day-to-day planning and delivery, but they also need to develop and grow the language so that it relates to ECE more specifically. Pedagogical leaders are at the forefront of building a strong bank of professional knowledge about how to teach children and not simply accept a watered-down version of primary school teaching.

Developing Pedagogical Leadership at LEYF

Like many ECE settings, LEYF's approach to developing pedagogical leaders is built on a combination of noticing staff with interest, ability and enthusiasm and then building in learning opportunities including training. According to the OECD report in 2012, it is not the staff's qualification level per se that most influences child development and pedagogy but their capacity to provide a stimulating environment. However, better qualified staff were found to be more capable of providing such environments and experiences, indicating that higher levels of education for ECE staff better prepare them to provide quality pedagogical environments. Hence at LEYF, we developed a LEYF pedagogy module as part of the BA early childhood degree in partnership with the University of Wolverhampton.

> LEYF has enabled me to develop my skills, knowledge and understanding through continuous training including the 'My LEYF' digital learning platform, Workplace Facebook and reading about action research conducted by other staff. LEYF works as a big family where you are continuously encouraged to express and strive to learn and achieve more not just for yourself but for the children as well. LEYF has also provided us with the opportunity to interpret strands of the pedagogy through action research.
>
> (LEYF Teacher)

However, where staff in the role of pedagogical leaders often come unstuck is not in their teaching of children but in how they try and facilitate their colleagues' learning and help them make changes to their practice. It is not a simple task of transferring learning knowledge. They must help colleagues to own their decisions and avoid complacency and *taken-for-granted practices* by embedding a pattern of behaviour that encourages and celebrates creativity, innovation and change. Successful pedagogical leaders are those who can bring learning alive and make the implicit explicit. People frequently make simple things complicated but doing the reverse and simplifying the complicated is central to the role of the pedagogical leader.

> Pedagogical leaders make learning visible to others.
>
> (Waniganayake et al., 2017, p. 118)

At LEYF, we have found that the most effective ways of doing this are through:

- Coaching
- Leading pedagogical conversations
- Action research

Coaching

Coaching is so important at LEYF that we have written a full programme available throughout the organisation. The coaching model was designed to empower others to think for themselves, recognise their own learning styles, identify issues for development, resolution or change and work out the solutions. We consider workplace coaching as the combination of skills, processes and knowledge which help people make the maximum impact while also building their confidence to respond to the continuous change that is driven by children and the wider context.

> At LEYF, coaching is a supportive rather than a directive approach that relies on asking questions. It's more of a pull approach and it helps us to find the solutions to our own questions and evaluate the consequences of possible decisions before we make them.
>
> (LEYF Teacher)

Leading Pedagogical Conversations

Alongside coaching, the pedagogical conversation is the most useful means of engaging staff to make their thinking explicit, understand relevant connections and extend their practice. Zeldin summed it up when he said that:

> Educators able to initiate and sustain such dialogue require special talents, wisdom, confidence and rich education, in the best sense of the word.
>
> (Zeldin, 1998, p.128)

People like to talk and deep conversations are often the place where shared understanding and new thinking emerges. However, Moyles (2002) found that many staff were reluctant to engage in pedagogical conversations because they found it difficult to articulate or describe in any detail the specifics of their practice and why it was important to them. They were stronger on the 'what' and 'how' but less confident on 'why'. The LEYF pedagogical conversation is structured to address this by using the keywords 'because' and 'so' in the conversation. Therefore, the better the pedagogical leaders are at engaging and modelling constructive conversations, the more they can build their colleagues' confidence to talk to other colleagues and strengthen their abilities to articulate the why.

How we conduct pedagogical conversations is based on a commitment to a parallel pedagogy. Pedagogical conversations are a key learning tool for both adults working in ECE and for the children that they work with. When LEYF teachers engage children in conversations, they are also developing the child's capacity to reason about 'the why' through the terms 'because' and 'so'. Doing this will also build children's cognitive confidence to be able to reason out what is happening for them and their learning.

Pedagogical leaders help to build relationships through conversations in which people are ready to listen to and work with each other. As Freire (1970) says, the focus lies upon coming to some greater understanding rather than winning the argument. Therefore, good pedagogical conversations need to be led by staff who are confident and emotionally intelligent and can respond sensitively and respectfully. By using the conversation to explore the complexity of delivering the pedagogy in clear and understandable terms, the pedagogical leader will help build confidence in practice.

Through their research, Pascal and Bertram (2002) highlighted the urgent need to build cultures of professional inquiry in ECE. Participation, active involvement, dialogue and shared knowledge typify the culture of such inquiry as well as having systems in place to monitor and keep track of agreed actions. However, at LEYF, we recognise that personal inquiry often starts with a conversation that gets you thinking. Kline (1999) says that thinking for yourself remains a radical act, so the pedagogical leader needs to create an environment which celebrates the importance of thinking carefully and deeply.

> The best condition for thinking, if you really stop and notice, are not tense. They are gentle. They are quiet. They are unrushed. They are stimulating but not competitive. They are encouraging. They are paradoxically both rigorous and power nimble.
>
> (Kline, 1999, p. 37)

Action Research

A culture or professional inquiry is advanced at LEYF through action research (a full exploration of action research at LEYF is offered in Cuttler and Corlett's chapter in this volume). The LEYF pedagogical leader is encouraged to develop an action research plan in response to thoughtful questions posed by them or elicited from colleagues. Pedagogical leaders can lead the process by shaping the research through questions such as:

- What do we know already?
- What theory do we use to inform what we do?
- How does it work for the children, families and communities?
- What don't we understand?
- What research have we done on the matter?
- What have others learned from their investigation?

Research is both specific and broad. For example, one pedagogical leader coached the staff in the Baby Room to consider whether the routine was sensitive and flexible enough to balance staff worries about health and safety with the sense of fun and risk babies need to develop. The result included a set of observations, interviews and professional reflections which led to changes to the environment and some practice improvements that resulted in changes to all Baby Rooms across the organisation.

A similar piece of research was led by another pedagogical leader after she read the national findings about white working-class boys not doing well in education (Impetus-Pef, 2014). She responded by looking at the LEYF cohort tracking data and discussed the findings with all the deputies across the organisation. The result was that every nursery examined their tracking data of boys and found that while they were progressing well against the baseline in most areas, they were below in maths. The result was an organisation action research project, called Boys Outside which looked at how we could improve how we taught maths to boys. We focused particularly on the outdoors given the research on how boys can learn better outdoors. The results led to a marked improvement in the children's mathematical confidence and in the staff's ability to extend and differentiate more successfully, as well as a positive acceptance of the power of action research in delivering a rich pedagogy.

> At LEYF, there is no emphasis on hierarchy and this is evident when observing the relationships between staff and their management teams – this enables the

learning to take place at a deeper level making my pedagogical leadership more credible and effective. An apprentice is as much of a pedagogical leader as the manager but we all possess different strengths. Across LEYF, we have a shared vision of the child at the centre of all decision making which meant I could lead research with people from all across the organisation towards a shared common goal.

(LEYF Teacher)

Driving action research requires an understanding of the cycle of change. Pedagogical leaders need to be willing to investigate, observe and question, find a means of being comfortable with uncertainty and open to new ideas. Therefore, pedagogical leaders need to be able to apply the theory of change with all the behavioural change patterns if and when they want to promote changes to drive learning with quality outcomes at its heart (the relevance of change management models for pedagogical leadership is explored more fully in Perkin's chapter in this volume). Every new idea and every conversation may result in a change, however small. Good pedagogical leaders lead change by understanding it, explaining it and applying the changes fairly and reliably.

Conclusion

From the research at LEYF it has become clearer to me that there are seven important tasks that the pedagogical leader needs to do. These are:

- Be able to articulate the pedagogy of the setting with confidence and use the language of how we teach ECE with assurance.
- Be great teachers themselves, constantly seeking to develop their practice through further professional development and open-minded inquiry.
- Support other colleagues to improve their practice through coaching formally and informally.
- Engage others in deep pedagogical conversations that are transformative.
- Lead and partner with other colleagues to improve practice through action research.
- Put action research central to the work of the pedagogical leader as a means of improving reflective practice and driving a cycle of continuous improvement.
- Be prepared to engage in exploring the importance of practice with academic colleagues to develop stronger and more collegiate understanding.

There remains a need for a clear national vision for a highly professional and qualified ECE workforce with the capacity to provide quality ECE to every child. We must focus on extending both organisational and pedagogical leadership skills in a more systematic way, with the top priority being a coherent career progression pathway for ECE professionals.

References

Anders, Y. (2015) *Literature Review on Pedagogy*. Paris: OECD.

Boe, M., & Hognestad, K. (2017) Directing and Facilitating Distributed Pedagogical Leadership: Best Practices in Early Childhood Education. *International Journal of Leadership in Education*, 20(2), 133–148.

Bruner, J. (1983) *Child's Talk*. Oxford: Oxford University Press.

Freire, P. (1970) *Pedagogy of the Oppressed*. London: Bloomsbury.

Goffee, R., & Jones, G. (2006) *Why Should Anyone Be Led by You? What It Takes to Be an Authentic Leader"* Boston, MA: Harvard Business School Press.

Harrison, L., & Ungerer, J. (2005) *What can the Longitudinal Study of Australian Children Tell Us about Infants' and 4 to 5 Year Olds' Experiences of Early Childhood Education and Care?* Australian Institute of Family Studies. Family Matters No.72 Summer 2005. https://impetus.org.uk/assets/publications/Report/Impetus-PEF_Digging-Deeper1_June_2014.pdf

Impetus PEF (2014) *Digging Deeper: Why White Working Class Boys Underachieve and What Can Be Done About It*. Available at: https://www.impetus.org.uk/assets/publications/Report/Impetus-PEF_Digging-Deeper1_June_2014.pdf (Accessed July 2021).

Horgan, G. (2007) *The Impact of Poverty on Young Children's Experience of School*. Available at: https://www.jrf.org.uk/report/impact-poverty-young-childrens-experience-school (Accessed 27 February 2021).

Kline, N. (1999) *Time to Think*. London: Ward Lock, Cassell Illustrated.

Knudsen, E. (2004) Sensitive Periods in the Development of the Brain and Behavior. *Journal of Cognitive Neuroscience*, 16(8), 1412–1425. https://doi.org/10.1162/0898929042304796.

Litjens, I., & Taguma, M. (2010) —*Revised Literature Overview for the 7th Meeting of the Network on Early Childhood Education and Care*‖. Paris: OECD.

Male, T., & Palaiologou, I. (2015) Pedagogical Leadership in the 21st Century: Evidence from the Field. *Educational Management, Administration and Leadership*, 43(2), 214–231.

Moyles, J., Adams, S., & Musgrove, A. (2002) *SPEEL: Study of Pedagogical Effectiveness in Early Learning*. London: Department for Education and Skills.

Oakeshott, M. (1972) Education: The Engagement and Its Frustration. In Fuller, T. (ed.) (1989) *The Voice of Liberal Learning*. New Haven, CT and London: Yale University Press.

OECD (2012) *Starting Strong 111: A Quality Toolbox for Early Childhood Education and Care*. Paris: OECD Publishing.

OECD (2015) *Early Childhood Education and Care Pedagogy Review*. England: OECD.

O'Sullivan, J. (2018) Extending Practice: The Role of Early Childhood Services in Family Support. In Miller, L., Cameron, C., Dalli, C., & Barbour, N. (eds), *The SAGE Handbook of Early Childhood Policy*. London, pp. 321–339.

Pascal, C., & T. Bertram. (2002) *Early Years Education: An International Perspective*. Qualifications and Curriculum Authority.

Putnam, R. D. (2000) *Better Together*. New York: Simon & Schuster.

Rogoff, B. (2003) *The Cultural Nature of Human Development*. Oxford: Oxford University Press.

Shonkoff, J., & Phillips, D. (2000) *From Neurons to Neighborhoods: The Science of Early Childhood Development*. Washington, D.C.: National Academies Press.

Simpson, D. (June 2015) *A UK–US Investigation of Early Years Practitioners' Opinions about Child Poverty. Teesside University*. Retrieved August 2017 from https://www.tees.ac.uk/docs/DocRepo/.../Simpson%20 report.pdf

Stephen, C. (2010) Pedagogy: The Silent Partner in Early Years Learning. *Early Years*, 30(1), 1–14.

Sutton, L., Smith, N., Dearden, C., & Middleton, S. (2007) *A Child's-Eye View of Social Difference*. York: Joseph Rowntree Foundation. Available at: file:///C:Users/mona5/Downloads/2007-children-inequality-opinion.pdf (Accessed 27 February 2022).

Sylva, K. et al. (2004) *The Effective Provision of Pre-School Education (EPPE) Project: Final Report; A longitudinal; Study funded by DfES 1997–2004*. London: Institute of Education, University of London/Department for Education and Skills/SureStart.

Waniganayake, M., Cheeseman, S., Fenech, M., Hadley, F., & Shepard, W. (2017) *Leadership Contexts and Complexities in Early Childhood Education*. Sydney NSW: Oxford University Press.

Zeldin, T. (1998) *Conversation: How Talk Can Change Your Life*. London: Harvill Press.

Trauma-responsive Pedagogical Leadership in ECE

What It Is and Why It Matters

Julie Nicholson

Introduction

Children, families and early childhood professionals are living in a world where the risks and realities of experiencing trauma are growing exponentially. Poverty, natural disasters, community violence, racism, child maltreatment, the health pandemic, climate and war-related displacement, among other factors, are creating an urgent need for trauma-responsive early childhood environments. As a result, to be truly effective in supporting children and adults impacted by trauma, pedagogical leadership will increasingly involve learning how to create and sustain early childhood programmes that reduce stress and prevent harm through the implementation of trauma-responsive practices. This chapter outlines what trauma-responsive pedagogical leadership would look like and the rationale that underpins it.

Trauma-informed or Trauma-responsive?

Although the more familiar and commonly used term in professional literature is 'trauma-informed', I prefer the commitment to 'trauma-responsive'. Building awareness of trauma and its impact (to be trauma-informed) is an essential first step, but not sufficient. Pedagogical leaders must go beyond building awareness and understanding of trauma and resilience to apply this knowledge in their everyday leadership practice. To be trauma-responsive is to take intentional actions for positive change including shifting mindsets, beliefs, language, communication and programme policies and practices.

Trauma-responsive leaders create environments that provide young children with stability, safety and caring relationships that buffer their stress and its potential negative impact on their developing brains and bodies. Trauma-sensitive environments are also critical for the early childhood workforce as many have their own trauma histories and are at risk of empathic distress as a result of working with a growing number of children and adults impacted by trauma. Empathic distress refers to a 'strong aversive and self-oriented response to the suffering of others, accompanied by the desire to withdraw from a situation, disconnect from those who are suffering, and adopting depersonalising behaviours in order to protect oneself from excessive negative feelings' (Hofmeyer, Kennedy, & Taylor, 2020, p. 234). Pedagogical leaders can use their knowledge of trauma-responsive practice to create environments that prevent early educators from experiencing empathic distress which will not only benefit the educators' physical and mental health but could also improve workforce morale and job retention.

Central to trauma-responsive practice is an understanding of the neurobiology of stress and trauma and the concept of *state dependent functioning* (Perry, 2020b). State dependent functioning represents the phenomenon that our internal state is continually shifting along an arousal continuum from a state of calm → alert → alarm → fear → terror. Our lower brains are continually receiving input externally (through our senses; what we hear, see, smell, taste) and internally (in our bodies) and monitoring to determine if we are safe or in danger. Anytime our brains perceive a threat, we move up the arousal continuum shifting from a state of calm into a state of alert, alarm, fear or terror.

Three factors are most likely to increase stress for adults and children and move their internal states from calm and alert to fear and terror. First, *novelty*. This describes those events or experiences that are unfamiliar to us and activate our stress-response systems. Secondly, *unpredictability*. This is when we experience a high degree of uncertainty or constant change and our brains cannot make any predictions about what is coming next and our stress is elevated. Thirdly, *a perceived lack of personal agency and control*. This describes the time when we do not feel a sense of control in our lives. Our stress increases significantly, and we are more likely to experience fear and anxiety. Consequently, the foundations of trauma-responsive practice includes consistent, responsive relationships (being in the presence of people we are familiar with and trust buffers stress and helps us feel safe), predictable environments (consistent people and routines reduces uncertainty and helps us feel safe) and opportunities to have agency and control (when individuals perceive that they have opportunities to influence the conditions in their lives – having 'voice and choice' – their feelings of stress and trauma are reduced).

Pedagogical leaders who understand trauma-responsive practice recognise the power of mirror neurons and that both stress and calmness are contagious. Human beings are neurobiologically wired to be relational and we absorb the emotions of the people around us. Because of cells called mirror neurons, we are instinctively and unconsciously able to understand what another person is feeling or experiencing (Acharya & Shukla, 2012; Conkbayir, 2017). It is our mirror neuronal system that allows us to empathise with the feelings of anxious, distressed, excited, jubilant and mourning parents, colleagues and children. Our emotional state is 'mirrored' by the neuronal systems of others with whom we are interacting and the same is true in reverse. The mirror system of one person alters their emotional and physical state to match the emotional and physical state of the person with whom they are interacting. An example of this is when we see someone crying and feel sad knowing that they are hurting, or we sense someone is stressed and this creates our own feeling of internal distress or the spontaneous way we smile when we see a baby smiling at us. This process of taking-in another's emotional state happens at a subconscious level, which means individuals are neither aware of this process nor in control of it.

> I talk to my staff about being a mirror. I am basically saying when someone comes at you with a lot of escalated energy, we don't want to absorb that energy but instead, if we stay calm, they will then begin to absorb that calm. In this way, we can lead them to more regulation rather than dysregulation.
> Drew Giles, director of Educator Programs, Franklin-McKinley School District at Educare, Silicon Valley

Connecting this understanding of mirror neurons with state dependent functioning, pedagogical leaders understand that as the internal state of one person shifts up and down the arousal continuum (calm → alarm; terror → alert), others around them are likely to find their arousal levels shifting too. Therefore, trauma-responsive pedagogical leaders are keen observers, continually aware of shifts in their own and others' emotional states and behaviour as these are valuable signals about how they feel and what they need.

Leading When the Cortex Is/Is Not 'Open for Business'

When staff, parents, family members or other adults are calm and regulated, have their basic needs met (e.g. they are not hungry or thirsty, too hot or cold), are not multi-tasking or managing significant demands on their attention and are in familiar environments where they feel a sense of safety and belonging with people they trust, they are capable of engaging the full range of their cognitive reasoning and capabilities. They have their cortex, as Bruce Perry describes, 'open for business' (Perry, 2020b). When pedagogical leaders guide and support individuals and teams to be in a calm and regulated state of arousal they will be able to:

- Reflect on their beliefs, behaviours, intentions and impact.
- Identify their sensations (physiological bodily responses to stress) and emotions.
- Think abstractly, logically and creatively.
- Learn and retain new information.
- Relate to time in complex ways (e.g. they can think about the here and now as well as think back historically and dream into the future).
- Consider different perspectives, solutions and ideas when thinking through how to solve a problem or address a complex situation.
- Self-regulate strong emotions and behaviour.
- Act in alignment with their own or the programme's values and/or mission.
- Consider the consequences of one's beliefs, decisions and/or behaviours.

Many of these cognitive functions are needed to be responsive, attuned and effective early childhood professionals. If pedagogical leaders want to reflect on an interaction they had with a child, they need their cortex fully online and engaged. If directors want their staff members to learn a new social emotional curriculum or if educators are discussing the benefits and drawbacks of adopting a new enrolment policy, pedagogical leaders can use their knowledge of trauma-responsive practice to create the conditions that support thoughtful, intentional and effective professional learning and decision-making for themselves and their colleagues.

When our brains detect information that could be a potential threat to our safety (e.g. we are cold or hungry in the presence of an unfamiliar person or environment), the body's stress-response system is activated and a chain reaction of survival responses are automatically triggered in our bodies (e.g. heart starts racing, pupils are dilated and blood is shunted away from the limbs to protect vital organs). These physiological responses impact our thoughts, feelings and behaviours as certain systems in our brains are essentially on while others are turned off (or greatly reduced in their functioning) in order to support our survival. Among the most critical of these shifts for pedagogical leaders to understand is this reality: the greater the perceived threat (whether internal or external), the less access adults will have to their cortex and the more primitive systems will take over in order to prioritise survival.

What will pedagogical leaders observe when adults' stress-response systems are activated and they have less cortical capability? One answer is what Perry (2020b) describes as *state dependent regression* where adults functionally regress, acting less like adults and more and more like young children. State dependent regression looks like adults who are reactive, emotional, anxious and hard to reason with, more sensitive to sound, light and touch and quick to misread the positive intentions of others. Adults whose stress-response systems are activated will find it challenging to focus on time outside of what is happening 'here and now'. Consider the implications of this limitation: How can early childhood professionals improve their professional practice without being able to reflect and consider how they are impacting others? The truth is, they can't. At least not very effectively. So the capacity of pedagogical leaders to respond sensitively to others' perceived threats and the subsequent physiological and emotional responses is vital.

When people and groups are stressed, especially when their stress-response systems are continually activated and scanning the environment for danger, they become emotionally and physically exhausted. It is draining for the brain and body to be vigilant in this internal state of activation and survival. Pedagogical leaders will observe productive employees and dedicated parents and families showing signs of emotional, physical and psychological depletion and fatigue. Their ability to focus and their level of productivity in their jobs will suffer as they struggle to acquire new knowledge and skills and find it challenging to focus on even the most mundane and simple tasks and responsibilities. As stress is increased significantly by novelty, uncertainty and conditions that reduce people's feelings of control, adults whose internal states are higher on the arousal continuum (alarm, fear, terror) will be very unlikely to embrace new initiatives or changes in programme personnel, policies and practices. Maintaining the status quo – even if problematic – is likely to feel safer as it is familiar, predictable and leaves people feeling that they have more agency and control (though this may not actually be the case).

Creating the Conditions That Support Regulation

Given the significant impact on adults' functioning when their stress-response systems are activated and the reality that a high percentage of adults and children experience toxic stress and trauma, what intentional actions for positive change should early childhood pedagogical leaders take? To align teaching and caring practice with the core values and ethical responsibilities at the centre of the early childhood profession – such as reflection, inquiry, humility, attunement, respect, partnership, responsivity, continuous learning and improvement – adults need to be regulated and have access to their cortex. Therefore, it is critical that pedagogical leaders learn the different pathways to regulation. That is, the strategies adults (and children) can use to shift their internal state by reducing their stress and decreasing the factors that increase perceptions of threat both internally (in their bodies) and externally (in the environment). *Trauma-responsive pedagogical leaders adopt and live by a mantra, 'the key to attuned, responsive, equitable and high quality practice is regulation.'*

What are the pathways to regulation and how can pedagogical leaders integrate them into early childhood programmes? Perry (2020a) describes four main pathways to shift state dependent functioning from an aroused and activated state (alarm, fear and terror) to a more regulated state of calm and/or alert. The four pathways are relational regulation plus top-down regulation, bottom-up regulation and dissociative (intentional disconnection) regulation.

Because of our relational neurobiology, that is, the ways in which our brains have evolved to be wired for social connection (Perry & Szalavitz, 2011), relational regulation is the most powerful pathway to buffer stress and guide people back to a state of calm. Adults and children feel safest when they are with others with whom they experience mutual feelings of care and respect and who provide them with a sense of authentic belonging. Being in the presence of others we care for, love and respect significantly increases our ability to tolerate and manage adversity, to cope and build resilience as well as to heal from the impact of trauma. The reverse is also true: when people are in environments where they do not feel respected, cared for, or have a sense of belonging and support, they are more vulnerable to the negative impacts of stressors and less likely to build resilience and heal from trauma. Pedagogical leaders who use relational pathways to regulate children and adults:

- Take time for connections and personal check ins during staff meetings instead of rushing right into 'business'.

In our staff and leadership meetings, we start with connectors so we can learn about each other. Our staff find these motivating because it allows them to slowly switch gears and mindfully transition into the meeting . . . it's a great way to build those relationships and really be present with one another. And then, at the end of our meetings we have time to do 'Aha's, appreciations and apologies so that staff have a safe place where they can connect, share and/or apologise to one another in our leadership group or in our teaching group. We're not just doing the celebrations – the appreciations and the 'Aha's, but also creating a safe place for people to feel like they can apologise because we are human and sometimes we reflect on our reactions and realise they might not have been what we wanted or intended them to be. I want them to know that they don't have to let these things steam and fizzle. We can talk about them together and then move on. (Director of Educator Programs, Franklin-McKinley School District at Educare, Silicon Valley)

- Take time for brief and regular connections with people they trust and respect throughout the day to regulate themselves and others. These connections can be as short as sending a brief text, email or popping their head in someone's office to wave hello. They encourage colleagues to bring photos of loved ones (people and animals) to work and make a habit of pulling them out to look at (even if only for a few seconds) when sensing signs of stress as just seeing their faces will create a calming effect in their body.

I have to say, you know, me and Kristina and I are constantly texting and checking in with each other, that really, really helped me just to have that, that beyond supervisor supervisee relationship, that trust. And I think that the level of collaboration, the level of trust that we both have and respect, we both have for each other, we hold each other up. (Mitchell Ha, assistant program director, Hayward Unified School District Early Learning Program)

- Bear witness to people's worries and concerns. They create spaces to listen to others without jumping in to try to 'fix' the problem. They understand that often just being present with someone and allowing them time and space to talk about their fears or worries or just to metabolise a stressful experience (e.g. letting them cry and 'feel' or process big emotions) reduces their stress and decreases their feelings of isolation.

One of my Family Advocates called and texted me repeatedly that the mom she supports just told her she was experiencing domestic violence. I could tell she was worried and feeling dysregulated and needing support and guidance. I called her immediately reassuring her I am here for her and we will work on this together. When we talked it was so important that I let her unload her worries, thoughts, feelings. I could feel the steam of built-up tension slowly dissipating as we talked. As she calmed, I slowly began to ask questions such as, 'Is mom safe, does she have a plan, what community resources can we think of that might support her?' Together we came up with a comprehensive support plan to keep mom and her child safe, to connect her to community resources and to ensure she has the emotional support she needs. (Rhonda Paxton, preschool site supervisor)

- Put people first. They communicate to staff, families and community partners that they are never too busy to connect with them, that people, relationships and connection are their top priorities.

People need to realise that it doesn't matter what position you're in within an organisation. You have to see and put people first and you have to take a pause and really listen to people and what they need. People always say, 'Oh, I know you're super busy. I don't want to bother you.' But we set the tone from the beginning that we are never busy enough that we cannot stop. Paperwork can wait, you can't. Take a pause and really put people first. (Kristina Adams, program director, and Mitchell Ha, assistant program director, Hayward Unified School District Early Learning Program)

Top-down Approaches to Regulation: 'Using Your Cortex (Thoughts) to Regulate and Calm'

One of the pathways to regulation that calms an activated stress-response system is a 'top-down' approach. This pathway reduces stress through calming thoughts. For example, telling yourself that you are safe, that you can manage something stressful, that you may feel scared or perceive you are in danger but in reality, you soothe yourself with reminders that you are *actually* safe. Top-down strategies engage the cortex – our thinking and reasoning – to de-escalate stress and return people to a state of calm. Top-down strategies are useful for the pedagogical leader's toolbox in some contexts. However, the fact that they require the 'cortex to be open for business' means that they are not a realistic or effective approach when someone's internal state is already activated at the level of alarm, fear or terror. Once a child or adult is already dysregulated and primitive brain systems have activated a comprehensive survival response, top-down regulation strategies are not recommended because they are not as effective as other pathways. Pedagogical leaders who use top-down regulation strategies guide children and adults to:

- Think of 'grounders' (people, places, objects, activities or locations that they associate with safety, belonging and calm) whenever they feel their stress-response systems activated. Using grounders provides people with agency and control by giving them something they can do if they start to feel their stress-response activated.
- Think through different solutions (and the benefits and limitations associated with each) to a challenge or problem. This reduces uncertainty and provides them with feelings of agency and control as they see 'options' for acting to address the problem.
- Share encouraging mantras, sayings or affirmations at team meetings or write them on signs and post in appropriate places throughout the programme ('You got this!', 'This too shall pass!', 'QTIP: Quit taking it personally'). In essence these sayings support people to feel less alone and to remember that they have strengths, coping skills and forms of resilience that have always helped them manage adversity and will continue doing so.
- Reframe critical self-talk and distorted thinking patterns. For example, shifting a thought from, 'This is the end of the world.' to 'This is just a moment in time. We can get through this.' This final example is the essence of Cognitive Behavioural Therapeutic approaches that help people disrupt mind loops of negative thinking that are more likely to occur in conditions of stress when the brain and body perceives threat and filters all communication and behaviour through this lens.

Bottom-up Approaches to Regulation: 'Using Patterned Repetitive Somato-sensory Activities to Regulate and Calm'

Bottom-up approaches are the most effective and direct way of regulating an activated stress-response system (Perry, 2020a). Bottom-up approaches are efficient regulatory strategies as they directly reach the parts of our brain responsible for calming and regulation. Repetitive, somato- (i.e. movement) sensory (sight/sound/touch etc.) activities activate the brain's core regulatory networks and help people calm their stress-response systems when activated.

Pedagogical leaders can use *Bottom-Up* regulation strategies to quickly and efficiently increase feelings of calm and regulation for children and adults. Repetitive somato-sensory activities can be integrated into early learning programmes to support young children throughout the day or at stressful times for children with histories of trauma (e.g. transitions, naptime, drop-off and pick-up). They can also be used to support adults' regulation by integrating them into short breaks throughout meetings and trainings or when people are working on complex tasks. They can help 'open the cortex' just before a high-stakes decision is made, or bring people back to calm during an emotional or difficult conversation and/or interactions.

Somoto-sensory activities are important tools for pedagogical leaders who can use them to reduce stress and increase people's cognitive capacities including their attention, logical thinking, reflective capabilities and empathy. And the good news is that these activities can calm and regulate children and adults in a short amount of time (listening to thirty seconds of music, taking five deep breaths, stretching or walking briskly outside for five minutes during a break). Examples of Bottom-Up regulation strategies include:

- Rocking back and forth (in a rocking chair or while standing or sitting in place);
- Walking or running (e.g. brief walks at a break to get fresh air);
- Swimming and riding a bike or tricycle;
- Jumping (e.g. on a trampoline or in place);
- Petting a dog or other pets and animals;
- Listening to music, dancing, singing, chanting or humming;
- Taking deep breaths and doing breathing exercises;
- Stretching, yoga, Tai Chi or Qi Gong;
- Drumming and rhythmic use of musical instruments;
- Mindfulness activities.

Dissociative Approaches to Regulation: 'Proactive Intentional Disengagement to Regulate and Calm' (Perry, 2020a)

Dissociative approaches to regulation are the most common way that people regulate and calm themselves when impacted by stress. Although dissociation is often associated with mental health challenges and a protective response for individuals impacted by trauma, this usage is referring to a more universal process we all experience in our brains (although we are often not consciously aware of it happening). Dissociative pathways to regulation happen when the brain has a momentary withdrawal from a focus on the external (outside) world to instead, tune inward. Taking a momentary break from all the stimulation and sensory input entering the brain has the effect of reducing stress for the individual. During these dissociative moments, people may find that time seems frozen, their feelings of hunger, tiredness or pain are no longer in their conscious awareness, they might even feel like they are 'observing' themselves in a manner that can feel like watching a movie of their own life (The Child Trauma Academy, 2011, p. 4). Pedagogical leaders can work with adults and children to teach them about this pathway to regulation or model what these strategies look like in practice. Examples of Dissociative or Intentional Disengagement Regulation strategies include:

- Daydreaming or mind-wandering (create opportunities for children and adults to wander a school garden while engaging all their senses, play soothing classical music during a 'brain break' for five minutes to support mind-wandering in the middle of a long meeting);
- Disengaging/tuning out for brief moments while engaging in a task/meeting/interaction/class and so on (e.g. reduce the amount of time devoted to lecturing or 'talking at' people and increase time for engagement and interaction to reduce the frequency of people's brain's intentional disengagement);
- Guided imagery.

  Let's go on a journey together in thinking about our dream early learning programme that is adequately funded and resourced: Imagine you are employed at Sunshine and Stars child-care programme. Staff in this centre are attuned to the needs of children, families and their fellow educators. The philosophy and core values places the collective community at the heart of programme outcomes and the environment is healing centred. All classrooms are able to freely select from the top notch state of the art vendors when enriching the indoor/outdoor environment whose play materials are both trauma-sensitive and culturally responsive to the children served in the programme. The program has its own internal substitute pool so educators are able to easily schedule vacations and medical appointments knowing classroom coverage is not a concern. Continuous program quality improvement focuses on educator voice in all decision-making. Educators and families serve on the Senior Leadership Team to inform programmatic goals, fiscal stewardship, organisational operations, as well as family and community supports. What thoughts come to mind imagining working in this environment? What feelings? (Nicholson, Kurtz, Leland, Wesley, & Nadiv in press).

- Prayer, chanting, meditation and self-hypnosis

  I start my mornings with a quiet meditation, a practice I began as a child inspired by my family's cultural practices as citizens of the Cree and Cherokee nations. I have prayer points that I pray on every single day. I pray for the world, I pray for things that come up in the news, I pray for my family, I pray for my work family and my colleagues. I begin those prayers with a gratitude prayer, and thank you, and an affirmation that the day is going to be good, that there will be blessings in the day. – (Karen Tapia, director, California Early Childhood Mentor Program; Nicholson et al., 2019)

Trauma-responsive Pedagogical Leadership in Early Childhood: Buffering the Impact of Stress and Trauma by Creating Environments That Regulate and Calm

Drawing upon knowledge of the neurobiology of stress, state dependent functioning and pathways that support stress reduction and regulation, pedagogical leaders in early childhood can create environments that buffer stress and support children, families and the workforce serving them to feel safe, supported and regulated. In a world where the risks and realities of experiencing trauma are growing quickly, advancing pedagogical leadership and the understanding and implementation of trauma-responsive policies and practices in early childhood environments is important. Key to pedagogical leadership is the capacity to regulate yourself and support others to regulate themselves. Greater levels of regulation in turn provide a foundation for the healthy attachments, risk-taking, engagement, empathy and joy that characterise thriving centres of ECE.

References

Acharya, S., & Shukla, S. (2012). Mirror neurons: Enigma of the metaphysical modular brain. *Journal of Natural Science, Biology and Medicine*, 3(2), pp. 118–124. Doi: 10.4103/0976-9668.101878.

Aguilar, E (2018). *Onward: Cultivating Emotional Resilience in Educators*. San Francisco, CA: Jossey Bass.

Bethell, C., Davis, M., Gombojav, N., Stumbo, S., & Powers, K. (2017). *Issue Brief: A National and across State Profile on Adverse Childhood Experiences among Children and Possibilities to Heal and Thrive*. Johns Hopkins Bloomberg School of Public Health. Retrieved from https://www.cahmi.org/wp-content/uploads/2018/05/aces_brief_final.pdf

Brandt, K. (2020). *Reflective Supervision*. Bruce Perry office hours. Retrieved from https://vimeo.com/406307258

Child Trauma Academy Staff (2011). *Neurosequential Model of Therapeutics: Clinical Practice Tools*. Retrieved from https://www.comtrea.org/files/users/melaniecole/ChildTraumaAcademyClinicalPracticeTools-Psychoeducation.pdf

Conkbayier, M. (2017). *Early Childhood and Neuroscience: Theory, Research and Implications for Practice*. New York: Bloomsbury Academic.

Hofmeyer, A., Kennedy, K., & Taylor, R. (2020). Contesting the term 'compassion fatigue': Integrating findings from social neuroscience and self-care research. Collegian, *27*, 232–237.

Nicholson, J., Driscoll, P., Kurtz, J., Wesley, L., & Benitez, D. (2019). *Culturally Responsive Self-Care Practices for Early Childhood Educators*. New York: Routledge Press.

Nicholson, J., Kurtz, J., Leland, J., Wesley, L., & Nadiv, S. (in press). *Trauma-Responsive Practices for Early Childhood Leaders: Creating and Sustaining Healing Engaged Organizations*. New York: Routledge.

Perry B. (2020a). *Understanding Regulation. NN COVID Series 5*. Retrieved from https://youtu.be/L3qIYGwmHYY

Perry B. (2020b). *Understanding State Dependent Functioning. NN COVID Series 2*. Retrieved from https://youtu.be/PZg1dlskBLA

Perry, B., & Szalavitz, M. (2011). *Born for Love: Why Empathy Is Essential and Endangered*. New York: Harper Collins.

Resick, P.A., Monson, C.M., & Chard, K.M. (2017). *Cognitive Processing Therapy: A Comprehensive Manual*. New York: Guilford Press.

Thomas, M.S., Crosby, S., & Vanderhaar, J. (2019). Trauma-informed practices in schools across two decades: An interdisciplinary review of research. *Review of Research in Education*, *43*, 422–452.

5

Pedagogical Leadership in Practice with Babies

Mandy Cuttler

Introduction

Research clearly demonstrates a correlation between pedagogical leadership and high-quality learning experiences for children, ultimately impacting on children's outcomes (Siraj-Blatchford and Manni, 2008). However, there is a lack of clarity as to what comprises effective pedagogical leadership. Leadership in early childhood education (ECE) is complex. O'Sullivan (2015) explains that there is no clear definition of leadership, emphasising that 'the current leadership debate highlights the complexity of the role, which in turn reflects the complexity of the sector' (O'Sullivan, 2015, p. 3). This is also reflected by the Ofsted Early Years Inspection Handbook (2019) used by settings in England which outlines eleven criteria leaders must meet to be judged 'Outstanding', incorporating engagement with children, engagement with parents, support for staff development, support for staff well-being, management of resources and adherence to statutory responsibilities. Within this context, research on the theoretical underpinnings and practical application of pedagogical leadership in the Baby Room of ECE settings is notable by its absence. The exclusion of children in this age group from discussions about ECE practice is not a new phenomenon. Baby Room professionals have long felt as though their work is invisible or less highly valued than that of their colleagues working with older children (Goouch and Powell, 2013).

This chapter aims to consider this further by exploring pedagogical leadership in the context of the Baby Room. The term 'baby' will be used to refer to children below the age of two. I will consider (1) the lack of appreciation for the complexities of pedagogical leadership within baby provision, and how this does a disservice to our Baby Room professionals and children, (2) what pedagogical leadership with babies looks like in practice and (3) how pedagogical leadership with babies can be advanced.

Pedagogical Leadership with Babies: The Missing Story

Despite the fact that 35 per cent of children under two receive formal childcare in England (Department of Education, 2019), there is little literature considering pedagogical leadership in the context of under twos provision. Working with babies requires a specific knowledge base and skill set, and therefore requires a particularly thoughtful consideration of pedagogy and subsequently pedagogical leadership. In their first two years of life, young children's rate of development is staggering; they learn new skills, the architecture of the brain develops rapidly, and they begin to learn about themselves and the world around them. Yet, ECE remains beset with unhelpful distinctions drawn between care and education, and nowhere is this more prevalent than in work with babies. It often follows that 'education' is associated only with older children and 'care' with the youngest. Shin (2015) argues that referring to professionals working with babies as 'caregivers' contributes to an underappreciation of professionalism in the Baby Room:

> Care is often times situated in the affective domain and involves feelings, emotions, and personal traits that early childhood practitioners should possess, rather than intellectual acts they should perform. The commonly held 'gentle smiles and warm hugs' view of caring fails to capture the complex and challenging aspects of our work and undermines the pedagogical approach to teaching and the intellectual aspect of caring.
>
> (Shin, 2015, p.497).

Although this perspective is understandable, and further research indicates that Baby Room professionals themselves feel as though they are viewed as carers rather than educators (Goouch and Powell, 2013), it is undeniable that work with very young children incorporates an element of caregiving. Work with young children should absolutely be situated in the affective domain, as the development of young children is dependent on attachments formed with nurturing, tuned in and responsive caregivers. Shin (2015) marries the need for work with young children to be considered as both caring and pedagogical through advocating 'a pedagogy of care'. Her research outlines that caring is 'both an emotional and intellectual act' (p. 505) and demonstrates that caring experiences are also learning experiences, while learning experiences are enhanced by a caring approach.

Consider the nappy changing procedure, mealtimes or an adult reading a book with a baby. All of these are caring processes and must be carried out with nurture which is responsive and attuned to the babies' needs. These are also learning experiences. The approach to working with babies, including the carrying out of care routines, should be informed by pedagogical values. Our pedagogical approach must be based on our view of the child. A caring pedagogy which views young children as active participants in their environment with rights and agency will be evident in both the approach to caregiving and the experiences offered to children. In practice this may be enacted through a nappy changing process that invites active participation from children and learning experiences that are aligned with the interests of the children. When we view caring experiences through a pedagogical lens and learning experiences through a caring lens, it becomes apparent that care and learning cannot be considered separately.

Although it is clear that a pedagogy of care must be centred on the building of relationships between babies and adults, an analysis of the available literature reveals conflicting perspectives on the nature of these relationships. Page (2015) found that some professionals strived to form relationships with children characterised by a parental type of love, while others responded that they did not feel a substitute parental relationship to be appropriate. Additionally, this study found that a significant proportion of ECE professionals were reluctant to show physical affection towards the children due to concerns about how this would be perceived. This finding demonstrates an insecurity among professionals who work with babies in ECE about both the nature of their role and the interactions that comprise their day-to-day experiences. This lack of clarity is demoralising, disempowering and needs to be resolved by building a collaborative vision of pedagogical leadership for working with babies and understanding what this looks like in action in the Baby Room. The following section describes an emerging vision of pedagogical leadership with babies and the principles underpinning this. It is offered as a starting point for more explicit dialogues about the nature of Baby Room pedagogical leadership.

Building a Vision of Pedagogical Leadership with Babies

The Sound Foundations report (Mathers et al., 2014) presents an overview of research on what constitutes high-quality early years provision for children under three. In this report three areas of pedagogical practice are highlighted to be particularly important in supporting the development of the youngest children:

> Play-based activities and routines which allow children to take the lead in their own learning, support for language and communication and opportunities to move and be physically active.
>
> (Mathers et al., 2014, p.16)

It is long established that play is the most appropriate way to support the holistic learning and development of young children. However, it is reasonable to assume that the nature of the play experiences offered to the youngest children will differ from those offered to older children.

Mathers et al. (2014) outline two forms of play which are particularly supportive of young children's development: the first of which is 'floor-based play'. This is play which enables children to use their senses to investigate objects in their environment. A nursery environment that provides free access to resources through the use of low-level shelves and where children are freely able to move around is one which supports floor-based play. Mathers et al. (2014) also emphasise the importance of symbolic play, in which children – typically during the second year of life – begin to experiment with representing the world around them and their everyday experiences. They might use objects around them to represent other things (e.g. a banana becomes a telephone) and enact activities that they typically see (e.g. adults talking on the phone). Mathers et al. (2014) suggest that symbolic play may be the foundation for children's emerging private speech – or 'self-directive talk' to use Vygotsky's term – that can then be used for problem-solving and self-regulation. Such private speech is the basis for the development of more complex thinking and communication.

It is clear that the pedagogical approach adopted when working with babies must be thoughtfully considered. An environment lacking pedagogical leadership could become one where the experiences offered to the youngest children are not considered more deeply than meeting their basic physical needs. This would deprive children of the benefits listed earlier, the opportunity to engage in symbolic play, to engage in repeated activities which support cognitive development and to explore a range of sensorially stimulating resources. This deep consideration of pedagogical practice with babies has the additional benefit of creating a virtuous cycle. Where we critically reflect on our pedagogical practices with babies, we deepen our understanding of how young children learn. Based on this we adapt our approach, reflect on the impact of this and repeat the cycle.

The second element highlighted by Mathers et al. (2014) is support for language and communication. Considering this from a pedagogical perspective also opens up possibilities which will ultimately have a positive impact on the development of our youngest children. It is well established that reciprocal interactions are central to children's developing language skills, (Whitehead, 2010). If we consider language merely as a means to an end, we might limit our interactions with children to that which is necessary to achieving an objective. A pedagogy that is rich in language emphasises the benefits of reciprocal interactions and encourages professionals to provide a narrative for young children's activities that will ultimately have a positive impact on their communication development. This is supported by the findings of the National Institute of Child Health and Human Development (NICHD) that the language support provided by professionals during children's first year correlated with their cognitive and language skills at fifteen, twenty-four and thirty-six months (Huntsman, 2008).

Mathers et al. (2014) also emphasise the importance of supporting young children's physical development through enabling them to play on the floor, crawling, rolling, pulling up and having 'tummy time'. Once babies start walking, they can begin to experiment with more gross motor physical skills including running, jumping and hopping. When considering how to facilitate such explorations, the pedagogical leader must consider how they strike a balance between providing physical support and enabling children to take physical risks. The following is an example of how this balance can be achieved:

Six babies and two ECE professionals are on an outing to the local park, where it has been raining. One of the children puts his foot on the bottom of a grassy hill then stops, making eye contact with his keyperson. The keyperson approaches the child and asks if he would like to go up the hill. He nods and the adult encourages him to proceed, reassuring him that she is close by. He resumes walking up the hill cautiously, looking back at the adult several times. Each time she smiles and praises his efforts. While he is walking up the hill the adult remains close to him but does not provide physical assistance. Halfway up the hill the child stops abruptly. The adult asks if he needs help and he nods in response, so the keyperson takes his hand and together they walk to the top of the hill.

Here we can see that the professional is actively encouraging the child to take a risk and challenge his physical skills, while remaining close to ensure he feels emotionally and physically safe. When later discussing this interaction, she emphasised that he was on a grassy hill and the likelihood of him becoming hurt was minimal considering both the soft surface and her proximity. It is worth noting that it is not solely the environment that provides the child with the opportunity and confidence to challenge himself, the bond with his keyperson plays a central role.

Enabling babies to make smaller movements, such as reaching for objects, pulling them closer and orienting the body and the head are also essential. It is vital that children explore these movements in a range of environments both indoors and outdoors. Professionals are sometimes reluctant to provide very young children with opportunities to explore the outdoor environment, particularly in cold or wet weather conditions. However, being outside provides children with a range of sensory experiences that cannot be replicated indoors. These include rolling, touching and stretching on different terrains; feeling the rain on their faces; feeling the wind in their hair; listening to trees rustling in the wind; and grasping flowers and blades of grass. Adopting an approach which enables young children to have these opportunities necessitates pedagogical leadership which facilitates a shared understanding of their importance. Very young children often spend large amounts of time in car seats, buggies, slings and play pens, rather than on the floor freely exploring or moving themselves around as much as possible. An approach informed by pedagogical understanding will result in a room layout which provides children with ample floor space to crawl, roll and stretch, furniture placement which provides support for children who are cruising and learning to take steps independently and a shared understanding of the value of outdoor play in all weathers.

Another consideration is the stability of care. Debate on the appropriateness of group care for babies is ongoing; however, what is clear is that the importance of forming attachments with consistent adults cannot be overestimated.

> available studies all support the conclusion that instability of care can negatively affect children's socio-emotional and language development, the security of their attachments with caregivers and their interactions with peers.
>
> (Mathers et al., 2014, p.18)

In English ECE settings it is a requirement of the early years foundation stage (EYFS) (Department for Education, 2017) that all children have a keyperson, to provide them with a secure relationship and ensure their care is tailored to their individual needs. Yet too often the role of the keyperson is seen as predominantly involving the completion of observations, assessments and other administrative duties. Consideration of the rationale of the keyperson approach from a pedagogical rather than operational perspective highlights the seminal role this person plays in the development of young children. This will inform the structural approach to putting this into practice, for example with time set aside for keypeople to spend one-to-one time with their children. Such an approach is crucial, as Jarvis (2020) explains that the quality of the attachment between a young child and their main carers plays a fundamental role in their ongoing emotional development.

A further area where strong pedagogical leadership is crucial is in how we work with parents. The decision to place a child in non-familial care is often an emotionally charged one (Vincent and Ball, 2001) which requires a particularly high level of empathy and sensitivity on the part of the ECE professional. Parents may experience guilt, challenged by the need to return to work due to financial reasons (Moylett, 1997), or worried that that their baby's relationships with adults in the ECE setting will surpass their own (Page, 2011). It is imperative that the pedagogical leader strives to develop a culture which opens dialogue with parents about any anxieties they may have, such as discussing the importance of secondary attachments and reassuring parents that they are irreplaceable. This can also be linked back to earlier discussions about the pedagogical leader's responsibility to look beyond the classroom when considering their approach.

Growing Pedagogical Leadership in the Baby Room

Having established the impact of pedagogically informed practice on the development of our youngest children, the chapter now presents the views of those working with children under the age of two in positions of pedagogical leadership, exploring the ways in which they develop pedagogical leadership in the Baby Room. While writing this chapter, several ECE professionals working in London Early Years Foundation (LEYF) were invited to share their perspectives. Their interpretation of pedagogical leadership was predominantly aligned with the views of Male and Palaiologou (2012, 2015) that pedagogical leadership is complex, multifaceted and goes beyond what happens inside the nursery.

> We have a leadership model which shows how many different elements there are to pedagogical leadership. Leading learning environments, leading your own and others' learning, leading with parents, leading in the community just to name a few. I like that because sometimes we think of the room leader as the person who makes sure the room runs smoothly, which of course is part of it but really oversimplifies the role of the room leader. In the baby room you have to make sure that your team understand how babies learn, the importance of

attachment, how to make sure care routines are respectful and nurturing, how to interpret babies' views, because these issues are not explored enough in the Level 3 qualifications.

(Baby Room leader)

As well as emphasising the multi-layered role of the pedagogical leader, this leader discussed the specific skills and knowledge needed to be an effective Baby Room leader. She also highlighted the inadequacy of current qualifications in equipping professionals with the knowledge and skills to work with babies. This is reflective of Goouch and Powell's (2013) research.

The professional who made the statement earlier dedicates a great deal of time to upskilling her team and favours a coaching approach. When prompted to elaborate on her view about the benefits of adopting a coaching approach she explained:

> For me this is the best approach, as people who work with children should be empowered to take control over their own learning. I can tell my team what they don't know and fill in the gaps, or I can encourage them to identify gaps and fill these themselves. Which approach is most empowering, and will embed their learning more?

Here she makes an interesting point, alluding to the fact that pedagogical leaders need to understand not only how children learn but also how adults learn. This is even more relevant in the case of the Baby Room since adults working in this context are less likely to have specialist knowledge and understanding about babies, because of the disappointingly narrow focus of pre-service training and qualifications. This view is consistent with Coughlin and Baird's (2013) emphasis on the pedagogical leader's role in guiding adults as well as children.

A deputy manager I interviewed discussed the value of pedagogical conversations in supporting her team to become reflective practitioners, which ultimately supports the development of their skills and enhances the quality of their practice:

> How do I teach my team? Through consistent and reflective pedagogical conversations. For example, if they prepare a learning experience for the children we will talk about their rationale for that particular experience, how it includes the children's interests and supports their development, the teaching approaches they will be using and why. It's too easy to fall into the habit of operational rather than pedagogical conversations. Don't ever underestimate the importance of conversation as a teaching exercise!

(deputy manager)

As highlighted here, dialogue is an effective strategy to facilitate critical reflection. Moyles (2002) agrees that dialogue is a valuable tool for encouraging reflective practice, making implicit knowledge explicit and enabling teachers to interrogate their own practice and its theoretical underpinnings.

Having discussed what the role of the pedagogical leader entails, conversation turned to markers of high-quality Baby Room leadership and what this looks like in practice. As previously mentioned, literature explicitly linking pedagogical leadership to practice when working with babies is very limited. However, the professionals whom I spoke to were eloquent about what pedagogical leadership in a Baby Room should look like in practice. A clear vision of pedagogical leadership with babies is a vital step in its development.

> Pedagogical leadership with babies needs to be as reflective and responsive and dynamic as with any other age group. The needs of the children change, therefore so must our approach. We must never do things in a particular way because that's the way it has always been done. We need to be critically reflective, challenge ourselves and our peers and be continually responsive to the needs of the children. But it is different with babies because babies can't tell you verbally what they need, so as a leader it is my role to create a culture where my team understand the importance of knowing their children well and reading their cues.
>
> (Baby Room leader)

> The close bonds between the adults and the children are obvious, just by watching the interactions. Professionals know their children and the children are comfortable with them. The room will include floor space for physical movement and cosy areas for a child to spend one-to-one time with their keyperson. And lots of language. Conversation with babies is so important. Experiences offered will be sensorially stimulating with children given the freedom to explore at a level that is comfortable to them.
>
> (Baby Room leader)

This response is aligned with the emphasis in Mathers et al. (2014) on play experiences, communication and physical development opportunities.

The issue of working with parents was raised too and one professional was very clear about her responsibilities to include parents in the learning environment and pedagogical approach.

> As the leader you need to make sure that your team understand the weight of the decision to use childcare, and role model sensitivity towards the parents. If a parent calls 10 times a day whilst they are building a relationship with us, we

must not dismiss them as an overly anxious parent but understand that they are seeking reassurance that they have chosen the right people to trust with the most important little person in their whole world. It is important that they feel as though they are as much a part of the nursery community as their child. This is a key part of our pedagogy; it doesn't begin and end at the nursery door.

(Baby Room leader)

Another professional agreed that working with parents is a central role to their leadership, elaborating on their role:

parents often feel worried when they see their child start to bond with us. They worry that their child will love us more, want us rather than them when they are upset. It is my responsibility to ensure my team are knowledgeable, confident and sensitive enough to explain the importance of that bond and reassure them that the child's parent will always be the most significant adult to the child.

(Baby Room leader)

This experience is reflective of Page's (2011) findings relating to parents' anxiety about the decision to use non-familial childcare, particularly regarding feelings of apprehension about their child forming a close attachment with another adult. This reiterates the importance of ensuring pedagogical considerations are outward facing and involve consideration of the formation of relationships with various stakeholders.

Pedagogical leadership with babies also needs to be responsive to the lack of understanding and research on this. Thus, part of being a pedagogical leader with babies is creating a stronger sense of voice for the role of working with babies in ECE. This might involve advocacy and community leadership roles, so that there are opportunities to speak out about the experiences of enacting pedagogical leadership with babies. It can also be developed through action research. We must empower our Baby Room professionals to address the gap in our understanding of pedagogical leadership with babies. They need to do this themselves, to carry out research within their own settings and share this with the wider sector to advance understanding of the pedagogical nuances of work with the youngest children. Spaces must be created for reflective dialogue within and across teams working with this age group, to enable them to engage in pedagogical conversations and begin to see themselves as a community of practice (Wenger et al., 2002).

We also need to look carefully at the professional development opportunities that exist relating to pedagogical leadership with babies. A coherent approach to pedagogical leadership with babies requires knowledgeable professionals with a deep and reflective understanding of how babies learn. Goouch and Powell (2013) highlighted the sparsity of professional development opportunities available to Baby Room teachers, and it appears that little has changed. An evaluation of the training provided by three local authorities in London reveals a breadth of training pertaining to school readiness, the EYFS, literacy and mathematical learning (with a focus on pre-school) but very little that equips teachers with the skills and knowledge to be effective Baby Room leaders. This is particularly concerning given the commonly held view that the current early years qualifications do not adequately prepare teachers for working with babies (Gouch and Powell, 2013). Again, this absence of babies from training can give the impression that the work professionals in this age group do is less skilled and less valued. This was a perspective shared by one of the ECE professionals here:

> our internal training academy has lots of training, which is tailored towards those working with under 2s, however if this wasn't the case I am not sure what CPD I would do. When we look at the training offered by our local authority it is usually related to safeguarding or tailored towards pre-school teachers. Does that mean that teachers working with babies need less knowledge or skills?
>
> (LEYF Baby Room professional)

Given the impact of the first two years of a child's life and the complexities of working with under twos, this is undeniably not the case, yet it is clear how a lack of inclusion of baby-specific training could create this impression.

Conclusion

In conclusion, the stark absence of work with babies in the literature on pedagogical leadership must be urgently addressed. It is undeniable that those working with babies require a specific set of knowledge and skills to be able to support the development of children in this age group and that this involves an understanding of not just interactions with the babies but also considerable insight into supporting others adults to develop their practice and working closely with families to create the best conditions for babies to flourish. The commonly held perspective of Baby Room professionals as carers as opposed to educators could be viewed as a contributory factor to the absence of babies from the research: however, it is neither possible nor desirable to omit caring practices from discussions about pedagogy with babies. The proposal of a 'pedagogy of care' (Shin, 2015) which highlights the inextricable nature of the intellectual components of teaching and the high level of care provided by those working in this age group is a proposal that should be explored in more depth (Male and Palaiologou, 2012, 2015).

Following from this chapter's contribution, the ECE community needs to focus more on the experiences of those working in the Baby Room, gathering stories of what high-quality pedagogical leadership looks like when working with babies and the practices that help to develop it. A practical step that ECE settings can take towards this is to integrate action research into the work of those in the Baby Room so that professionals working with babies can simultaneously strengthen their professional confidence and contribute to building a broader knowledge and understanding of this topic.

References

Coughlin, A.M., Baird, L. (2013) 'Pedagogical leadership', Available at http://www.edu.gov.on.ca/childcare/Baird_Coughlin.pdf (accessed 18 February 2021).

Department for Education (2017) 'Statutory framework for the early years foundation stage', Available at https://assets.publishing.service.gov.uk/government/uploads/system/uploads/attachment_data/file/596629/EYFS_STATUTORY_FRAMEWORK_2017.pdf (accessed 17 January 2021).

Department for Education (2019) 'Childcare and early years survey of parents in England', Available at: https://assets.publishing.service.gov.uk/government/uploads/system/uploads/attachment_data/file/853358/CEYSP_2019_Report.pdf (accessed 15 January 2021).

Goouch, K., Powell, S. (2012) 'Orchestrating professional development for baby room practitioners: Raising the stakes in new dialogic encounters', *Journal of Early Childhood Research*, 11(1), pp. 78–92.

Goouch, K., Powell, S. (2013) *The Baby Room: Principles, Policy and Practice*. Maidenhead: Open University Press.

Huntsman, L. (2008) *Determinants of Quality in Child Care: A Review of the Research Evidence. Literature Review*. New South Wales, Australia: Centre for Parenting & Research: New South Wales Government.

Jarvis, P. (2020) 'Attachment theory, cortisol and care for the under-threes in the twenty-first century: constructing evidence-informed policy', *Early Years: An International Research Journal*, advance online publication, available at https://www.tandfonline.com/doi/full/10.1080/09575146.2020.1764507 (accessed 1 February 2021).

Male, T., Palaiologou, I. (2012) 'Learning-centred leadership or pedagogical leadership? An alternative approach to leadership in education contexts', *International Journal of Leadership in Education*, 15(1), pp. 107–118.

Male, T., Palaiologou, I. (2015) 'Pedagogical leadership in the 21st century: Evidence from the field', *Educational Management Administration and Leadership*, 43(2), pp. 214–231.

Mathers, S., Eisenstadt, N., Sylva, K., Soukakou, E., Ereky-Stevens, K. (2014) 'Sound foundations: A review of the research evidence on quality of early childhood education and care for children under three: Implications for policy and practice', Available at https://www.suttontrust.com/wp-content/uploads/2019/12/1sound-foundations-jan2014-3-1.pdf (accessed 13 February 2021).

Moyles, J., Adams, S., Musgrove, A. (2002) *SPEEL: Study of Pedagogical Effectiveness in Early Learning*. London: Department for Education and Skills.

Moylett, H. (1997) '"It's not nursery but it's not just being a home": A parent and childminder working together' in Abbott, L., & Moylett, H. (eds.) *Working with the under 3's: Responding to Children' Needs*. Maidenhead: Open University Press. pp. 11–34.

Office for Standards in Education (2019) 'Early years inspection handbook for ofsted registered provision', Available at: https://assets.publishing.service.gov.uk/government/uploads/system/uploads/attachment_data/file/828465/Early_years_inspection_handbook.pdf (accessed 19 January 2021).

O'Sullivan, J. (2015) *Successful Leadership in the Early Years*. London: Bloomsbury Publishing.

Page, J. (2011) 'Do parents want professional carers to love their children?', *Journal of Early Childhood Research*, 9 (3), pp. 310–323.

Page, J. (2015) 'Professional love in early years settings: a report of the summary of findings'. Available at: https://pleysproject.files.wordpress.com/2017/06/pleys-report_singlepages.pdf (accessed 10 February 2021).

Shin, M. (2015) 'Enacting caring pedagogy in the infant classroom', *Early Child Development and Care*, 185 (3), pp. 496–508.

Siraj-Blatchford, I., Manni, L. (2008) *Effective Leadership in the Early Years Sector. The ELEYS Study*. London: Institute of Education.

Vincent, C., Ball, S.L. (2001) 'A market in love? Choosing pre-school childcare', *British Educational Research Journal*, 27 (5), pp. 633–651.

Wenger, E., McDermott, R., Snyder, W.M. (2002) *Cultivating Communities of Practice*. Boston, MA: Harvard Business School Press.

Whitehead, M (2010) *Language and Literacy in the Early Years 0–7* (4th ed.). London: Sage Publications.

6

Plan-Do-Review

What Can We Learn from Change Management Theories about Pedagogical Leadership?

Helen Perkins

Introduction

Pedagogical leadership is more than supporting teaching and learning. It includes supporting other professionals in implementing the curriculum and striving for continuous quality improvement. Pedagogical leaders influence children's experiences by nurturing family engagement and embedding the setting's mission, vision and values. This chapter offers an exploration of pedagogical leadership in early childhood education (ECE) in the context of leadership and management theories. It identifies the theories that are most relevant, examines how such theories can be adapted in ECE contexts and shares examples of ECE students learning to work with these theories in order to extend their own pedagogical leadership practices.

Context

In this chapter, I reflect on my work with students as a lecturer in Early Childhood Studies at an English university. I lead a level 6 (third year undergraduate) module: Leading Quality in Early Childhood. The aim of this module is to prepare our students for the workplace. It is anticipated that as early childhood graduates, they will take up leadership roles in the future. The module is the final step of the three-year work-based practice journey for our undergraduates. As they progress through their degree, they have been developing their practice in a range of early childhood settings with children aged from birth to eight years, working towards the Early Childhood Graduate Practitioner Competencies (ECSDN, 2018). Throughout their degree, placement has provided the space to connect theory with practice. As they enter their final year, we complete that journey by preparing our students to lead pedagogy and practice. However, many have limited experience of taking the lead, and feel inexperienced in leading people. The module focuses on traditional business models of leadership and change management theory to provide the students with a framework to plan and lead a change in pedagogy in their setting. For the students, this often feels quite unsettling and definitely out of the students' comfort zone. Having identified an area for development, they are tasked with planning and implementing the change following the theoretical concepts offered in the module. Examples of these plans are presented as case studies, showing how students use structured and reflective approaches to plan and implement their change.

Introducing ECE Students to the Language of Leadership

The business world offers many examples of leadership styles. It is recognised in research on ECE leadership that finding a leadership style is dependent on the personality, experience and knowledge of the leader (Rodd, 2006). While there are many types of leaders, an effective pedagogical leader must have a lexicon of leadership, understanding the many languages of leadership and how and when to use them. With our students we have reflected together on three leadership styles (autocratic, democratic and laissez-faire) and how they apply these leadership styles given their roles and positionality in their specific ECE settings.

According to Fullan (2004) pedagogical leaders need to be fluent in the language of leadership if they are to be responsive to the needs of a team given the many different contexts and also considering the stakeholders involved in the situation.

To build a more nuanced understanding of leadership with our students, we draw on the research of Daniel Goleman looking at emotional intelligence. As part of this research, Daniel Goleman identified six leadership styles. Our students explore the characteristics and potential impacts of each leadership style.

In particular, we explore how each leadership style can have a different effect on people who are being led. We ask students to reflect on their own experiences of leadership, either in their placement or in any previous employment. They can use Goleman's taxonomy to step back from the experience of interacting with a leader to identify what kind of leadership it represents and the potential and pitfalls of this kind of leadership. It is often the case that they see a leader in an authoritative, 'telling' role, in a position reinforced by traditional management hierarchies. This new knowledge that it is acceptable, even desirable, to adapt leadership approaches to a given situation requires a shift in their thinking about leadership. They are encouraged to open up their understanding of leadership so that they look beyond traditional management hierarchies and see opportunities for pedagogical leadership in ECE that employ more democratic or coaching styles.

Exploring Leadership Practices with ECE Students

Acknowledging that there are different ways of being a leader, we then introduce the different ways of doing leadership. In particular, we look closely at transformational, situational and distributed leadership. *Transformational leadership* is a valuable tool for driving change, though it relies on the individual's specific personality traits (Bass and Avolio, 1994). Transformational leaders are often described as charismatic, inspirational and motivational; they are respected and trusted (French and Raven, 1959). Transformational leadership therefore relies on the leader's ability to transform others, to move beyond self-interest and to work towards what is best for the organisation, and in the case of ECE, the children and families. A transformational leader should be able to *walk the walk* and act as a role model.

There is a body of research that suggests transformational leadership is the preferred leadership style used by women. Traditionally feminised values, which include building relationships, communication, consensus building, power as influence and working together for a common purpose, make this approach relevant for leaders in ECE, as the workforce is mainly female, and its values congruent with feminist values and philosophy (Salter et al., 2010; Butz and Lewis, 1996; Stogdill, 1974).

Many students find this approach attractive as they see it as making a significant difference in practice. In reality, often their student-volunteer status can be a barrier to taking this approach. They perceive, in many cases correctly, that they do not have the power or authority to take the lead. The next section looks at distributed leadership, moving away from the valorised individual and looking at a team-centred approach.

Distributed leadership is an approach to action and influence, centred on the coordination, communication and collaboration involved in leading practice (Gronn, 2000). In contrast to the traditional approaches to leadership, which come from the business world and are adapted for use in ECE settings, distributed leadership has travelled from the world of education and become more prevalent the business world. There has been a move away from a single leader overseeing everything to a more distributed approach. Rather than focusing on the skills and traits of one individual, distributed leadership draws on the skills within the team or organisation (Goleman et al., 2002).

The pedagogical leader may not be the manager or the room leader but one who takes the lead in pedagogical practice. A distributed approach can lead to a more committed workforce as staff feel valued for their knowledge and expertise. Taking this approach provides an opportunity to develop leadership skills within the team. There are inhibiting factors to taking a distributed approach. Some staff may not wish to take on the responsibilities of leading. With responsibility comes accountability which can add to people's workload. It is important to pay attention to these factors to ensure there is fair distribution of tasks as well as appropriate recognition and reward.

Situational leadership involves the leader adapting their style of leading to suit the current work environment and the needs of the team. This model was conceived by Blanchard and (Hersey and Blanchard 1969) when researching organisational behaviours in the 1960s. This model acknowledges that there is no one *best* style of leadership; successful leaders are those who adapt their style to the ability and willingness of the individual or the team. The determining situational factors depend on the specifics of the task, the relationship with the team member, the individual's maturity level (their level of expertise in the task or role) and the level of authority needed to be exerted by the leader.

Thus, in acknowledging that leadership is a mechanism to bring about change; the next section will introduce models of change and how they can be used to improve pedagogical practices.

Understanding Pedagogical Leadership as Managing Change

With ever changing policy, changing governments and changing practice, ECE professionals are used to expecting change! However, while ECE professionals are often subject to changes demanded by others, they may be unfamiliar with the means through which they can initiate and implement change for themselves.

In developing pedagogical leadership among our students, we focus on the benefits of understanding models of change that, while generated in business and management contexts, can be helpful for bringing about pedagogical change in ECE settings.

Key to pedagogical leadership is the capacity to reflect on learning processes and seek ways to improve children's experiences, and this involves leading and motivating the whole ECE team. When looking to make a change, using a model to plan the change is supported by a large body of research concerning the processes needed to implement change successfully and make it 'stick' (Rodd, 2006; Kotter, 2012; Lewin, 1951). We introduce students to Lewin's (1951) three-step model for change, 'Unfreeze – Change – Refreeze', moving from the current state, through the transformation to the desired future state and then 'refreezing' the new ways of working into everyday practice. Although this approach is over sixty years old, we find that it is still relevant to today's ECE students and that it can help them to plan and implement pedagogical change. We also work with Kotter's (1996) eight-stage model, which builds on Lewin's work, breaking the process of change management into smaller steps. He found that all eight steps needed to be present and in the right order for the process to be successful. He cautioned that moving onto the next step before enough time has been spent on the preceding step will only give the illusion of progress.

Common to all models is a continuous cycle from the initial identification of an issue, encouraging others to 'buy in' to the idea and embedding the change as part of the routine. We have found that Kotter's model is particularly useful for those new to taking a leadership role.

Examples of Students' Observations and Reflections

To explore further how our ECE students have used leadership theories and models of change in order to develop their own pedagogical leadership, it is helpful to take a closer look at the students' own observations and reflections of this process. Using what they have learned about leadership styles, leadership practices and models of change, students submit a detailed plan and a supporting essay, analysing their planned approach to leading change. I have chosen two excerpts from these essays to analyse and comment upon. Together they show both the potentials and the pitfalls of working with theories that have originated in the business world and applying these to the development of pedagogical leadership in ECE professionals typically without an official leadership role in a setting.

Example 1 – Introducing Child-centred Pedagogy

An Excerpt from M's Assignment

I aim to change the reception classroom environment to create a child-centred space in which we can change the current teacher led practice to child-initiated pedagogy. The teaching is curriculum and assessment led. The school's Ofsted report identified the need for a more child centred pedagogy in the Foundation Stage. When conducting observations for my Early Childhood Graduate Competencies evidence, I used the Leuven scales and ECERS assessment tools to identify children's levels of engagement and enjoyment. My observations identified missed opportunities for children to learn through child-initiated play. The first step was to present the evidence for making a change firstly with the manager, and then with the team.

Kotter (1996) and Lewin (1951) stress the importance of justifying the need for change. In a staff meeting, I presented the observations and related this to the Ofsted Report. I also shared the research on child-initiated play. Staff had time to consider the evidence and discuss the possibilities, challenges and limitations in making a change.

As the leader I needed to 'set the stage' by being clear and specific in justifying how the change will improve outcomes for children, families and staff. At this stage of the process, I used a 'visionary' leadership approach (Goleman, 2000) to motivate staff towards aligning the vision for the change with the setting's vision statement, 'Dream it, Believe it, Become it'.

It was important to understand how staff felt about the change. The team had been working in the previous way for quite some time, so any changes could come as a shock to staff who had been working there for a while and had set ways of working. This was a barrier to implementing change, because if staff did not buy into the change because of fear of new ways of being or not feeling convinced of the benefits, then it would make the transition more difficult. The potential for conflict and challenge should be anticipated (Aubrey, 2011). Tuckman (1965) describes this stage as 'storming', when tensions arise which can create a hostile environment and divisions within the group. At this point I used my 'emotional intelligence' (Goleman, 2000) and employed an 'affiliative' style of leadership to build a bond of trust with the team, showing empathy and to find out what motivated specific individuals; different people have different motivators such as extra responsibility or need for recognition (Maslow, 1943/2019; Herzberg, 1966).

As a transformational leader, taking a democratic approach, practitioners were encouraged to get involved and choose an area or action they would like to concentrate on. My challenge was to engage a long serving member of the team because I believed if she would buy in to the idea, then others would follow. I had heard that she was a very good artist. Away from the group I talked with her about this, sharing what I had seen in my other placements,. I explained that I was not very creative myself and sought her advice on how she thought we could develop a creative area. Once the tensions had been smoothed, she agreed to develop that area and a clear strategy was be put in place.

There was another team member who was very keen to create a home corner, with real world artefacts and equipment. She agreed to take the lead on this and engaged parents and the children in creating the space. Her enthusiasm encouraged others to participate. Another recalled reading about 'loose parts play' on a Facebook page. She did some research and worked with a colleague and a parent on developing a construction area, incorporating loose parts.

With the children, I also used a 'democratic' style of leadership, asking them for their opinions on the environment and if they had ideas to contribute (Hart, 1992; Goleman, 2000). I invited parents to contribute by means of a questionnaire and to invite those that may have additional skills and ideas to offer, to put themselves forward and to involve them as part of the change.

In Kotter's model, the next stage is where the change starts to take place and Tuckman (1965) would call this 'norming' when the leadership is accepted, and people are co-operative and open to the change. It is the role of a good leader to recognise these strengths in others in the context of the change and environment, known as situational leadership (Hersey and Blanchard, 1969). Also, empowering individuals to be aware of their own strengths and weaknesses and establishing collective responsibility is suggested to maximise the impact on quality (Rodd, 2006; Lindon and Trodd, 2016).

A further barrier was to encourage staff to let children take the lead. A staff development session was provided by the University as part of their support for settings who take students on placement. As a follow up, it was suggested that staff did observations to see how the children were using the new areas. The findings were positive. This gave staff the momentum to consider making other areas in the room more accessible to the children. The findings provided what Kotter refers to as 'a short-term win'. Parents, carers and staff brought equipment and resources home.

A regular meeting and a newsletter were established for parents to get involved and an ideas tree collated the children's ideas.

Progress was monitored through weekly observations using the environmental and wellbeing scales and the Leuven levels of involvement scales (Laevers, 2015). In the long term, staff would hopefully see an improvement in children's engagement, behaviour and learning focus.

Commentary

M's assignment highlights the potential of using theories of leadership and change that have originated in business contexts as a starting point for developing pedagogical leadership. In particular it shows how the models help the student to plan her next moves. Rather than feeling 'stuck' and unsure of what to do next, the models provide a structure for moving forward. Because of this structure for moving forward, the reflection on these models and approaches also help to give the pedagogical project some momentum. For example, when the student realised – through reflecting on the leadership and change management theories – that she needed to identify and work with a key figure to 'win over' the team, she shifted fluently into a problem-solving mindset rather than allowing herself to remain disheartened and stuck with the status quo.

On the other hand, M's assignment also suggests some areas for further development when working with students to extend pedagogical leadership and change management by engaging with leadership theories from a business context. In particular, working with the theories of leadership and change management does not enable this student to reflect on a deep level about the impact of the pedagogical shift she is trying to enact. There is no space to consider what exactly she means by child-centred learning and to unpick its nature as a contested term with many interpretations. There is no space to examine whether child-centred learning is actually what is needed in this situation, and what it means for different stakeholders in the situation. In short, there is no impetus from the change management theories to engage with the nature of the change on a more critical level. Only discussions about pedagogy can achieve this level of criticality. This would highlight the need to ensure that leadership and change management theories from the business world do not 'take over' the pedagogical elements of ECE leadership. A deep understanding of pedagogy, founded on critical engagement, is essential.

Example 2 – Developing a Model for Children's Transitions

An Excerpt from J's Assignment

In my dissertation, I investigated the transition process from Reception to Year One. Research findings show how transition processes are often seen as negative but have also revealed the importance of parent partnership to support children through all transitions. Hornby and Blackwell (2018) found that in settings using strategies such as workshops the transition process was more successful and seamless and that parental involvement is a crucial component in facilitating transitions. The setting's vision is 'remain family orientated' and 'strive to work in partnership with our parents and third parties' however the Ofsted report identifies that partnership could be improved. Bronfenbrenner (1979) argues that learning is optimised by supportive links such as home and school and children's ability to adapt to new situations depends on the extent to which parents and teachers cooperate; this underpins my own values as both a practitioner and undergraduate.

The plan was to develop a successful transition model. In contrast to the existing approach, in which transition was addressed in the last week of the academic year, I proposed that transition takes place over an extended period of time and includes parents. (If successful, it was proposed that the model be extended to become a whole school approach).

The first action was to meet with Senior Management and relevant staff well in advance to discuss and evaluate current policies for transition and partnership. I discussed with the manager if we could work together to lead the change or if she could nominate one member of staff to lead with me in a coaching role as I have no experience of taking the lead. We discussed timescales and resources available to implement the change. It was agreed that the Deputy and I would work together.

I visited other settings to observe how they promoted parental engagement and how they approached relevant transitions. I also researched available training opportunities relating to parental involvement and transitions to prepare for the next step.

We then arranged a staff meeting to inform staff of the proposal. In the meeting I shared the research and literature on effective transitions. Staff were encouraged to comment, challenge and offer ideas. We explored the ways in which the team could contribute to this change, identifying areas of expertise as well as concerns and development needs. I used a distributed leadership approach as the whole team is integral to the change and will lead at the various phases of the change. I used a visionary leadership style to motivate people towards change and build relationships. However, having a vision may not work for all team members and barriers may arise (Newstead and Buck, 2013).

There were concerns about additional workload. Goleman (2000) suggests that when dealing with people who put barriers in the way of change, a different style of leadership is required. I used an affiliative style when required as this style creates harmony and heals rifts in a team. We discussed the issues. In this instance the Deputy responded, identifying how time could be found. She used an authoritative style, rallying the staff by highlighting the long-term benefits of an effective transition on their future workload. I detected a hint of a commanding style, exerting her positional power, albeit gently. This allowed us to move forward.

Given the evidence shows parent partnership as key, we held a parent meeting where parents were invited to give their views. Parents have a relationship with their child's teacher and teaching assistants; therefore, their skills and expertise were employed to take the lead at this stage. Children's views fed into the final plans and were acknowledged in the documentation.

A small working party was established including staff, children and parents. Reviewing the feedback from the initial meetings a plan was created which included:

- *A series of weekly transition workshops and transition workshop packs to be sent home to parents that are unable to attend.*
- *Staff chose which workshops they wanted to lead.*
- *Parents and children agreed to lead sessions where they felt best able to contribute.*

The working party fed back to the whole staff team for confirmation and clarity of communication. A newsletter was prepared and sent to all parents with a short rationale for the transition workshops and inviting them to participate.

The final stage in Lewin's model is to refreeze: to make the change stick. Some argue that the refreezing step is outdated due to a continuous need for change but without the refreeze step there is a high chance that people will revert to the old way of doing, this stage is crucial to embed the change. Monitoring and evaluating the plan is essential. Regular staff meetings were held where staff shared successes and raised any worries. When support was needed, I observed the Deputy adopt a coaching style of leadership to support and develop staff confidence. Feedback from parents was sought via questionnaires included in the transition packs and the parent forum. A box was placed in reception for parents and staff members to put suggestions in, if they were not comfortable talking in person. These received responses and the plans were refined. I was disappointed not to be able to follow up as my placement ended.

Commentary

Example 2 highlights some other ways that working with leadership and change management theories from the business world can influence the development of pedagogical leadership practices among students. In particular, the student clearly developed an awareness of others' leadership styles through the language used on the module. For example, he was conscious of when the manager shifted to a more authoritative style and when the deputy showed a coaching leadership style. This suggests the student is therefore more reflective about leadership and what it means (and looks like and feels like) to be led by others. This can help the student to navigate future professional contexts where managers and those in more official senior positions engage various styles of leadership. Rather than passively experiencing these leadership styles, he can respond to them more dynamically and with more understanding.

This example also shows us that effective self-reflection about the development of leadership may involve more than just knowing about different theories and models of leadership. Although the student mentions that he has adopted various leadership styles he offers very limited discussion of how he did this and what it felt like. This is something for us to consider embedding further in the students' learning experience, challenging them to probe further how exactly they put the theory into practice. For example, how did the student show a commitment to distributed leadership, as stated? What did this look like? One way to achieve this greater level of reflection might be to encourage students to observe and reflect on their own micro-interactions. For example, if they were able to capture just a five-minute interaction between themselves and other team members, relating to the change they are attempting to introduce and manage, they could look more closely at how they are leading (through what they say and their nonverbal communication) and how this relates to the theories they have come across. This is still about linking theory and practice, but it positions practice first and theory as the tool to deeply reflect with, as opposed to using theory always as the starting point for practice (or intentions about practice).

Students Reflecting on Their Pedagogical Leadership Development

At the end of the module, we ask students to reflect on what they have learned through the module's content, tasks and assignments. In analysing these reflections, we find that there are six common themes running through their reflections. These are:

1. Leadership is complex: you need to be able to adapt your style and approach to individuals' needs;
2. Preparation and planning for change is essential;
3. Having a good idea is not enough; you have to be able to motivate a team to embed a change in practice;
4. Power can be used in many ways but using it appropriately is essential;
5. Co-construction and cooperation are the key to making things happen;
6. Accepting help is not a weakness.

Conclusion

This chapter has discussed the key leadership and change management theories that we use to support pedagogical leadership development among students of ECE. As a pedagogical leader, the challenge is not only understanding pedagogy but also knowing how to influence and motivate colleagues when introducing pedagogical change, particularly when this involves others who may have more experience (longevity) working in early childhood education and care or may be in more senior, managerial roles. Like any theory, leadership and change management models are just that: a theory. They are dependent on the individual taking the lead, the individuals being led and the context. The daily experience of children in early years settings and the overall quality of provision depends on all professionals having appropriate skills and knowledge and a clear understanding of their roles and responsibilities. The need for expertise in leadership is more relevant than ever before but many of the current ECE qualifications in England (and indeed, around the world) do not include an explicit focus on leadership development. If we are to create a professional workforce, a professional sector and offer quality provision then understanding how to lead people, pedagogy and practice is essential.

References

Aubrey, C. (2011). *Leading and Managing in the Early Years*. 2nd ed. London: Sage Publications.

Bass, B. M., & Avolio, B. J. (1994). *Improving Organizational Effectiveness Through Transformational Leadership*. Thousand Oaks, CA: Sage Publications.

Bronfenbrenner, U. (1979). *The Ecology of Human Development: Experiments by Nature and Design*. Cambridge, MA: Harvard University Press.

Butz, C. E., & Lewis, P. V. (1996). Correlation of gender-related values of independence and relationship and leadership orientation. *Journal of Business Ethics*, 15(11), 1141–1149.

ECSDN (2018). *Graduate Practitioner Competencies*. Accessed 27.02.2022: https://www.ecsdn.org/competencies/

French, J. R. P., Jr., & Raven, B. H. (1959). The bases of social power. In D. Cartwright (Ed.), *Studies in Social Power* (pp. 150–167). Ann Arbor, MI: Institute for Social Research.

Fullan, M. (2004). *Leading in a Culture of Change*. San Francisco, CA: Jossey Bass.

Goleman, D. (March/April 2000). Leadership that gets results. *Harvard Business Review*, 78(2), 78–90.

Goleman, D., Boyatzis, R. & McKee, A. (2002). The emotional reality of teams. *Journal of Organizational Excellence*, 21(2), 55–65.

Hart, R. A. (1992). *Children's Participation: From Tokenism to Citizenship*. Florence: UNICEF International Child Development Centre.

Hersey, P., & Blanchard, K. H. (1969). *Management of Organizational Behavior: Utilizing Human Resources*. Hoboken, NJ: Prentice Hall.

Herzberg, F., (1966). *Work and the Nature of Man*. Cleveland, NY: World Publishing Company.

Hornby, G., & Blackwell, I. (2018). Barriers to parental involvement in education: An update. *Educational review*, 70(1), 109–119.

Gronn, P. (2000). Distributed properties: A new architecture for leadership. *Educational Management & Administration*, 28(3), 317–338.

Kotter, J. P. (1996). *Leading Change*. Boston, MA: Harvard Business School Press.

Kotter, J. P. (2012). *Leading Change*. Boston, MA: Harvard Business Review Press.

Laevers, F. (2015). *Making Care and Education More Effective Through Wellbeing and Involvement. An Introduction to Experiential Education*. Belgium: Research Centre for Experiential Education – University of Leuven.

Lewin, K. (1951). *Problems of Research in Social Psychology*. New York: Harper and Brothers.

Lindon, J, & Trodd, L. (2016). *Reflective Practice and Early Years Professionalism 3rd Edition: Linking Theory and Practice*. New York, NY: Hachette.

Maslow, A. H. (1943/2019). *A Theory of Human Motivation*. Delhi: General Press.

Newstead, S., & Isles-Buck, E. (2013). *Essential skills for managers of child-centred settings*. London: Routledge.

Rodd, J. (2006). *Leadership in Early Childhood*. 3rd ed. Maidenhead. Open University Press.

Salter, C. R., Green, M., Duncan, P., Berre, A., & Torti, C. W. (2010). Virtual Communications, Transformational Leadership and Implicit Leadership. *Journal of Leadership Studies*, 4(2), 6–17.

Stodgill, R. M. (1974). *Handbook of Leadership: A Survey of Theory and Research*. New York: Free Press.

Tuckman, B. W. (1965). Developmental sequence in small groups. *Psychological Bulletin*, 63, 384–399.

7

Pedagogical Leadership

Comparing Approaches and Practices in England, Greece and Sweden

Ioanna Palaiologou, Eleftheria Argyropoulou, Maria Styf, Catarina Arvidsson, Amanda Ince and Trevor Male

Introduction

Conceptualising leadership in ECE is complex. Previous research suggests that there is a tendency to try to theorise leadership by borrowing styles, models and types of leadership from other levels of education (e.g. Murray and McDowall Clark, 2013). It has been argued (e.g. Nicholson and Maniates, 2016) that due to the nature of ECE, there is a need to develop conceptualisations of leadership that are specific to the field. Moreover, some (e.g. Mathers et al., 2014) argue little attention has been given to the role of pedagogical leadership and its impact on the quality of ECE. Instead there is a focus on either the functions or the structures of leadership. Here, 'functions' refer to administrative, managerial and educational aspects of leadership while 'structures' refer to types, approaches or models of leadership that exist.

In this chapter, we argue that these functions and structures should be seen as inseparable elements of pedagogically driven leadership. To achieve this, previous work by Palaiologou and Male (2019) has suggested that leadership is best thought about as a pedagogical praxis (= theory, actions, reflections). Our new transnational research develops this conceptualisation further and in this chapter we explore how formal accountable leaders think about their leadership and whether this ties into the notion of 'pedagogical praxis', where pedagogical leadership is inextricably intertwined with the functions and structures of leadership.

The following discussion is based on a qualitative study in three countries with relatively limited research on ECE leadership: England, Greece and Sweden. In these three countries, the field of ECE presents many complexities which include multi-professional identities, a wide range of qualifications among the people working in the sector and diverse discourses (e.g. care versus education, playful learning versus preparation for formal schooling). In this transnational study, we aim to:

1. Identify underlying ideologies and pedagogical leadership practices in ECE in each country;
2. Identify and compare boundaries and challenges in pedagogical leadership in ECE across the three countries;
3. In light of the findings, revisit and develop the construct of pedagogical leadership, particularly in relation to the idea of pedagogical praxis.

The chapter begins by discussing our theorisation of leadership as pedagogical praxis. Then it moves to explain the study and the context of each country. It continues with key findings highlighting the complexities of pedagogical leadership in each national context. Finally, in the discussion of the findings, we argue that the (re)conceptualisation of leadership as *praxis* can successfully address the continuing ideological and practical concerns which permeate ECE.

Moving beyond Leadership of Learning and Teaching to Pedagogical Leadership

Associating leadership with pedagogy has attracted much interest in ECE, with a recent OECD report (Douglass, 2019) concluding that the discourse about leadership is dominated by explorations of pedagogical practices intended to ensure quality of classroom/playgroup interactions with young children. The term 'pedagogical leadership' has been used widely to refer to practices which support learning and teaching (e.g. Douglass, 2019; Heikka and Waniganayake, 2011). In studies such as these, the main focus is leadership for learning for both children and teaching teams (Carroll-Lind et al., 2016). Pedagogical leadership is thought to depend on the 'co-construction of learning through active involvement, dialogue and shared knowledge [. . .] based on] relationships with parents, professionals and the wider community' (Murray and McDowall Clark 2013, p. 292). In turn, this construct has been extended in some studies to refer to creating a work culture where staff are supported through peer learning to implement the curriculum and assessment (Cheung et al., 2019; Eskelinen and Hujala, 2015; Whalen et al., 2016) and establishing partnerships with the families and the community. In that sense, pedagogical leadership is viewed as participatory, collaborative and not the responsibility of one administrative person, but as shared activity and a responsibility of all staff involved in teaching and learning (Waniganayke, 2003; Murray and McDowall Clark, 2013).

Building on these ideas, Palaiologou and Male (2019) and Male and Palaiologou (2015, 2017) extended the construct of pedagogical leadership to include more complex relationships, defining pedagogy as an interconnected triangular relationship between the (1) learning environment, (2) learners and (3) educators, who all interact within the ecology of the community in which they operate. This means that pedagogy is as much about the organisational aspects of administration, management and accountability as it is about the direct interactions between children and adults. Thus, they conceptualise leadership within education as a complex relationship system that includes a diverse range of professionals, services, families, children and infrastructures (i.e. pedagogical praxis). They argue that we must move beyond a focus on just the learning and teaching (what happens in the classroom or playroom) to embrace the community and the influential factors that are internal (e.g. values, culture, customs) and external (e.g. global economy, policies, national curricula). They conclude that:

> *pedagogical leadership is rooted in its specific context and pays attention to its own environment through engaging with the historicity, culture and subjective perspectives/realities of the contexts that are involved. Thus, the ECE community (researchers and practitioners) should seek their own end purpose (telos), rather than trying to bridge 'theory' (sophia) from disparate and different communities.* (Palaiologou and Male, 2019, p. 31)

In the research discussed in this chapter, we were therefore interested in how the context of each community studied – including participant lived experiences and local and national ideologies and practices – shaped leadership as pedagogical praxis.

The Context of the Study

In all three countries, ECE presents challenges due to the variety of service providers and qualifications of those working in the sector. ECE can be offered by the state or private sector or through a hybrid model and that brings challenges in terms of finance, resources and diverse qualifications of the workforce.

In England, ECE provision is a complex picture comprising a mix between maintained (government funded) and private, voluntary and independent (PVI) settings. There are a range of qualifications among the workforce with the agreed minimum to work with children in an unsupervised capacity as Level 3. This equates to university entrance requirements. It also serves as the baseline for formal leadership roles and responsibilities. The reality is that leaders hold a variety of qualifications from Level 3 through to graduate and postgraduate. Consequently, given these various qualification routes and levels there are debates about the suitability of different qualifications and how these relate to quality and the core purposes of ECE. Understandably the variety of both providers and qualifications leads to confusion about the scope of formal leadership roles.

In Greece, ECE provision happens through child-care centres, supervised by the Ministry of Work, Social Security and Social Solidarity. These host children from birth to four years where attendance is not compulsory. These centres can be privately owned with fees or municipal (owned and run by the Borough) with fees; moreover, there are twenty-four centres all over the country owned by the Greek Manpower Employment Organization without fees for less privileged children. All such centres tend to employ graduates called Vrefonipiokomoi (infant carers) who have rich leadership roles. There are also preschools that host children aged four to six years where attendance is compulsory. These are similar to child-care centres, but have to follow a national curriculum and are supervised by the Ministry of Education, Research and Religious Affairs. The preschools are staffed by university graduates who have been trained to be early years teachers (known as 'Nipiagogoi'). There is no specific policy for preparing them as formal leaders, however, and a lack of pre-post or in-post training. This dichotomy in provision where the notion of pedagogical leadership is contextualised is to be found mainly in preschools.

Meanwhile, in Sweden the preschool (for children from one to five years) has in many ways been regarded as unique with care always positioned in relation to learning (internationally referred to as Educare). This way of looking at learning and the perception of the child as a subject in one's own learning has been part of the special nature of the preschool. Since December 2013, professional certification is required for school and preschool teachers on permanent contracts. The purpose was to raise the status of the teaching profession, support professional development and thus increase quality in education. From first of July 2019, the title of 'preschool manager' was changed to 'principal' and it became mandatory to participate in the national school leadership training programme. In the revised Education Act (2010:800), the head of the school and the principal of the preschool have the same assignment: that is, the principal of the preschool is to lead and coordinate the pedagogical work. In the school it is the principal's mission to evaluate the school's performance according to the curriculum whereas in preschool it is the principal's task to evaluate the quality of the provision.

The Study

We conducted a small-scale qualitative study to explore the conceptualisation and practice of pedagogical leadership in each of the national contexts outlined earlier. In England we conducted semi-structured interviews with a smaller number of participants, while in Greece and Sweden, researchers used the letter method which can be thought about as an intermediate between an interview and an open questionnaire.

In each national context, we explored the following themes in relation to pedagogical leadership (see Table 7.1):

- Views on leadership in ECE;
- Description of leadership practices and roles;
- The key challenges of leadership in ECE.

Findings

Comparing responses within and between the national contexts, we identified three characteristics that required further attention and reflection. These were:

1. Differences among participants in their understanding of pedagogy;
2. Confusion regarding the functions of their leadership role: administrative, management and educational;
3. Confusion regarding the structures of their leadership role: that is, the styles, models and approaches required to lead ECE, and particularly in relation to pedagogical leadership.

Table 7.1 Overview of the Methods and Participants

Countries	Methods	Participants	Ages	Education	Status
England	Interviews (either face to face or via phone – approximately 30 minutes each)	11 (10 female and 1 male)	25–45 years	2 (postgraduate status) 4 Practitioners (non-graduate level) 3 (studying at graduate level for Early Childhood Studies degree)	2 head teachers (primary and nursery) 7 managers in private ECEC settings.
Greece	The letter method	25 (24 female and 1 male)	22–60 years	23 graduates from four years university (responsible for children ages 4–6 years) 2 graduates from ATEI (responsible for children 0–4 years)	23 early childhood teachers (νηπιαγωγοί) 2 principals
Sweden	The letter method	16 (15 female and 1 male)		Graduate level	Principals Assistant principals

Differences among Participants in Their Understanding of Pedagogy

Most of the participants across all three countries considered themselves to be pedagogical leaders. However, when asked to identify what pedagogy meant, they tended to refer only to children's educational outcomes as in the following example from Sweden:

> As a leader in pre-school, I have a great responsibility to ensure that education is of good quality and that it helps to compensate the children's homes. For this, I need to work with my colleagues, in the design of goals and in the follow-up, that I learn with them about new pedagogical research and about the new curriculum, that we have a working way for systematic quality work and accurate pedagogical discussions. (Principal)

For some, the terms 'pedagogy' and 'education' seemed to be interchangeable as the following extract from England suggests:

> What I mean about pedagogy is how we educate the children . . . I am not sure how they differ. (Manager)
>
> It is about leading activities for children's learning. (Practitioner-room leader)

On the other hand, one manager in England argued that 'formal schools are about pedagogy because they are educational contexts, whereas early years is about play'. Thus, the idea of pedagogy was detached from an understanding of quality ECE.

Greek ECE participants emphasised the importance of building healthy relationships with children and colleagues as core to pedagogy:

> It is important for me to ensure that ECE teachers maintain an amiable and fruitful contact with each child . . . it is the only way to help children progress. (ECE centre head)
>
> Leadership in early childhood settings is a type of its own, it cannot be conceived as in primary or secondary [school], it is closer to the pedagogical notion and away from standards and exams [. . .] it is relations and good climate with parents, colleagues, the community, [. . .] all for the children's benefit. (ECE teacher)

The selected extracts highlight differences in the interpretation of pedagogy (and therefore pedagogical leadership) in each context. If conceptualisations of pedagogy diverge in this way it can create tensions in the enactment of pedagogical leadership, as the rest of the findings indicate. Data revealed that the meaning of the pedagogy was limited to learning and teaching rather than the body of knowledge that orients contextually educational purposes, practices and relationships within its community:

> In our setting my role as leader is to make sure that our pedagogy, meaning how we act with children, is of high quality and we allow play as means of learning and development. (England, manager)

> We lead activities and how those spark interests in the children and we can build on that to develop the children with the EYFS, that is what leadership means to me. (England, manager)

> Leadership is when you are respected for the learning and help you offer to young children. (Greece, ECE teacher)

There Appeared to Be Confusion Regarding the Functions of Their Leadership Role: Administrative, Management and Educational

Another key finding more evident in the English and Greek data was that participants found it difficult to define what leadership means and even more difficult to relate their definitions of leadership to an understanding of pedagogy.

In the Greek data nine out of twenty-five participants showed confusion in terms of how management, administrative duties and pedagogy came together in the ECE leader's role:

> My role is mainly auxiliary; we have no leading role in preschool. We have full cooperation and understanding with our colleagues and the parents. (Early Childhood teacher)

> I have no leading role as a director. I have the duties and roles which derive from the Official Job Description, according to the Ministry Laws. (Early Childhood teacher)

> I am responsible for the absence leave taken by my colleagues, I am also responsible for financial matters and for the organisation and implementation of innovative programmes. (Principal)

In the English data there were similar responses among leaders in ECE PVI settings, but the language was different among head teachers who were running a nursery within the primary school. The difference is illustrated in the following extracts:

> Leadership is challenging when running a setting that is a business at the same time. As a manager, I run the business, try to continue quality, look after the

> safety of the children, communicate effectively with parents and make sure that I have high quality staff and deal with stressful situations. (Early Years manager with Level 3 qualification in a PVI setting)

> Leadership for me is to make sure that everything in my school runs smoothly. Valuing my staff, make sure that children's wellbeing is safeguarded and every child has opportunities for learning. (Head teacher of a primary school)

There appeared to be less confusion about the functions of leadership among Swedish participants. This may be because the role is more clearly defined by the Educational Act. However, in practice, the participants felt that sometimes their role was not clear and that it was a challenge to balance administrative, managerial and educational duties:

> My leadership emerges in interaction and in confidence in my employees. During the three years as head of preschool, I have put great emphasis in building relationships with all my employees. (Principal)

> As I see it, it is the principal's role to build an external framework for preschool development. By setting up development areas for the entire preschool's activities, a general direction is set out. It is then up to the pedagogues in each department to form an activity that is in line with the desired general development based on the children's group's need for care, development and learning. (Principal)

Confusion Regarding the Structures of Their Leadership Role: That Is, the Styles, Models and Approaches Required in Leading ECE, and Particularly in Relation to Pedagogical Leadership

Across the countries, participants were aware of different styles of leadership. Generally, they wished to be seen as democratic, fair and collaborative leaders, but felt that in reality this was not always possible. They found themselves moving between different styles depending on the situation they had to face, as in the following example from the Swedish data:

> I am the manager and leader, which means that I lead people in groups and get the privilege of watching them grow. Sometimes I need to govern more and make sure that laws and rules are followed. (Principal)

As Sweden has a clear policy and training on what a leader's role is in the preschool the participants felt more comfortable in identifying their style. However, in reality they moved between different styles and approaches depending on the context. The English and Greek participants were less able to clearly articulate their leadership style, perhaps due to the limited leadership development and guidance provided in these contexts, although they all prioritised the importance of communication for effective leadership.

> I feel to be a good leader you need to communicate with the staff and parents, to guide staff effectively, to care for children and make sure that you have knowledge of different issues: administration, curriculum and able to deal with any situation fairly. (England, manager)
>
> Responsibility, initiative, a democratic profile, practical communication skills, diplomacy, to be dynamic. (Greece, Early Childhood teacher)

Discussion

The findings suggest an (imperfect) divide between the Swedish context on the one hand and the English and Greek contexts on the other hand. In the latter contexts, the majority of participants either do not recognise themselves as leaders or state that they have no leading role. However, in the cases where they say they recognise that they have a leading role, they seem to confuse its functions with those of administration and downplay the relationship between leadership and pedagogy. Pedagogy is seen as an extension of the teaching role, rather than as something interwoven with management, administration and accountability.

On the other hand, in the Swedish context the formal leadership role is clearly defined by the Educational Act. Participants were clear that key to leadership of ECE was taking responsibility for the quality of educational activities. However, the Swedish participants did recognise that achieving a balance between administrative duties and pedagogical leadership was sometimes a challenge.

Our research demonstrates that being a pedagogical leader is a complex assignment and an act of balancing between being an administrative authority that creates processes in the organisation and someone who creates a good learning environment for both teachers and children, with trust and collaboration as key elements. Laying the foundations for this complex assignment at a national level is essential. In England and Greece, formal leaders struggled to develop leadership as pedagogical praxis, because they felt unsure about the interconnectedness of leadership and pedagogy. In some cases, they struggled even to define pedagogy. This is likely to relate to the lack of policy guidance, pre-service training and in-service professional development for the ECE workforce, particularly with regards to leadership development. On the other hand, these challenges were less obvious in Sweden where there is clear guidance on the leader role and more training available. However, leaders in Sweden still encountered practical challenges when it came to enacting their leadership role.

To conclude, progressing pedagogical leadership depends on both the implementation of policy shifts (more training and clear guidance on ECE leadership in the Greek and English contexts, similar to what currently occurs in Sweden) and more reflection and engagement about the meaning of pedagogical leadership.

We argue that in ECE we must revisit the discourse of what we mean by pedagogy and pedagogical leadership, on the basis that many ECE professionals acting in formal positions of leadership feel uncertain about what these terms mean and what they look like in practice. On a micro level, leaders cannot be limited to carrying out an administrative role, but need to be given the support to embrace all of the pedagogical complexities involved in the leadership role. At a macro-level, pedagogical thought needs to be reinvigorated to include historicity, culture, lived complex realities and identities and positioned as the body of knowledge that orientates ECE and subsequently leadership.

References

Caroll-Lind, J., Smorti, S., Ord, K., and Robinson, L. (2016). Building pedagogical knowledge in early childhood education, *Australian Journal of Early Childhood*, vol. 41 (1), pp. 28–35.

Cheung, A. C. K., Keung, C. P. C., Kwan, P. Y. K., and Cheung, L. Y. S. (2019). Teachers' perceptions of the effect of selected leadership practices on pre-primary children's learning in Hong Kong, *Early Child Development and Care*, 189(14), 2265–2283, DOI: 10.1080/03004430.2018.1448394.

Douglas, A. L. (2019). *Leadership for Quality Early Childhood Education*, OECD Education Working Paper 11.

Eskelinen, M, and Hujala E. (2015). Early childhood leadership in Finland in light of recent research, in Waniganayake, M., J. Rodd, and L. Gibbs (eds.), *Thinking and Learning about Leadership: Early Childhood Research from Australia, Finland and Norway*. NSW, Sydney: Community Child Care Cooperative.

Heika, J., and Waniganayke, M. (2011). Pedagogical leadership from distributed perspective within the context of early childhood education, *International Journal of Leadership in Education*, vol. 14 (4), pp. 4995–512.

Male, T., and Palaiologou, I., (2015). Pedagogical leadership in the 21st century: Evidence from the field, *Educational Management Administration and Leadership*, vol. 43 (2), pp. 214–231, DOI: 10.1177/1741143213494889.

Male, T., and Palaiologou, I. (2017). Pedagogical Leadership in action: Two case studies, *International Journal of Leadership in Education Theory and Practice*, vol 20 (6), pp. 733–748, DOI: 10.1080/13603124.2016.1174310.

Mathers, S., Eisenstadt, N., Sylva, K., Soukakou, E., and Ereky-Steves, K. (2014). Sound foundations: A review of research evidence on quality of early childhood education and care for children under three: Implications for policy and practice. Available at: https://education.gov.scot/improvement/research/sound-foundations-a-review-of-the-research-evidenceon-quality-of-early-childhood-education-and-care-for-children-under-three-implications-for-policy-andpractice-2014/.

Murray, J., and McDowall Clark, R. (2013). Reframing leadership as a participative pedagogy: The working theories of early years professionals, *Early Years*, vol. 33(3), pp. 289–301, DOI: 10.1080/09575146.2013.781135.

Nicholson, J., and Maniates, H., (2016). Recognising postmodern intersectional identities in leadership for early childhood, *Early Years*, vol 36 (1), pp. 66–80.

Palaiologou, I., and Male, T. (2019). Leadership in early childhood education: The case for pedagogical praxis, *Contemporary Issues in Early Childhood*, vol 20 (1), pp. 23–34.

Waniganayake, M. (2003). Distributed leadership, in M. Ebbeck and M. Waniganayake (Eds.), *Early Childhood Professionals Leading Today and Tomorrow* (p. 34). Philadelphia, PA: Maclennan and Penny.

Whalen, S., Horsley, H., Parkinson, K., and Debra, P. (2016). A development evaluation study of a professional development initiative to strengthen organizational conditions in early education settings, *Journal of Applied Research on Children: Informing Policy for Children at Risk*, 7(2), 9.

8

Pedagogical Leadership among Directors and Deputies in Early Childhood Settings in Australia, Finland and Norway

A Summary of a Small-scale Study

Leena Halttunen, Margaret Sims, Marit Bøe, Karin Hognestad, Johanna Heikka, Manjula Waniganayake and Fay Hadley

Introduction

Pedagogical leadership in this chapter is understood as a broad concept enacted within early childhood education (ECE) centres. Involving several actors, who can vary according to the country or local context. The extent to which the distribution of leadership can influence core pedagogical tasks and programme quality is not yet fully understood in the early childhood sector in Australia, Finland and Norway. Although in these three countries there are other leaders in ECE centres who are responsible for leading pedagogy, this paper focuses on how pedagogical leadership is shared among centre directors (Ds) and deputies (DDs). Although there is some research on the centre director's role in pedagogical leadership (Heikka and Suhonen, 2019), the role of a deputy director is vague and under researched. In addition, there is no research about how directors and deputies collaborate as partners when leading pedagogy. It is also yet unknown if the establishment of the roles of director and deputy director creates the right conditions for cultivating pedagogical leadership.

This chapter examines the practices of pedagogical leadership among Ds and DDs across three countries to explore the impact of different contexts on practice. The following sections offer a brief note on the lack of research about deputy leadership and a broader consideration of pedagogical leadership in ECE settings. This is followed by an explanation of the contexts in which the research was conducted. Our findings about pedagogical leadership are then highlighted in each context and discussed in relation to each other. Overall, we argue that pedagogical leadership must be understood in context and cannot be considered a singular, universal construct.

Deputy Leadership

The enactment of leadership practices among deputy leaders is a forgotten area of educational research (Cranston et al., 2004). There is a lack of research about deputy principals in school education, although the tradition of the deputy position is older and more established than in the early childhood sector (Barnett et al., 2012). Consequently, research on deputy leadership in early childhood is extremely limited. Our previous research suggests some tensions in tasks performed by ECE centre directors and deputies in Australia, Finland and Norway (Halttunen et al., 2019).

We found the nature of allocating leadership roles and responsibilities within each setting to be highly localised, particularly within Australia and Finland where there were no legislative guidelines about the appointment of deputies as is available in Norway. In this chapter, we go further in exploring the pedagogical aspects of the work of these directors and deputies in each of the three countries. As a pioneering study, however, the goal is not to compare these three nations, but to ascertain insights about current developments in pedagogical leadership in ECE.

Pedagogical Leadership

Directors (D) and deputy directors (DD) have multiple responsibilities including those of line management, administration and pedagogical leadership. Pedagogical leadership means leading professional work towards organisational goals (Heikka and Waniganayake, 2011). Research indicates that effective pedagogical leadership results in teachers feeling greater commitment (Heikka et al., 2021), improved quality of ECE (Douglass, 2019; Melhuish et al., 2006; Sylva et al., 2010) and improved well-being of children (Fonsén et al., 2020). Pedagogical leadership includes leading the daily pedagogical activities and curriculum work in ECE settings. It also includes leading pedagogical reflection and assessment as well as enhancing pedagogical and professional development in line with core values and ethical practices (Bøe and Hognestad, 2017; Corrick and Reed, 2019; Heikka et al., 2019). A pedagogical leader has the responsibility to support and inspire educators and shape a learning organisation (O'Sullivan, 2009; Stremmel, 2019). Pedagogical leaders can do this in several ways, for example, by influencing the curriculum decisions and facilitating and directing pedagogical discussion of the educators (Waniganayake et al., 2017).

Classical conceptualisations of pedagogical leadership (e.g. Sergiovanni, 1998) focus on teaching and learning. Contemporary research is based on understanding early childhood pedagogy as a holistic phenomenon, integrating education and care, and the community aspects of leadership. Heikka and Waniganayake (2011) considered that the term is connected not only with children's learning but also with the capacity building of an early childhood professional, and the values and beliefs about education held by the wider community. According to O'Sullivan (2009), pedagogical leadership is enacted by different facets of service and the relationships within the wider community.

In a narrower sense, pedagogical leadership can be understood as the work of people who hold managerial positions at the upper levels of the organisations and who are seen to have the responsibility for setting education goals (Atkinson and Biegun, 2017; Soukainen, 2013). However, leading an ECE centre is a joint task that involves centre directors and other leadership stakeholders, such as deputy directors and teachers. Pedagogical leadership is separately enacted by formal and informal leaders but interdependently through organisational contexts. Leadership structures, routines and tools mediate distributed leadership functions. Interdependence between the stakeholders involved in leadership is crucial for the achievement of organisational goals (Spillane, Halverson and Diamond, 2001; Spillane, 2006).

According to Heikka (2014), Heikka and Suhonen (2019) and Heikka et al. (2021), distributed pedagogical leadership functions include, first, the enhancement of shared consciousness of visions, goals and values for ECE within the centre. It also means the distribution of responsibilities for pedagogical leadership as well as distributing the enactment of pedagogical improvement within ECE centres. This can be promoted by focusing on the roles and responsibilities of the Ds and DDs in pedagogical development and negotiating how they facilitate the learning and expertise of educators aligned with centre goals. The authority is shared as the Ds work independently but interdependently as supporters of educators in the centre. It is also important to enhance the DD's participation in decision-making and enhancing efficient and participatory decision-making among all staff in a centre (Heikka et al., 2013). Well-planned, goal-oriented and regularly assessed strategies assist in achieving cooperation (Heikka et al., 2013). In addition, competences required from the directors include both knowledge of ECE and broader leadership skills (Muijs et al., 2004). It is clear from the literature that there are different ways in which pedagogical leadership is perceived and enacted, and this variation is accompanied by different understandings of the responsibilities of both Ds and DDs in leading pedagogy. Exploring the contexts in which the different understanding operates will help to clarify the concept of pedagogical leadership, which ultimately may lead to improvements in practice.

The Contexts

In Australia, in 2012, the *National Quality Framework* (NQF) established the legislative framing of all ECE services in Australia, including introducing the idea of 'educational leadership' (Australian Children's Education and Care Quality Authority (ACECQA), 2019). This term is used widely in this country, rather than the alternative term, 'pedagogical leadership' as used in this paper. However, pedagogical leadership was not clearly articulated in the NQF and for some years was interpreted and enacted in different ways (Harrison et al., 2019, Sims and Waniganayake, 2015, Waniganayake and Sims, 2018). This confusion continues to blur the boundaries between pedagogical leadership and line management responsibilities.

It is not uncommon in Australia for centre owners to be untrained, yet they operate as line managers, while another staff member (usually, but not always, one with an ECE degree rather than a vocational diploma – Harrison et al., 2019) takes on the pedagogical leadership role. However, where managers have an ECE diploma or degree qualification, they will often perform the pedagogical leadership role together with managerial responsibilities, creating their own synthesis of line management and pedagogical leadership.

Regulation 118 of the NQF specified that the service 'must designate, in writing, a suitably qualified and experienced educator, co-ordinator or other individual as educational leader at the service to lead the development and implementation of educational programmes in the service'

(https://www.legislation.nsw.gov.au/view/whole/html/inforce/current/sl-2011-0653). Educational leadership was further articulated in Quality Area 7, Standard 7.2.2 in the NQS, as a role responsible for supporting and leading the 'development and implementation of the educational program and assessment and planning cycle' (ACECQA, 2011 (updated 2020)).

Seven years after the introduction of the concept, a substantive guide around the expectations and requirements of the role was introduced (ACECQA, 2019). Here it is argued that educational leaders play a central role in supporting a culture of continuous improvement, empowering centre staff to strive towards practice that consistently delivers the best outcomes in terms of children's learning and well-being, and communication with families and the community. The implication is that such improvements are reflected in quality assessment and service accreditation.

In Finland, pedagogical leadership is enacted by diverse ECE stakeholders, including the Ds and ECE teachers and municipal level ECE leaders. Teachers' engagement in pedagogical leadership is essential because the implementation of national curriculum reforms requires the commitment of teachers as developers of ECE pedagogy (Act on Early Childhood Education and Care 540/2018 (Varhaiskasvatuslaki 540/2018), Finnish National Agency for Education (EDUFI), 2018). The Finnish Education Evaluation Centre (FINEEC) (2018) launched quality indicators for ECE according to which leadership of ECE should be planned and goal-oriented. High-quality pedagogical leadership comprises evaluation and development and taking care of educators' professional learning.

The municipalities and private ECE organisations in Finland are free to decide the procedures of pedagogical leadership, resulting in considerable variation in leadership practices and arrangements. The qualification requirement for the ECE centre D was a bachelor's degree in ECE until 2018 when the qualification requirement was raised to a master's degree (Act on Early Childhood Education and Care 540/2018). Until then, notions of ECE leadership in national policy documents were limited. In 2018, FINEEC stated that the aim of ECE leadership is transferring pedagogical goals into ECE practice. Distributed leadership is emphasised as a strategy for high-quality pedagogy. However, teacher leadership is also considered important. The *National Core Curriculum for Early Childhood Education and Care* (2018) states that 'the head supports the community's development into a learning community where competence is developed and shared. . . . The head is also in charge of ensuring that shared working practices are made visible and regularly examined and assessed' (p.31). These national documents do not, however, use the term 'pedagogical leadership', but rather focus on describing the responsibilities of the leaders.

In Norway, pedagogical leadership is understood in relationship with the roles assigned to leaders. The Kindergarten Act (The Norwegian Ministry of Education and Research, 2005) states that centres must have *adequate* pedagogical and administrative leadership. The D has the overall responsibility for the tasks required by law and *National Framework Plan*. This concerns both the direct tasks of the D, and the responsibility of the D for all the centre's tasks, including those performed by the other staff. Centres must have a D who is an ECE teacher with a bachelor degree or another education qualification at a tertiary level relevant for working with children and including pedagogical expertise. One of the government's strategies is to increase the effectiveness of ECE leaders and their capacity to lead based on a leadership qualification at a master's level. For this purpose, leadership education programmes for Ds and DDs are offered by Norwegian higher education institutions (The Norwegian Ministry of Education and Research, 2017). These consist of a three-semester, master's level course (thirty credits) completed while working part-time.

Pedagogical leadership includes collaboration with the owner, teacher leaders and other staff as well as with relevant institutions. It contains following up on the planning, documentation, evaluation and development of the pedagogical content and working methods and ensuring that all staff are involved in this work. Expanded governance of ECE, in particular through extensive capacity building such as pedagogical leadership (The Norwegian Ministry of Education and Research, 2018), emphasises that Ds have an increasing responsibility for pedagogical leadership.

Depending on size of the centre, ECE centres may have a full-time DD position or less, to meet the requirement of *adequate* pedagogical and administrative leadership (over 100 children = full-time deputy position). In the *Framework Plan* for the content and tasks of kindergartens (The Norwegian Directorate for Education and Training, 2017) including pedagogical leadership responsibilities of the owner, D and pedagogical leaders are clarified and emphasised. The DD is not a formal leadership position described in the *Framework Plan*. That is, the DD's roles and responsibilities and how they enact their leadership is not clarified in the plan. A DD is appointed by the owner to assist the director of an ECE centre.

In order to understand more about the roles of Ds and DDs across the three contexts, we engaged ten Ds and seven DDs in semi-structured interviews. Participants were all women, ranging between thirty-one and sixty years. The majority (n = 10) were highly experienced ECE practitioners with twenty years or more employment in the sector.

Theoretical Underpinnings of the Study

The theory of practice architectures was initially developed by Kemmis and Grootenboer (2008) and is built on the practice theory of Schatzki (2002). For the purpose of this study, we used the definition introduced by Kemmis et al. (2014). Practices are understood, communicated and enacted within a cultural and organisational culture that has its own history and materiality and can be examined through an analysis of participant 'sayings', 'doings' and 'relatings', which reflect already existing, external cultural-discursive, material-economic and social-political arrangements. This theory has been applied in previous studies focusing on ECE leadership (Barnes et al., 2019, Hognestad and Bøe, 2015, Rönnerman et al., 2015, Rönnerman et al., 2017).

According to Kemmis et al. (2014), cultural-discursive architectures are the resources in practice that create, construct and enable the language, knowledge and ideas used in the practice and in sayings about the practice. Cultural-discursive conditions are mediated through language in a semantic space, for example languages, discourses, cultures and thoughts. Through material-economic architectures, the resources that make possible or hinder the actions in practice are made visible. Material-economic conditions are expressed through actions in a physical space, such as time, material, room and the artefacts. Socio-political architectures contain dimensions such as power, hierarchies and solidarity between participants in a practice. Relationships can be shaped through roles, experience, competence and education of participants as well as through political architectures. Practice architectures allow us to understand the conditions that enable and constrain the DDs leading practices through their own expressions, described activities and how they relate to the D and other staff in a practice.

Findings

We outline the key elements arising from the data analysed for each country, reflecting practices associated with pedagogical leadership in Australia, Finland and Norway.

From Australia:

- There was a strong association between improving pedagogy and improving documentation of children's learning in the data from both Ds and DDs. Interactions with children were not identified as elements in improving pedagogy.
- There was an absence of an explicit link between pedagogy and leadership evident in the ways in which leadership and pedagogy were discussed separately.

- Leadership matters focused on macro-level functions connected with staff support and relationships with families.
- There was a lack of clarity between leadership and management roles, and for DDs, there was confusion between their role as a DD and their role in working directly with children.
- There was evidence of a clear hierarchy with DDs ceding power to Ds (and consequently, sometimes feeling powerless) accompanied by a lack of clarity around the division of responsibilities.

From Finland:

- Both Ds and DDs emphasised that the role of the DD focused more on administrative tasks and not pedagogical leadership. Ds did not expect to share pedagogical leadership with their DDs.
- Ds' direct pedagogical leadership activities were, for example, being responsible for structures which supported pedagogical development, bringing new pedagogical knowledge and ideas, being an example for the staff and visiting teams.
- DDs were indirectly sharing pedagogical leadership through being members of the leadership team. They joined the team meetings and discussions but did not have a leading role in pedagogical leadership at the centre level.
- DDs' relatings with the staff were not directly related to pedagogical leadership but more focused on taking care of the well-being of others. They valued being present and close to the colleagues which made them more able to sense what was going on at their centre.
- DDs were at the same time teachers of a group of children. They were active pedagogical leaders in their own team and in their role as the ECE preschool teacher who is responsible for the pedagogy of the team.

From Norway:

- DDs acted as leaders at the Ds' leadership level participating in pedagogical leadership activities and pedagogical improvement.
- How pedagogical tasks were shared between Ds and DDs depends on the Ds' workload, needs and wishes. However, division of pedagogical work was shared through a negotiating process between them.
- DDs acknowledge the Ds' positions as overall leaders, and they felt comfortable not being accountable for the whole centre leadership functions. DDs relate to the D as an assistant.

- Pedagogical collaboration involved tasks that facilitated pedagogical improvement. While the Ds had the overall pedagogical responsibility for thoughts and visions, the DDs acted as a bridge between visions and everyday practice.
- Collaboration was built on a trusting relationship and mutual support.

Discussion and Conclusion

Our findings indicate clearly that pedagogical leadership is enacted differently across the three countries in the study, indicating that the concept is fluid, and its enactment is somewhat dependent on the cultural/economic/social/political context in which it is operating. The Australian data pinpoints that pedagogical leadership is aimed at improving quality as identified in the quality assessment process defined in national ECE policy. In this context, pedagogical documentation is seen as crucial and pedagogical leadership tends to focus on the inspection and improvement of this documentation. In Finland and Norway, pedagogical work is understood as enhancing quality where both directors and teachers have a significant role. In Finland, the DDs' actions in leading pedagogy merely took place when they were working directly with children as teachers. In Norway, the DDs lead at the centre level in collaboration with the D.

Compared to Finland and Norway, the Australian data demonstrated a completely different approach. Here Ds and DDs positioned themselves as key pedagogical leaders whose role was to ensure that teachers implement the correct pedagogical approaches. The data suggests perceptions of a hierarchy, with Ds positioned at the apex. DDs are positioned below them, with the consequent responsibility functioning as a channel between staff, families and the D. This hierarchy brings with it an assumption that Ds, at the apex, are the experts when it comes to pedagogy, with DDs following them and staff in positions where their pedagogical knowledge is perceived as sufficiently limited as to require supervision, mentoring and correcting.

The Finnish data demonstrated the importance of pedagogical leadership being shared across all those who work with the children and families. In Finland, teachers with at least a BA degree in ECE studies are expected to lead pedagogy with their group of children. In this context, it is therefore understandable that Ds may take more of an overview role in relation to pedagogical leadership. They ensure that all those working in the centres have access to the latest information, and that the work environment creates the right context (processes and structures) to support their teachers to lead their own pedagogy effectively. Perhaps because of this distributed leadership around pedagogy, there appears to be little for DDs to undertake in terms of pedagogical leadership. Rather their leadership roles, as in the case of Australia, tend to focus more on administrative work. It is worth noticing that in Finland, there is a tendency to have, for example, a separate position for a pedagogical leader who works at the centre level leading pedagogy.

If Finland is positioned at one end of a continuum of distributed pedagogical leadership and Australia at the other end, it might be argued that Norway fits somewhere between. Here the DD appeared to take a stronger hands-on role around pedagogical work and staff work with the DD in teams. The D appeared a little more distanced, functioning to provide an overview of the ways in which the pedagogical work of the leadership teams meets required national standards in each country. Norwegian DDs also appeared to be more involved in pedagogical work than the Finnish DDs. There appeared to be more flexibility for the leadership dyads to negotiate their roles in Norway than in Finland or Australia. In the latter, this is likely related to the stronger sense of hierarchy evident in the Australian data that may preclude perceptions of DDs' capability to take on what might be perceived as a higher level of responsibility. In Finland and Australia, this may be because the role of the DD appears to be more strongly identified with administration rather than pedagogy.

This study demonstrates that there is not a universally understood concept of pedagogical leadership, nor a universally enacted structure that defines the roles of the D or the DD in pedagogical leadership. It is crucial to remember that cultural-discursive, economic-material and social-political differences between countries will always create different contexts into which ideas are enacted. Cultural-discursive arrangements are resources to make possible the language and discourses. This leads us to consider how official documents or daily discussions interpret and justify the work of those with a leadership position. Material-economic arrangements are resources enabling and constraining activities. A critical question is, for example, do DDs have time for sharing pedagogical leadership with the D or other staff at the centre? Kemmis et al. (2014) note that these three arrangements and practices do not appear separately. It seems that social-political arrangements including aspects of power and solidarity have a significant role in what actually happens in practice. There is a need to consider the resources existing within centres, what relationships are possible and if organisational functions, roles and rules support or restrict the relationships and work related to pedagogical leadership. Seeking to determine a universal constant that operates independent of these influences is not useful as it is the richness of different contexts that provides opportunities for learning.

Pedagogical leadership is better understood in the context in which it is enacted, rather than seeking to determine a global universal approach. However, examining understandings of pedagogical leadership in different contexts creates opportunities to challenge one's own perspectives, and perhaps broaden understanding and change practices towards what might be considered more desirable outcomes.

References

Atkinson, K. & Biegun, L. 2017. An uncertain tale: Alternative conceptualizations of pedagogical leadership. *Journal of Childhood Studies*, 42(4), 61–68.

Australian Children's Education and Care Quality Authority 2019. *The Educational Leader Resource*. Canberra: Australian Children's Education and Care Quality Authority.

Australian Children's Education and Care Quality Authority 2011 [updated 2020]. *Guide to the National Quality Framework*. Canberra: Australian Children's Education and Care Quality Authority.

Barnes, K., Hadley, F. & Cheeseman, S. 2019. Preschool educational leaders: Who are they and what are they doing?. *Australasian Journal of Early Childhood*, 44, 351–364.

Barnett, B. G., Shoho, A. R. & Oleszewski, A. M. 2012. The job realities of beginning and experienced assistant principals. *Leadership and Policy in Schools*, 11, 92–128.

Bøe, M. & Hognestad, K. 2017. Directing and facilitating distributed pedagogical leadership: Best practices in early childhood education. *International Journal of Leadership in Education*, 20, 133–148.

Corrick, G. & Reed, M. H. 2019. Pedagogical leadership: challenges and opportunities. In: Cheeseman, S. & Walker, R. (eds.) *Pedagogies for Leading Practice: Thinking about Pedagogy in Early Childhood Education*. London: Routledge.

Cranston, N., Tromans, C. & Reugebrink, M. 2004. Forgotten leaders: what do we know about the deputy principalship in secondary schools? *International Journal of Leadership in Education*, 7, 225–242.

Douglass, A. L. 2019. *Leadership for Quality Early Childhood Education and Care*. OECD Education Working Papers 211. OECD Publishing.

Finnish Education Evaluation Centre (FINEEC) 2018. *Varhaiskasvatuksen laadun arvioinnin perusteet ja suositukset [Guidelines and Recommendations for Evaluating the Quality of Early Childhood Education and Care]*. viewed 8th December 2020, from https://karvi.fi/app/uploads/2018/10/KARVI_vaka_laadun-arvioinnin -perusteet-ja-suositukset.pdf.

Finnish National Agency for Education (EDUFI) 2018. *National Core Curriculum for Early Childhood Education and Care*. Helsinki: Finnish National Agency for Education.

Fonsen, E., Lahtinen, L., Sillman, M. & Reunamo, J. 2020. Pedagogical leadership and children's well-being in Finnish early education. *Educational Management, Administration and Leadership*. Published online 20 October 2020, 1–16: https://journals.sagepub.com/doi/10.1177/1741143220962105

Halttunen, L., Waniganayake, M. & Heikka, J. 2019. Teacher leadership repertoires in the context of early childhood education team meetings in Finland. *Journal of Early Childhood Education Research*, 8, 143–161.

Harrison, L., Hadley, F., Irvine, S., Davis, B., Barblett, L., Hatzigianni, M., Mulhearn, G., Waniganayake, M., Andrews, R. & LI, P. 2019. *Quality Improvement Research Project Commissioned by the Australian Children's Education and Care Quality Authority (ACECQA)*. Sydney: Australian Children's Education and Care Quality Authority.

Heikka, J. 2014. *Distributed Pedagogical Leadership in Early Childhood Education*. PhD, University of Tampere.

Heikka, J. & Suhonen, K. 2019. Distributed pedagogical leadership functions in early childhood education settings in Finland. *South East Asia Early Childhood Journal*, 8, 43–56.

Heikka, J. & Waniganayake, M. 2011. Pedagogical leadership from a distributed perspective within the context of early childhood education. *International Journal of Leadership in Education*, 14, 499–512.

Heikka, J., Waniganayake, M. & Hujala, E. 2013. Contextualizing distributed leadership within early childhood education: current understandings, research evidence and future challenges. *Educational Management, Administration & Leadership*, 41, 30–44.

Heikka, J. Pitkäniemi, H., Kettukangas, T. & Hyttinen, T. 2021. Distributed pedagogical leadership and teacher leadership in early childhood education contexts. *International Journal of Leadership in Education*, 24 (3), 333–348.

Hognestad, K. & Bøe, M. 2015. Leading site-based knowledge development: A mission impossible? Insights from a study in Norway. *In*: Waniganayake, M., Rodd, J. & Gibbs, L. (eds.) *Thinking and Learning about Leadership: Early Childhood Research from Australia, Finland and Norway*. NSW, Australia: Community Child Care Co-operative Ltd.

Kemmis, S. & Grootenboer, P. 2008. Situating praxis in practice: Practice architectures and the cultural, social and material conditions for practice. *In*: Kemmis, I. S. & Smith, T. J. (eds.) *Enabling Praxis, Challenges for Education*. Rotterdam: Sense Publishers.

Kemmis, S., Wilkinson, J., Edwards-Groves, C., Grootenboer, P. & Bristol, L. 2014. *Changing Practices, Changing Education*. Singapore: Springer.

Melhuish, E., Quinn, L., Hanna, K., Sylva, K., Sammons, P., Siraj-Blatchford, I. & Taggart, B. 2006. *Effective Pre-school Provision in Northern Ireland (EPPNI) Summary Report*. Belfast: Department of Education Northern Ireland.

Muijs, D., Aubrey, C., Harris, A. & Briggs, M. 2004. How do they manage? A review of the research on leadership in early childhood. *Journal of Early Childhood Research*, 2, 157–169.

O'Sullivan, J. 2009. *Leadership Skills in the Early Years: Making a Difference*. London: A & C Black.

Rönnerman, K., Edwards-Groves, C. & Grootenboer, P. 2015. Opening up communicative spaces for discussion 'quality practices' in early childhood education through middle leadership. *Nordic Journal of Studies in Educational Policy*, 3. https://www.tandfonline.com/doi/full/10.3402/nstep.v1.30098

Rönnerman, K., Grootenboer, P. & Edwards-Groves, C. 2017. The practice architectures of middle leading in early childhood education. *International Journal of Child Care and Education Policy*, 11, 8.

Schatzki, T. R. 2002. *The Site of the Social: A Philosophical Account of the Constitution of Social Life and Change*. Pennsylvania, PA: Penn State University Press.

Sergiovanni, T. J. 1998. Leadership as pedagogy, capital development and school effectiveness. *International Journal of Leadership in Education*, 1, 37–46.

Sims, M. & Waniganayake, M. 2015. The performance of compliance in early childhood: Neoliberalism and nice ladies. *Global Studies of Childhood*, 5, 333–345.

Soukainen, U. 2013. Superior's pedagogical support in distributed organisation of early childhood education. *In*: Hujala, E., Waniganayake, M. & Rodd, J. (eds.) *Researching Leadership in Early Childhood Education*. Tampere: Tampere University Press.

Spillane, J. P. (2006) *Distributed Leadership*, San Francisco: Jossey-Bass.

Spillane, J. P., Richard Halverson, R. & Diamond, J. B. (2001) Investigating School Leadership Practice: A Distributed Perspective. *Educational Researcher*, 30(23), 23–28.

Stremmel, A. J. 2019. Pedagogical leadership as ethical collaborative behavior. *In*: Cheeseman, S. & Walker, R. (eds.) *Pedagogies for Leading Practice*. Oxon: Routledge.

Sylva, K., Melhuish, E., Sammons, P., Siraj, I. & Taggart, B. 2010. *Early Childhood Matters: Evidence from the Effective Pre-school and Primary Education Project*. London, Routledge.

The Norwegian Directorate for Education and Training 2017. *Framework plan for the content and tasks of kindergartens*. Oslo: The Norwegian Directorate for Education and Training.

The Norwegian Ministry of Education and Research 2005. *Kindergarten Act*. Oslo: The Norwegian Ministry of Education and Research.

The Norwegian Ministry of Education and Research 2017. Kompetanse for fremtidens barnehage. Revidert strategi for kompetanse og rekruttering 2018–2022 (Competence for the future kindergarten Revised strategy for competence and recruitment 2018-2022). *Retrieved from*: https://www.regjeringen.no/contentassets/7e72a90a6b884d0399d9537cce8b801e/kompetansestrategi-for-barnehage-2018_2022.pdf

The Norwegian Ministry of Education and Research (2018) The Kindergarten Teaching Profession – Present and Future. Summary of a Report Developed by an Expert Group Appointed by the Ministry of Education and Research. https://www.regjeringen.no/en/dokumenter/the-kindergarten-teaching-profession--present-and-future/id2662934/

Waniganayake, M. & Sims, M. 2018. Becoming critically reflective: Australian educational leaders effecting change as street-level bureaucrats in a Neoliberalist policy landscape. *In*: Roopnarine, J. L., Johnson, J., Quinn, S. & Patte, M. (eds.) *Handbook of International Perspectives on Early Childhood Education*. New York: Routledge Press.

Waniganayake, M., Cheeseman, S., Fenech, M., Hadley, F. & Shepherd, W. 2017. *Leadership: Contexts and Complexities in Early Childhood Education*. South Melbourne: Oxford University Press.

9

An Organisational Approach to Supporting Pedagogical Leadership

Reporting on a Case Study with London Early Years Foundation

Mona Sakr

Introduction

Pedagogical leadership is most effective when it is enacted by all ECE professionals rather than just a select few with official management roles (Murray & Clark, 2013). Most research on pedagogical leadership in ECE so far has focused on its development outside of the practice context, for example through university-led training routes and external qualifications. We need to know more about what ECE settings can do to build pedagogical leadership amidst the pressures and relationships that characterise their everyday context. This chapter investigates how pedagogical leadership can be supported to flourish in ECE settings through an organisational approach, rather than external training or qualifications. It explores this through case study research with the London Early Years Foundation (LEYF) – a social enterprise group comprising thirty-nine nurseries across London. The thematic analysis of eighteen interviews across four LEYF nurseries suggests some of the key ways in which pedagogical leadership can be developed among ECE staff as part of the organisational processes that structure day-to-day activities and relationships within LEYF settings. The chapter presents four aspects of an organisational approach that are supportive of pedagogical leadership: (1) continuous improvement is conceptualised as the growth in pedagogical leadership capacity among staff, (2) in-house continuing professional development (CPD) focuses on pedagogical leadership, (3) career progression is explicitly related to the demonstration of pedagogical leadership and (4) staff have the opportunity to develop specialised pedagogical leadership by leading improvement initiatives and action research. I argue that some elements of these organisational foundations are available to all ECE organisations, regardless of size and resourcing, while others (such as the provision of CPD around pedagogical leadership) depend on smaller settings working together and the cross-sector support of larger organisations.

Pedagogical Leadership as 'Catalytic Leadership'

In the English context, the term 'pedagogical leadership' is quite closely related with the now defunct qualification early years professional status (EYPS). EYPS was a postgraduate qualification specifically for those working in ECE. Its creation was part of an attempt to drive up the levels of qualification in the ECE workforce. It has since been replaced by the early years teacher (EYT) status. One of the special aspects of the EYPS was its focus on the enhancement of quality ECE provision through pedagogical leadership, rather than formal management hierarchies. Those with EYPS were often brought into settings in roles that had no official seniority, and yet their training was in making and enabling change and improvements in pedagogy. Because of this, particular models of pedagogical leadership emerged that were distinct from an understanding of leadership in managerial terms.

The research of McDowall Clark (2012) contributed significantly to our understanding of the pedagogical leadership that could flow from the EYPS. She described this pedagogical leadership as 'catalytic leadership', which was the idea that particular professionals were able to improve practice through positively influencing the culture of the organisation. Through modelling, coaching and pedagogical conversations, the EYPs were able to generate a culture of questioning and curiosity, which in turn prepared the ground for change. They specialised in improving pedagogical implementation through the 'soft' means of inspiring and supporting others, without officially managing others. The EYPS qualification was thought to open up the possibilities of catalytic leadership because it acted as a model, helping these individuals to ask questions of their own practice, to be open to change, to be constantly attuned to future possibilities and potential improvements. Thus, the EYPS training was routed in creating spaces of critical, creative and collaborative reflection.

Regardless of official qualifications, deep reflective work seems to be the key component in international understandings of how to develop pedagogical leadership. Sims et al. (2015) suggest that leadership development initiatives can be either empowering or disempowering depending on the levels of reflection they encourage among professionals completing them. Empowering programmes focus on supporting practitioners to engage in reflection, challenge and insight – to develop their 'activist professionalism'. On the other hand, some leadership development can effectively be 'training in the dominant discourse' (p. 150). That is, leaders learn to 'play the game' set out for them. For example, they might not question for themselves the meaning of 'quality' in ECE, but simply accept that quality is whatever the government or regulatory powers say it is. They then focus on just dishing out more of whatever others have defined as quality ECE. In this kind of development, pedagogical leadership is inhibited because reflections lack depth with regards to 'how' and 'why' actions are carried out in the day to day.

Various studies have explored the potential of action research to develop pedagogical leadership. Henderson (2017) documented the use of action research in Australian ECE settings, arguing that the 'cyclical processes of learning, acting and reflecting' (p. 389) are key to the development of pedagogical leadership. The paper evaluates three action research projects in three ECE centres, as part of a wider professional development programme. Based on the evaluation, Henderson argues that the action research provided essential time for important relational work among ECE practitioners at all levels. The action research was an investment in the organisational culture, with dedicated time for learning together, which leads to 'moving from points of difference to engaging in genuine dialogue' (p. 394). Similarly, returning to an English context and the EYPS, Davis (2012) found that what mattered to EYPs was not a particular theory of leadership or change management, but the creation of a space for reflective discussion and intellectual stimulation.

Advancing What We Know about Organisational Approaches to Developing Pedagogical Leadership

Given the fragmented landscape of qualifications and training in the English ECE context (Elwick et al., 2018), the onus is often on ECE settings themselves to foster pedagogical leadership among their staff. We need to know more about how they might do this. In order to contribute to our knowledge, this chapter therefore shares conversations in the context of one ECE organisation (LEYF) in London and eighteen ECE professionals within LEYF regarding their pedagogical development. The professionals interviewed were working in various positions (ranging from apprentice to nursery manager) and across four of LEYF's nurseries. The conversations were structured around perceptions of leadership and leadership development more broadly, but the focus in this chapter is on the following questions within the dialogues:

1. How do professionals think pedagogical leadership is developed by LEYF?
2. What developmental activities and initiatives do they find particularly helpful in supporting pedagogical leadership to flourish?
3. How are these activities and initiatives managed within the everyday realities and constraints of an organisation like LEYF, where time and budgets are limited?

A quick note on terminology: in LEYF, all those working in the nurseries with the children are called 'teachers' regardless of qualification level or position. This is a conscious decision within the organisation to recognise the pedagogical purpose and contribution of those working 'on the floor'. In respect for this decision, the remainder of the chapter, when referring to LEYF staff, uses the term 'teacher' as opposed to 'professional' or 'practitioner'.

LEYF's Organisational Approach to Developing Pedagogical Leadership

The conversations suggested four ways in which LEYF develops pedagogical leadership:

1. Continuous improvement is conceptualised as the growth in capacity of pedagogical leadership among teachers;
2. In-house CPD experiences often focus on pedagogical leadership;
3. Career progression relates explicitly to the demonstration of and potential for pedagogical leadership;
4. Teachers have the opportunity to develop specialised pedagogical leadership; this builds confidence and passion across the organisation.

These themes are each outlined in the following paragraphs in more detail, with illustrative quotes from teachers.

Continuous Improvement Is Conceptualised as the Growth in Capacity for Pedagogical Leadership among Teachers

Continuous improvement is at the centre of all that LEYF does, and both managers and teachers voiced their commitment to improving practice every single day. There are a host of tools and practices that staff use as part of continuous improvement, which have been created by the central team at LEYF and embedded by nursery managers. Pedagogical leadership is built into these tools and resources. In the organisational context, using the tools and resources equates with showing pedagogical leadership.

For example, the LEYF Pedagogical Development Scale (LPDS) is used by nursery teams to reflect on their pedagogical practices and what next steps they would like to use. A detailed account of the LEYF pedagogy can be found in O'Sullivan's chapter within this volume. The teams are encouraged to actively use the LPDS tool as a demonstration of pedagogical leadership practice:

> We have the actual LEYF pedagogy development scale which relates to all seven strands of the pedagogy. So if you took 'spiral curriculum' for example, it would be broken down into satisfactory, good and outstanding, and within that what would you expect to see, what would you expect to be doing. So if you say you're good, what would be the next thing? And what would the teacher be doing? And then where could you progress? So it's all laid out like that for you, and we assess ourselves. (P5)

The development scale is used collaboratively, with teachers reflecting together on potential improvements:

> We have our sort of pedagogical goals – we're trying to focus on just a few things to get up to the next level. But it's never like 'we're going to do this', it's 'here are the goals, can we think about which ones we can realistically target'. (P10)

P10's manager explained that this collaborative approach was important for developing ownership and accountability:

> Sometimes it's good for them [the team] to reflect themselves and then see rather than you telling them. With you constantly telling they receive it in a particular way, rather than if they can reflect themselves and then they can identify the problems themselves. There's a sense of ownership there and accountability. (P15)

Improvement is intertwined across nurseries and individuals. The development scale for example is used both with teams (e.g. in team planning meetings) and with individuals (e.g. in individual supervisions):

> When I have supervision with my manager, I can speak to her about any concerns, and also hear what I'm doing well. And I like to hear what I'm doing well from her, I like her to acknowledge when I'm doing a good job, because it makes me feel good and know that I am on the right pathway. (P3)

> We have supervision. Just three weeks ago all of us had supervision. You tell her where you need support and she's definitely coming to make sure that yes you are improving on where you think you are lacking. (P14)

There is an effort to ensure that the language surrounding these developmental processes is supportive and positive, and that pedagogical leadership is seen as constant and ongoing; the work of pedagogical leadership is never done.

> The manager does support us, gives us ideas and opinions on what we can improve and what we're doing well, but also points out where we need to think a bit more about our activities in relation to the pedagogy. (P13)

> Our curriculum is spiral, it's constant and it's never-ending and I feel like LEYF is a bit like that as well. They never sit still for a minute, they're always 'ok, we've achieved this, what's the next step?' It's always doing something to further develop and develop. (P15)

In-house CPD Experiences often Focus on Pedagogical Leadership

In-house CPD experiences consistently start with and circle back to LEYF's values and pedagogy. When anyone joins the organisation, regardless of their role – whether they are a chef, teacher or finance officer in the Central Office – they complete a Level 1 qualification which outlines LEYF's social purpose, values and pedagogy. Further CPD designed for teachers brings pedagogy even more to the fore, meaning that pedagogical leadership is stressed as the heart of all individual and organisational development.

> I feel that when we go to our training, our Pedagogy Manager, he's brilliant, he's so excited all the time and that comes through and he gets us doing some really crazy stuff to inspire us. So just a couple of weeks ago I had a session, and it feeds me, it does, I came back and my team usually know when I have been on one of the Room Leader Workshops, they know that I'll come back with stuff, because they feed me. (P5)

> The training, the conferences, the rigorous monitoring from the Area Managers. It's just the culture. So, you know sometimes we have new people coming in and

the tone of how they speak and their body language and behaviour is different but after being in LEYF for a while, you see they have begun to absorb the LEYF culture and it all beginning to fall into place. (P15)

These responses suggest that training and explicitly developmental processes (such as mentoring or supervision) are not primarily about acquiring 'know-how' in the sense of technical knowledge. Instead, they are a transformative process in which the values and pedagogy of LEYF are increasingly taken up and embodied by the individual teacher, enhancing their capacity for pedagogical leadership. This is even more the case when we consider that staff are expected to share what they have learned through training with colleagues in their nursery:

With my colleague, we participated in a maths training and then we felt more confident to deliver the maths training within the nursery to the parents who feel that they were less confident to deliver maths to the children . . . you must be able to find something that you can take away for yourself and bring it back to your own setting. (P1)

Of course, these formal processes of induction, training and supervision do not have the same impact with all staff members. P8, who has been with the organisation for seven to eight months, expressed that although others in the organisation thought he had changed, he himself did not feel aware of these changes:

They said to me that I've changed a lot since coming here. . . . I don't know because personally I don't feel I've changed that much. (P8)

The same employee felt uncomfortable with the idea that he was a 'leader' in the organisation, or would develop leadership skills and roles over time:

I'm not really a leader . . . I don't feel that I would be suitable. (P8)

This might indicate that the 'LEYF-ification' process – in the sense of taking on the workplace culture and the commitment to pedagogical leadership – takes longer than seven to eight months to occur, or it might be that particular staff members feel unable or unmotivated to engage with these facets of the LEYF professional identity.

Career Progression Relates Explicitly to the Demonstration of and Potential for Pedagogical Leadership

The teachers generally felt optimistic about the opportunities for progression within the organisation. Even when they themselves were not committed to progressing to another formal role, they admired the journeys that they saw other employees going on. The journeys were conceptualised in terms of personal and professional development, rather than being seen as mechanistic movements through an organisation when vacancies arise. For example, participants explained:

> I've seen people that have started off as a trainee or an apprentice and they've gone off to become a teacher and after that they've moved on to be a room leader, or they've moved on to be a deputy, and they've moved onto manager, and they've moved onto other roles in the organisation. *It's just about how you want to channel yourself.* (P1; italics added)

> Here they take it step by step so there's practitioner, then there's room leader, then there's duty manager, then you can step up to be deputy. . . . And a lot of people that were apprentices, one or two of the girls that were in my class, are now deputies in LEYF nurseries. So it's amazing to see in such a short space of time that people can . . . there's lots of opportunities for that to happen. (P2)

> Yeah, if I stayed in the company I would definitely try to move forward. There is a way of going up. That's what I like about the company. *Because if you have a passion and you love what you do, you can move forward and people do it.* (P6 italics added)

As the foregoing comments show, opportunities for progression were surrounded by positive language: 'you can', 'I would definitely try', 'it's just about how you want to channel yourself'. Teachers talked about being encouraged by managers to attend training or apply for new roles; they did not have to ask for these opportunities, but these were regularly extended to them. This meant that progression was seen as the norm and staff encountered lots of reassurance and support in moving on to new challenges if it suited their personal circumstances, as the following quotes illustrate:

> I'm in the pre-school room, and there was a vacancy in the baby room and they encouraged me to apply to work there as Room Leader. But because I'm term-time, I thought I couldn't go there because the babies are full time, but they said 'no you can do it'. They reassured me a lot and encouraged me to go for the Room Leader post. (P9)

> We've got internal vacancies advertised before it goes out externally and you are really encouraged, 'why can't you try this?' and it boosts your career up which is really really nice. Here we are really encouraged, we are given the support to push your career to a limit. (P14)

The concrete invitations and encouragement to move forward professionally led to the development of a more intangible aspect of the culture among employees.

Many teachers discussed feeling that there was constant forward movement in the organisation and as a result, they did not feel stuck or limited in their role. They were excited about learning new things and engaging in professional development. In this sense, most of the staff interviewed demonstrated the commitment to professional development that was described by McDowall Clark (2012) as a key characteristic of catalytic pedagogical leadership:

> For me, I mean I've been in nurseries since I was 17 but I find that even now I'm still learning new things, which is really good so it doesn't get boring, you're not stuck in one place, you actually keep moving. I mean I know a lot of people do get stuck in one place, they're just in that rut, but I find that every day I'm just learning new things and they challenge me to take the chance, to go ahead and do that, and do this role, and I think it's really good, and they have that confidence as well. (P11)

> So she [the nursery manager] does help us and she does support us to progress, and it's obvious that she does want us to go forward in our career, she just doesn't want us to stay in the same level because if we stay in the same level for many years, we could get bored. We want to be challenged every day. For me I like to be challenged, I like to feel 'wow can I do this?' and then 'I'm going to do this because my manager says give it a try'. (P13)

Teachers Have the Opportunity to Develop Specialised Pedagogical Leadership: This Builds Confidence and Passion across the Organisation

Teachers, regardless of their level in the nursery, will take on particular roles and projects. This cultivates responsibility and ownership and accountability. With all of the structure at work in LEYF – the various tools and resources that staff are expected to know and work with – one might expect that staff would feel that their autonomy and freedom was constrained. The following responses challenge this perception, suggesting that the structures at work in LEYF create opportunities for independence and creativity:

> I feel like here I've got a lot of autonomy and I've worked in places where I haven't felt that and LEYF are very open to staff leading the way and what happens in the classroom and what happens in the nursery. (P5)

> I've been given a lot of freedom to coach and to lead people and to take the decisions in certain situations of what to do. (P6)

> I think it's giving you the – autonomy? – yes, because sometimes you go to your manager and you ask an opinion and she gives it back to you: 'what do you think?', 'how do you think this is going to happen?'. She sends it back to you but she's there to guide but you take the lead. . . . So she's giving you – not responsibility, but – a sense of control of the situation and that sense of 'I can do things, I can change things'. My opinions and my skills, my knowledge and understanding has been taken into account, because whatever I'm bringing it's been appreciated. And I'm conscious of that, to contribute to the day to day running of the nurseries. (P12)

One way in which staff develop increasing levels of independence and creativity is by taking on particular roles. These roles are pedagogical rather than organisational – so that they relate to areas of the pedagogy, which align with individuals' areas of interest and expertise:

> It [the organisation] can look at your skillset and there's an element of freedom and if you've got a strong project, or an idea you can take it forward. Like my philosophy has always been working with parents and somehow I've managed to shape that in this space in this nursery. (P4)

> The allocation of roles really helps you improve your input and then you feel I'm driving towards something higher, not just sitting back, but we do have a lot of input. She [the manager] supports us but she really lets you fill her role, that she is doing. It's not just leaving us at the back. We all drive together for the children, for the children. (P14)

One room leader also talked about allocating roles in relation to action research, which is a facet of LEYF's pedagogy:

> So, me as a room leader I would say to my team, who is going to research stuff for me this week? As an example, I've taken all the areas in the room and I've delegated to each member of staff, so for example if you are responsible for the construction area, I might ask, can you do some action research and find out activities and ideas for this age group? Or OK, we're going to do outdoor learning and one of the things that we really advocate is risky play, so come to me with some ideas about what can we do and so each member of staff is really encouraged to broaden their learning. (P5)

Discussion

The findings suggest four ways in which LEYF enables the development of pedagogical leadership across the organisation: (1) they use the language of pedagogy as a vehicle for making improvements every single day, so that continuous improvement processes become wrapped up in the practices and growth of pedagogical leadership, (2) they focus in-house CPD on the development of pedagogical leadership, ensuring that a majority of training experiences for staff focus on pedagogy, and that all use and embed the language of pedagogical leadership, (3) career progression is an important motivation for individual staff in the organisation, and the process of career progression is linked in the mind of staff to the demonstration of pedagogical leadership and (4) staff are encouraged to find particular pedagogical specialisms in which they can lead practice, and this helps to build confidence and passion among staff.

Some of these strategies are open to all organisations, regardless of size. For example, all organisations have the option to use pedagogy as part of their everyday language and to ensure that all professionals – regardless of their qualification level – are familiar with what the organisation's pedagogy is and how pedagogical leadership is demonstrated in concrete ways in an everyday context. All settings can encourage pedagogical specialisms and enable these through support for action research, or other processes that help practitioners to reflect on particular areas of pedagogical development.

Other strategies, such as the focus of in-house CPD on pedagogical leadership, are limited to organisations that have their own training programmes and packages. To make this strategy applicable in ECE settings, leaders need to think about their approach to managing CPD opportunities among staff and the extent to which the CPD they buy into prioritises pedagogical leadership. There is also the need to consider opportunities for partnerships across the sector, which might mean that smaller providers could 'tap into' the CPD driving pedagogical leadership in larger organisations. Linking career progression to pedagogical leadership is also more limited within smaller organisations where opportunities for progression are less frequent. However, while there may be limited opportunity for concrete progression in an organisation, other forms of individual professional development and appraisal – such as internal coaching and supervision – can be linked to pedagogical leadership.

This chapter presents findings from research with a single organisation. The findings are therefore not intended to be directly applicable to other organisations. They are, however, a starting point for reflection and dialogue at an organisational level with regards to pedagogical leadership. I hope that in highlighting the strategies and processes employed within LEYF, organisational leaders elsewhere are better able to conceptualise and articulate their own approach. Similarly, the findings shared here are by no means a comprehensive account of pedagogical leadership development. We need to continue to share good practice in this field and open up discussions about how these practices differ depending on organisational and national context.

Further research is needed in order to understand more about the development of pedagogical leadership in ECE organisations. While this chapter suggests a series of strategies according to what staff have said about what they do, we urgently need observational research to look at processes of pedagogical leadership development in action. Ideally, longitudinal research would allow us to see how pedagogical leadership emerges over time and not just how it is recounted at one particular moment in time. This would also enable us to understand the everyday 'messiness' of pedagogical leadership development, rather than relying only on the neat categories produced by a thematic analysis of interviews.

Conclusion

The chapter offers some insight into an organisational approach to facilitate and expand pedagogical leadership 'on the job' in ECE. Based on research with LEYF, the chapter suggests the importance of explicitly linking continuous improvement and career progression within an organisation to the demonstration of pedagogical leadership, as well as focusing CPD on pedagogical leadership and using distributed responsibilities and action research as a means for enhancing pedagogical leadership across all staff. While other organisations can learn from what LEYF does, the list of support mechanisms offered here is not presented as comprehensive or equally applicable in all contexts. The chapter is intended to act as an invitation for further dialogue and research about what ECE organisations can do themselves in the context of everyday practice, to foster stronger pedagogical leadership among their teams.

References

Davis, G. (2012). A documentary analysis of the use of leadership and change theory in changing practice in early years settings. *Early Years, 32*(3), 266–276.

Elwick, A., Osgood, J., Robertson, L., Sakr, M., & Wilson, D. (2018). In pursuit of quality: Early childhood qualifications and training policy. *Journal of Education Policy, 33*(4), 510–525.

Henderson, L. (2017). 'Someone had to have faith in them as professionals': An evaluation of an action research project to develop educational leadership across the early years. *Educational Action Research, 25*(3), 387–401.

McDowall Clark, R. (2012). 'I've never thought of myself as a leader but . . .': The early years professional and catalytic leadership. *European Early Childhood Education Research Journal, 20*(3), 391–401.

Murray, J., & McDowall Clark, R. (2013). Reframing leadership as a participative pedagogy: The working theories of early years professionals. *Early Years, 33*(3), 289–301.

Sims, M., Forrest, R., Semann, A., & Slattery, C. (2015). Conceptions of early childhood leadership: Driving new professionalism?. *International Journal of Leadership in Education, 18*(2), 149–166.

'If You're Going to Build a House Where Everyone Develops and Learns, You Can't Have Hoarders'

A Conversation about Pedagogical Leadership with Nichole Leigh Mosty

Nichole Leigh Mosty

What Does Pedagogical Leadership Mean to You? How Do You Think about It?

I think about it as seeing in action what you've learned about how people learn. If you are a good leader, you understand that people learn by doing and so you create opportunities for people to learn like this and you see people blossoming. Learning is something that is never static; it's something that is always developing. Pedagogical leadership needs to be like that too. You do not lead with a fierce hand. You learn by developing yourself and others constantly, by learning and teaching and learning and teaching.

Are There Particular Images That Come into Your Mind When You Think about Pedagogical Leadership?

I think about those instances when a group of people that you work with grasp something new. Whether you have just finished a lecture or a professional development course with your team and your people come back into the room with their new ideas. They have these great ideas, inspired by the lecture or the training. Over the weeks that come, I see them taking these ideas and placing them into their daily schedules and into action – into things that are actually happening day to day. You can feel it then. You've hit the right pulse and things are happening.

Of course, they might come to me and say, 'Nichole, that thing you told us, it is not working'. That is a part of it as well. It is about that development, the learning and questioning and realising what works and what does not and gaining the confidence to say, 'guess what, we need to do something else, this is not working for us'.

It Sounds Like It's a Lot about Giving People Time and Space to Reflect and Innovate

As a leader, your goal is not just about running a good centre or managing efficiently. It is not just about having your budget right. It is about development. These are human beings that we are working with. All the way down to the babies that we are working with. Everybody is in a state of development.

Educational centres, especially early childhood centres, are at the heart of a community. There are families, there is a neighbourhood and there are the schools. So development is something that always needs to be continuous. Like I said, it can't be static, it has to be always in motion. I think to myself sometimes, 'if Piaget came back now, and he looked at society as it is now, would he say the same things? Would he be happy to see people parroting what he said without thinking more carefully about whether it really applies to today's world and today's children?' I think he would be disappointed about us using his ideas so rigidly. We need to adapt and be part of the continual evolution of education.

Tell Us More about the Vision of ECE in Which It Is the Place Where the Whole Community Comes to Develop

For a lot of parents, young parents or parents new to the neighbourhood or even country, early childhood education (ECE) is their very first stop in understanding society and how it works. ECE is where they learn the norms that are expected of them. I have worked and visited many centres around the world and each centre is serving a different community and that matters. At each centre there are different emphases because the community is different, and things work differently. There are different families and there are different needs in the community and in the school. It's really important that people in leadership roles in ECE centres realise that.

We also have to recognise that the people who work in ECE centres are also members of those communities. The more room you give in your leadership for your staff to be active participants in the development of the centre, the more you open them up to do the same thing in their community. Empower them so that they can make a difference beyond the ECE centre and in the wider community.

So Pedagogical Leadership Is Like a Wave Carrying Everyone Forward

If you put the school in the Bronfenbrenner package, the leadership is the fabric that moves between the different layers of context. It connects all the levels. It brings you from the widest circle of society to the epicentre of the institution. If leadership doesn't strive to carry everyone forward, ECE won't evolve and move forward itself.

What Are Your Key Inspirations When You Think about Pedagogical Leadership?

Bronfenbrenner is definitely helpful. In education, we work in systems, and when I look at Bronfenbrenner, that's there. It just happens that way, the way we function, if you look at your centre, the crèche has a certain system and it connects to the next room that the children go to. Or schools that have outreach centres, the way it connects parents. There are always these connections between different layers of context, and the leader is working between those different layers and connecting them more effectively.

I'm also inspired by Gardner and his theory of multiple intelligences. That resonates because I've worked in such diverse environments and it's really important to keep seeing the multiplicity of needs and strengths. As a leader, you need to be able to pull on these needs and strengths in order to get things moving and progressing.

Is Pedagogical Leadership also about Your Own Reflection, as Well as Encouraging Others to Reflect?

Yes – that's probably one of the most important things to remember for anyone in any leadership role. And I really mean *any* leadership role. For example I'm no longer a leader in a preschool, I'm a mother and that means I'm a leader in my family, so I reflect upon the decisions I make as I lead my children forward in life.

You're always reflecting about what you do. It's something that you have to do in order to lead – you have to be able to reflect upon how you lead. The decisions you make, the good ones, the bad ones. You always have a choice to reflect on your mistakes and your successes. If you don't, you won't advance and you can't lead effectively. If you can't carry that off with yourself, how can you do it with others and support them to reflect?

In a leadership role, you'll have people that are very good at setting goals; but you'll have others who haven't discovered their inner leader yet and you have to help them to find it and learning to reflect is key to seeing one's strengths. You can only teach others to reflect if you have the humility to do it yourself.

Pedagogical leadership is about collaborative reflection. When I was working as a director of Curriculum and Professional Development in California, I worked with a wonderful woman who was so talented and clever, but she had no leadership skills. She did not know how to share her intelligence. She just did everything herself. You walked in and you might say, *'wow did you do that?'* and the other members of the staff would say, 'we weren't allowed to be a part of that'. My role as a leader was to explain to her, 'if you are just doing this for yourself, you are not leading. You have to share your talent so that we can all share the work and the joy'.

It took a lot of reflection. We broke down her responsibilities and thought about what others could be entrusted to do and we practised explaining aspects of the work to others. It was just a wonderful journey because it made me do the same. How could I explain things? I was teaching this person how to run a classroom, how to share tasks, how to organise a day so that you could get through sixteen different activities with just two hands. It made me think a lot about how I could be better at sharing and including others.

Pedagogical leadership comes when you are able to bring others into the story you want to tell and you can authentically involve them not just on a practical level but connecting them emotionally with what you are doing.

On a Practical Level, How Can We Support the Development of Pedagogical Leadership in Others?

What matters are the dialogues about others' visions and values and goals. We should never forget the importance of helping others to find out what their own goals are. So, it's not just about learning to reflect in general but about encouraging everyone to reflect on where they are and where they want to be in the future, where they see themselves and how they see themselves getting there.

Fewer and fewer centres have large numbers of trained teachers who have had opportunities to do this deep reflective work previously. Our in-service training must deliver that and therefore it is up to centre leaders to work with their staff in this way because the pedagogical health of the centre depends on meeting that need.

Isn't This Just One More Thing for Centre Leaders to Have to Do? Don't They Have Enough That They Have to Do Already?

You have to find people with the strengths to share the leadership. I call it shared leadership. You give other people responsibilities on the basis of their strengths. It frees you up to focus on professional development. Making sure that you're nourishing your staff with pedagogy, with educational theory, is essential. Then after the input, you give your team the opportunity to work with it and you step away and let it develop. Then you step back in to help them to reflect on what's working and what's not working and where they want to go next: 'Where do you see this new approach going? What materials do you need to take it to the next level?'

You Can't Do It All
I don't believe you can. If you walk away and your centre is still humming along, it's because of all those other leaders and all the leadership you've shared, all the things that you've empowered others to do under your direction and guidance. Then you've done your job as a leader. If you walk away and the centre implodes, because you never nourished or trusted your staff, and they haven't learnt to set long-term goals and how to reflect on the now and where they want to be later, then you haven't done your job as a leader.

How Do You Think We're Doing with Pedagogical Leadership More Broadly in ECE at a Local, National or International Level?
Just take the example of working in California. I was really sad to see how pedagogical leadership there had more to do with checking boxes and making sure that we were meeting statutory regulations. They weren't working as hard at developing professional skills among staff or the centre. They weren't encouraging people to continue their education or nurturing their love for the job. They weren't planning for the future.

Here, in Iceland, while there are some leaders who do that, I also see that things have been pulled out of the hands of a lot of leaders and are centralised. Of course, we need to have a national curriculum but we also need to have room for leaders to flourish and meet the needs of the communities they serve. Otherwise you're just working with checklists. What's happened here in Iceland is that municipalities can buy into a single large ECE provider. But then these particular centres end up working 'from the book'. I've hired a couple of people who worked in that way and I find that they have difficulty thinking outside of the box. They are always asking: 'What do I do now?' They're always looking for the book, asking me what the book says. I reply, 'we're writing the book now and we'll always be writing and re-writing this book'.

But with these big chains, the book doesn't change. There might be tweaks, but it doesn't evolve. It just is what it is, and there's someone who sits in their tower and thinks up the next edit or the next chapter. So we're not training our teams and our leaders to be problem-solvers, to be forward-thinkers.

Is It about Professionalism Then or Maybe a Lack of Professionalism?

I believe that professionalism lies within the elements that you hold dear as a leader and the passion you exhibit in your actions. Over time and through different leadership roles I have found that if I invest time in reflecting, I start to sense when there is a need for a change. You can actually feel that things need to evolve in your centre or among your staff. You can sense when conflict is coming and you know that something has to give. Maybe you sense something negative festering among the staff that needs to be addressed. Or you see something in society that is shifting, a changing population maybe, or new technologies, or a crisis – like Covid-19 now, and you understand that you need to get ahead of the curve.

Professionalism lies in allowing yourself to have this foresight needed to cultivate abilities in everyone. If you don't have foresight, if you don't get ahead of the curve, you'll always just be putting out the fires. A lack of professionalism is on display when leaders feel like they are continually putting out fires. But you know that there is a fire hazard before the fire happens. That is a significant part of leadership.

What Policies Help Centres to Generate That Kind of Leadership Approach?

We need policies that help us to set goals and aims, but it is really important that there is flexibility in those policies.

I believe education in general has run up against a wall in this area. If you remember Bush's 'No Child Left Behind' policy and Obama's ECE policies, which were essentially just a tweak on the same thing, these became about rewarding teachers for basically teaching to the test: check list policies. And now policy-makers have implemented tests that test how well teachers test. There's a lack of creativity.

Don't get me wrong. In education, as in life, people need parameters. It's how we feel secure, otherwise it's just anarchy. People need to feel safe and secure, but, you have to weave a certain amount of flexibility and collaboration into your approach of policy making.

Also policy-makers need to incorporate more collaboration outside of education. When I think about some of the best steps that I've made in leadership and development, it's when I've coordinated with a social worker, or someone in politics, to solve a problem. So maybe that's something that we need to think about in our education system: it's not just the department for education and making sure we hit our literacy goals, but daring to ask how can we collaborate with and utilise policy from our social affairs programmes? I think that leaders should be encouraged to do more of this. Nobody is going to slap your hand if you start working with environmental awareness, and you have actual people who work with nature in your school next to you.

Do We Need to Broaden Our Vision for Early Childhood Education?
We need to make education sexy. People think too much in terms of the checklists. Policy-makers need to say, 'this is our goal, we want to have everyone functioning within these OECD levels, but we want to give you the flexibility as a teacher to teach to children's learning styles'.

It's a really easy opt-out for a centre leader to have in their hand an A–Z compendium on how to do every single thing that happens in the centre, even down to changing a diaper. But it's not good enough and it doesn't work in the long term. Teachers need to be empowered to work things out for themselves.

To have flexibility, you need to have professionalism. You have to be ready to have answers. You have to know your pedagogy. And people have to be willing to share it. If you're going to build a house where everyone develops and learns, you can't have hoarders. Hoarders repel people from the vision, from wanting to take a part and having their own initiative. You have to build the house with lots of space for collaboration and reflection.

We need to foster systems where professionals are willing to work with action research and where they are continuously developing. When I was working in California I tried to use the term 'action research' with the team and everyone got scared because I used the word 'research'. I said 'let's take that out then and just use the model'. We set our plan. We reflect on our plan. We enact our plan. We reflect a little more. We change our plan.

You need processes where there is constant motion and growth. If a plan is too rigid, it means you go through the motions but there's no real motion, no real flow. But when you build something that has room for analysis and reflection and change, then you are expanding and growing.

And values, values, values. You've got to have your values. If we go back to those schools that really stand up, then right away you see things and you know their values. You see it when you walk through the school. A school here recently went through a value change and they decided on the new value of 'friendship'. I thought to myself, 'that's going to be tricky – how can you force people to make friends?'. But when I visited, I walked through the school, I saw it and I felt it. I saw it in the pictures, I saw it in the way people communicated. I saw it in the way adults guided other adults. I saw it in the way they had their website set up. Everything was set up on the basis that there was a possibility for friendship in every interaction on every single day.

So values are something that need to be made clear. You can have an educational plan, you can set the goals, but if you don't have any value behind that – how are you going to teach it, how are people going to feel when they learn it?

Is It Just about Organisational Values, or Should We Be Encouraging Individuals to Reflect on Their Own Values as Well?
Values set an imprint that you carry into all parts of your life. Things that I valued in the preschool at Ösp, such as community development, are now central to my work.

If you have staff who reflect on their own values and their own goals, this level of reflection can spill into the values of their community. Just before I left Ösp, we had set up our values, and we were progressing well, but there had been a change in staff and a change in policy that we needed to implement. We took a whole staff day to reflect on our values. We asked ourselves: 'Are we on the right path? Do we as individuals believe in the values we have set as a school? Do we need to change our values?' Having that discourse, it wasn't just about the school – it was about each individual. One of our values was play and we had such a deep discussion about that and the meaning of play as a value. Not only did play stay in as a value, it became a stronger value because each individual was afforded the chance to examine their personal values about play.

Individuals' values are essential because when you make them explicit, and you reflect on them openly, you are making it possible to enhance critical thinking and development. It opens up a discourse where change and development can happen.

I honestly believe that good leaders understand the value of change and development, for their institute, for themselves, for the people and hopefully empowering education. If education didn't change, we'd all still be out in Froebel's garden or Benedictine monks would be selecting just a few boys for their educational mission.

Change and development are especially important when you are in diverse communities because maybe you'll find somebody that on the surface of things doesn't share your values, but you'll learn – through talking about values – to respect the values of each other. And even for those staff members that you feel you never get anything out of – if you open up and listen to their values, you might find that thread of connection that enables you to develop something together.

11

Fostering Pedagogical Leadership through Action Research

A Practical Perspective

Mandy Cuttler and Nick Corlett *with* Mona Sakr

Introduction

This chapter considers what works to develop pedagogical leadership 'on the ground'. In this chapter, Mandy Cuttler, the London Early Years Foundation (LEYF) pedagogy manager, and Nick Corlett, senior nursery manager in LEYF, reflect on their experience of how action research can drive pedagogical leadership. LEYF is a large group of social enterprise nurseries in London which offer high-quality early childhood education (ECE) to 4,500 children and where over one-third of the places are subsidised to ensure children from disadvantaged backgrounds can attend. As an organisation it has a unique seven-strand pedagogy which interweaves action research into the strand described as 'leading for excellence'. The chapter was shaped by a discussion between Mandy Cuttler, Nick Corlett and Mona Sakr, in which Cuttler and Corlett provided examples which bring alive what action research can look and feel like in day-to-day ECE settings and how it can foster pedagogical leadership day to day.

This chapter aims to:

1. Introduce – from a practical perspective – action research as a key means of advancing pedagogical leadership in ECE organisations.
2. Explain how action research is used in LEYF and some of the choices that organisations need to make about the implementation of action research including scale, scope and the extent to which the emphasis is placed on collaborative or individual inquiry.

3. Explore the embedded systems that enable action research to flourish, and advance pedagogical leadership including opportunities to share ideas, talent fluency and coaching.

Action Research in ECE

There is a rich history of action research in the context of ECE and it continues to be a popular method of professional and pedagogical development. Researchers have highlighted how action research creates time and space for transformative reflection among professionals (Henderson, 2017; Davis, 2012). It can act as a tool to bring professionals together to look closely at what they do currently and the areas for potential improvement. It can grow professionals' awareness of their work, so that they are more open to both the possibilities for change and action and other ways of working (Cherrington & Thornton, 2013).

While action research is recognised as a powerful tool in the pedagogic work of ECE, organisations must make decisions about its implementation. In Kurt Lewin's initial work on action research, he outlined four different types of action research that placed the emphasis more or less on scientific methods, democratic participation and communication with a wider community (Adelman, 1993). These continue to be choices that organisations make with regards to the implementation of action research. ECE settings must think about why they are conducting action research – what the ultimate purpose is – how it will be structured and supported, who will do it, when they will do it, at what scale the action research will take place and how the findings will be communicated across the organisation.

The LEYF Action Research Approach

LEYF commits explicitly to being a learning organisation which supports the concept of continuous improvement. This means delivering high-quality ECE with the right staff and a strong pedagogy. At LEYF, high quality is understood as delivering ECE that is relevant and contextual to the lives of the child within the framework of social pedagogy. LEYF's social pedagogy is introduced in detail in O'Sullivan's chapter in this volume.

The LEYF pedagogy needs to be led by staff who can consistently understand, share, embed and improve it to benefit all the children, especially those from more disadvantaged families and circumstances. This means creating a culture of reflection, where professionals can be guided both by developing their theoretical understanding alongside their practical experiences and using action research to construct their new learning. Through many practical situations the ECE professional develops experiences which provide guidelines for their next practical action. Schon (1984) talks of people acquiring practical competence through reflecting on their own practice while they work and especially using conversations, dialogue and regular work opportunities such as supervision and action learning communities.

> The alternation between carrying out actions, reflecting on them and viewing them against theory and ethics – in order to act in the light of such reflection – can be seen as a necessary cycle for developing practice. It is important that such reflection should have a development orientation. Being interested in practice could mean trying to do more of what one already masters, or what has been seen to work in previous practice. There is something positive in learning from practice, but if it is solely on a practical level, it becomes problematic, as it will quickly lead to doing the same things over and over again. Workplaces that attempt to think in this way will probably be able to show some good working in the short term but the real spark will disappear after a while. Repetition will become mechanical and destroys creativity. . . . Few social pedagogues would agree that it's useful only to do more of what was done yesterday. They are keen to try to find and construct new ways of working.
>
> (Storo, 2013 pg. 44)

Pascal and Bertram (2002) noted that the ECE sector miss great opportunities by not developing a culture of professional inquiry. At LEYF we agree that we miss out on a wealth of experience and knowledge if we do not support staff working directly with the children and families to become researchers and be confident to question deeply about how and why things are done within a culture of reflection. Kline (1999) says that thinking for yourself remains a radical act, so creating an environment which celebrates the importance of thinking carefully and deeply for yourself is about building a radical organisation. LEYF designed a whole organisational approach so that action research to support a thinking and learning culture was embedded through the pedagogical principles, practice, processes and policies at every level of the organisation.

Action research in LEYF happens in three simple phases (as devised by Stringer, 1999) that offer a simple framework to help staff think intensely about everything they do. This includes helping them to understand and interpret current theories so they can be best applied to each child or situation intelligently. The phases are:

> **Look** – build a picture and gather information. Complete an action plan on which we define and describe the problem to be investigated, remembering the context and the role of the adult engaged in the process.
>
> **Think** – interpret and explain. Identify the means of research to collect the evidence necessary to interpret the situation. This includes researching and then reflecting on what people have been doing in order to analyse areas of success as well as any deficiencies, issues or problems. Identify the action necessary and agree the means of testing so it moves from action to concept.
>
> **Act** – test the research response to resolve issues and problems. Evaluate what we have learned. Judge the worth, effectiveness, appropriateness, and outcomes of those activities. Formulate the solutions and consider next steps.
>
> (Stringer, 1999: 18; 43–44;160)

In reality, this can mean developing an action plan to investigate a question from an individual apprentice asking whether the environment is effectively supporting the children to learn or from a manager asking the staff to explore an element of the service because it feels unsuccessful from her perspective, or a senior manager asking a group of deputies to explore how the concept of science is being developed at nursery level.

According to Cuttler and Corlett, this means of exploring the process of research can include one-to-one meetings, team meetings, area meetings, specific management meetings or formally organised action research, Sounding Boards and research hubs for a more collaborative action research. The latter approach is more often used to answer bigger organisational questions or for agreeing the organisational response to a government policy consultation.

Action research is also encouraged on a broader scale. There are often several action research projects in operation across the organisation led by staff who are interested in the issue, whether they are based in the Central Office or the nurseries.

Action research is always understood to be a cycle because any changes that are put in place need to be observed again, through the 'look' phase, to consider the impact or whether it has resolved the issue that prompted the action research in the first place. For example, Mandy and Nick describe the action research project on the use of bikes:

> We have a partnership with a social enterprise called Bikeworks. They donate bikes to us to give to the nurseries. Some of the nurseries have bike lending

schemes for parents as well. The purpose of the partnership is to encourage parents to support children to become more active. We are conducting an action research project on the impact of this initiative so that we can examine how staff use bikes in the nurseries and check parents' views on the use of bikes. This will generate data on how bikes are used, the views of staff and parents on how we use bikes and what they consider to be the benefits from using bikes. Our findings will be used to adjust what we are doing in order for it to have a greater impact. We also need to consider the replicability of the initiative and whether it is something that we can support other nurseries in LEYF to do, as well as the sector more broadly.

Ultimately, the purpose of the action research is to get staff to stop and reflect and consider the impact of what we are doing for the children, the staff, the environment and the wider community.

The LEYF pedagogy is monitored through the LEYF Pedagogical Development Scales (LPDS). This is the process where each of the seven pedagogical strands are considered by the nursery team and the team allocate themselves a score. This leads to the team agreeing an action plan to strengthen some areas, celebrate others and create a means of getting stronger and deepening confidence across the pedagogy. This process often leads to action research projects.

In addition, LEYF uses a digital system to track children's progress. This can be reported on either as a group or as an individual child. It is easy to identify patterns and then plan a response. For example, one action research project focused on the experiences of boys in the nurseries in outdoor areas. Most recently, Mandy and Nick described how the organisation is examining the impact of the Covid crisis on children's development and well-being. They noted that a decline in children's understanding of the world had been observed particularly given the reduction in the usual daily outings to local shops, parks, markets and visits to local services.

'Action Research Is a Thing'

At LEYF a lot of time is spent convincing LEYF staff that they already understand action research, and that in fact, they use action research as part of their practice without often realising it. Students reading for the BA in Early Childhood Studies which includes a module on the LEYF pedagogy, offered in conjunction with the University of Wolverhampton, start a module on action research often saying that they have never done action research before.

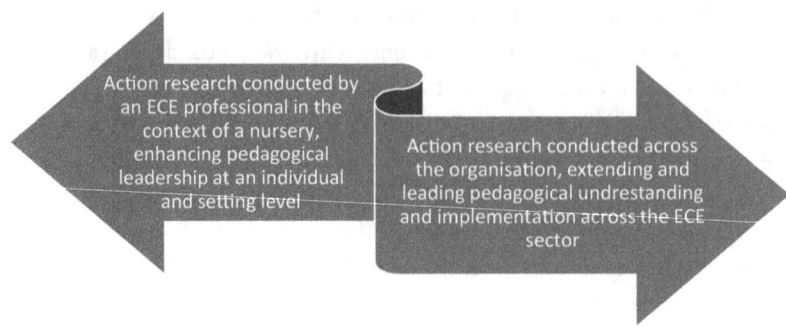

Figure 11.1 The spectrum of action research and pedagogical leadership.

I (Mandy) ask them: 'Have you observed something in your setting that's not working? Have you observed why it's not working and come up with some changes? Have you made the changes and then observed what happened as a result?' They say 'yeah we do that all the time'. They are doing action research but often not realising that it is action research.

We think it is important for them to see what they are doing as action research because it builds up their confidence as professionals. When they are able to label their reflective changes as action research through the action research cycle, they gain a stronger sense of themselves as professionals including better understanding of their potential to impact on others. Taylor (2017) suggests that incorporating action research into teaching is a lot about identity. Teachers need to build a narrative of themselves as researchers, because this gives them the confidence and the impetus to keep going with their research. So, when we support ECE professionals to see what they are doing in terms of action research, their commitment to reflectiveness and pedagogical leadership is heightened.

To support staff at LEYF to become confident action researchers, there is a training session on action research designed to increase awareness and understanding, and to encourage the staff to start using the language of action research (Figure 11.1).

Action Research and Pedagogical Leadership Are Community Processes

Depending on the tradition of action research to which you subscribe, there can be more or less emphasis on collaboration and community (e.g. Moran, 2007). At

LEYF, the model of action research is about community. Even though an idea may come initially from an individual, nobody is expected or encouraged to take forward that idea alone. Staff need to work together and understanding that we only really advance pedagogically when we work as a team. We cannot have the same impact if it is just one person beating the drum by themselves; it needs to be everyone together. This is why it is really important to get the 'why' of action research right, so that everyone can see and understand the need for change, rather than resisting change.

It is also vital that action research draws on the rich experience of everyone in the team. For LEYF, action research is not a theoretical pursuit and it is not about crafting a neat project. What matters most is that action research is part of practice. This means that dialogues among the team and agreeing whether to identify and agree that the action research project has the potential to make a difference to everyday practice in the setting or across the organisation. The founders of action research, Kurt Lewin and his many students were committed to democratic participation and this continues by making action research part of the routine work of the organisation.

Case Study: Green LEYF – Embedding Sustainability through Action Research

Nick Corlett

We are very much on our way to creating a sustainable culture within LEYF. It is not something that can happen overnight because sustainability needs to be embedded. It is not a case of turning off a light every now and again. It has to be part of your daily routine, and you need to have the children involved. It is a process of education for everyone, for children and professionals and families, so that when children go home they talk to their parents about why they do this and how we should do this.

In embedding sustainability, we approach it from various directions simultaneously. We are lucky that June (the CEO) is on board with it all and she wants to see it as an embedded part of every nursery in LEYF. But she knows that some people have a strength in this area and can help to move it forward, through their pedagogical leadership and using action research as part of this journey.

I come from Australia where sustainability is a core part of our early years curriculum. June, our CEO, could see that I was passionate about sustainability and that I wanted to lead on this. Her response was 'go for it'.

I see the task as inviting everyone to collectively look at how we can increase sustainability and what we think is the best way to do it. This means asking questions all of the time and listening to the questions that others have. Is it about education? Do we need to educate teachers who may have grown up in council flats with limited access to outdoors? How can we expect teachers to teach children respect for nature if they themselves have spent little time engaging with nature themselves?

To find out more about this – applying our action research approach – we hosted a nature pedagogy quiz for all staff to complete. We were amazed by the results. People struggled to name more than four birds that you can see around us in London. Someone even said a flamingo! This helped us realise that we cannot expect our teachers to educate our children on respecting nature and environment, when they themselves don't have the necessary knowledge.

To address this we developed a Level 4 qualification on sustainability in the early years. We have thirty-nine people enrolled on the programme from across the organisation. Everyone who completes the course will become an eco-champion in their nursery and they will learn how to cascade what they have learned to their colleagues, so that the impact ripples outwards and deepens downwards.

We use the cycle of action research to look further down the line at what difference this training has made and think about any changes that we need to make in order to support with the ultimate aim of embedding sustainability.

Through this approach, we also get the benefit of individuals and nurseries role modelling to one another. Some of the things that we have put in place at this nursery are posted on the internal social media platform called Workplace. This inspires others in the organisation and we see an emerging ripple effect with other nurseries trying the activities and posting photos and videos of their activities. For example another nursery recently posted photographs of them using the wormery with the children and doing cold composting. That sharing between nurseries is really powerful and brings pedagogical leadership alive.

Culture Is Key

Action research is a tool for developing pedagogical leadership, but it can only flourish in the right working climate. It cannot fix anything in an organisation where individuals are afraid to make mistakes or struggle to be open with one another. The LEYF organisation uses three things that enable action research to work for advancing pedagogical leadership. These are:

1. Sharing ideas – talking, thinking and conversations;
2. Talent fluency – knowing everyone's passions, interests and skillset;
3. Coaching – starting with individuals' strengths and building from there.

Sharing Ideas – Talking, Thinking and Conversations

Action research starts with ideas – it starts with people having ideas and then having the courage to share those ideas with others and see how they can develop over time and through conversation. In LEYF, people are encouraged to think and talk about ideas as much of the time as possible. Team meetings are structured to encourage participation, debate and discussion where everyone can be heard – from the apprentice to the setting manager.

In their work on humble leadership, Schein and Schein (2018) discuss the need for leaders to reframe personal challenges as collective challenges:

> Instead of heading into work wondering how you alone can solve the problem, what if you went to work committed to sorting it out with a partner, a group, a large or small work team? It's not up to you alone to solve the problem, to lead to greatness, to change the world. It is up to you to create a learning environment in which you and your group can cooperate in identifying and fixing the processes that solve problems, and maybe then change the world. (p. xiii)

In an approach where ideas are our currency and are always there to be shared and never just owned by individuals, action research to advance pedagogical leadership can start to come from everywhere. Whether it is a teacher seeing something isn't quite working and considering how best to change or somebody who has been on a training course excited to apply their new learning with the children. Somebody might have read an article about something and they've decided they'd like to put something into practice in their setting. One example shared by Mandy and Nick was the introduction of woodwork across the nurseries following a presentation from a well-known woodwork teacher at the annual conference. Ideas can come from anywhere.

> Mandy: Getting new ideas is engrained in an organisational culture. We are not a hierarchical culture, where all the ideas have to come from a manager. There's no sense of 'you'll do it this way because I'm the manager and I'm telling you to do it like that', that's not part of our culture. An apprentice can go to a manager and say 'I learned about something in class, and I'd really like to try it in our nursery' or 'one of the classmates mentioned something they're doing, can we see how it would work here?'

According to Mandy and Nick, that openness is part of the organisational culture at LEYF. Managers have to be humble and willing to see that others have good ideas and their job is not to implement all of the ideas, but instead to orchestrate the culture and the processes so that others can continue to generate ideas, share and then test them. As Schein and Schein (2018) explain, this is actually a more relaxed position for managers to be in since they can take some of the pressure off of themselves to do everything alone!

Talent Fluency – Knowing Everyone's Passions and Skillset

Talent fluency is an essential aspect of pedagogical leadership. If we want everyone to lead pedagogically, they need to feel that there are particular areas of expertise that they can contribute and others need to know this too. If someone has a passion for and expertise in woodwork, for example, they can develop their pedagogical leadership by sharing that information and then delegating to that colleague the responsibility for the advancement of this initiative across the organisation working at different levels.

Using action research is interconnected with this talent fluency. People can develop an awareness of what others' passions are and what they are knowledgeable about through action research projects. Someone can ignite a personal passion from leading or becoming involved in a small-scale action research project. Essentially, action research becomes a means by which the organisation can identify and collect information about the expertise, passions and talents that exist within the community that makes up that organisation. In their theory of social leadership, Guglielmo and Palsule (2014) argue that talent fluency is essential for helping everyone in an organisation to develop leadership capacities.

At LEYF, the introduction of dialogic reading started with an individual's passion which was allowed to flourish and is now the organisational approach to supporting reading at home. A particular teacher with a real passion for dialogic reading quickly became known as an expert across the organisation. She was asked to lead on the training for dialogic reading and she was released from her duties in her particular nursery to be able to share her expertise in this way. We have many similar examples including teacher-led development of Makaton and understanding schematic play.

It is important to remember that this started with a recognition of what someone in the organisation was able to contribute. Pedagogical leadership is about the whole team, not just the learning development team based in the Central Office; their role is to facilitate others' pedagogical leadership rather than own it across the organisation (this relates well to Leigh Mosty's argument about the need to avoid 'hoarding' if pedagogical leadership is to flourish, in this volume).

Coaching – Starting from Individuals' Strengths and Building from There

If you genuinely want everyone in an organisation, regardless of hierarchies, to engage in action research, a key focus of the organisation has to be building up confidence and the willingness to have a go and take a risk. This is where coaching comes in, and in particular, coaching that takes a strengths-based approach where individuals are noticed for doing well and this is the starting point for collaborative reflection and growth. When a culture of coaching takes off, then everyone is coaching one another – it is not just up to the managers to do the coaching. This resonates with our understanding of pedagogical leadership, since it is up to everyone to open up the possibilities for change and development, by working closely and supportively with others.

> Nick: We balance encouragement and active challenge. We have an Apprentice Manager whose role it is to see the little sparks and glimmers in the apprentices which they zoom in on. The manager notices something that an apprentice does well or seems to be excited by and it is her job to say 'you did that really well' or 'I see you enjoyed that'. She will encourage the apprentice to speak to the Nursery Manager about it and see where it might go from there, including the potential for developing an action research project on the topic. If the apprentice is hesitant, the Apprentice Manager will offer more support: 'let's speak to your manager together because I want to tell them what I saw because it's amazing.'
>
> We believe in nurturing passion at every level. The CEO models this kind of encouragement and it trickles down to all levels of management. She will say 'I saw this the other day and I remembered that you did this a couple of months ago, and so now I wonder if you could lead on it?' This can feel challenging, maybe even intimidating, but there is also a lot of personal development in those moments. You feel that if the CEO believes that you can do it, then probably you can do it.

We prompt everyone in the organisation to get involved. It is not as simple as just opening up the culture and making it possible for everyone to speak. Equity means helping everyone to engage and this can mean working with individuals to overcome their reticence. Not everyone feels that they have the automatic right to speak. If you simply open the floor and ask everyone to contribute, we see the same inequalities playing out in terms of who will come forward. It is up to us therefore to reach out and help everyone to engage in the discussions.

It is really important to avoid hierarchical behaviours. For example you may need to actively elicit the views of apprentices because they won't necessarily speak up without an invitation. But when you do that frequently enough, and they see that their views actually matter and this becomes a catalyst for genuine change.

This is another example of the coaching in action and it is the essence of pedagogical leadership – it is both about continuous pedagogical improvement and it is about the enhancement of horizontal leadership so that everyone in the organisation behaves like a leader.

Case study: Growing Confidence through Action Research

Mandy Cuttler

As part of my work, I support students to develop their action research through a module on the LEYF degree, offered in conjunction with the University of Wolverhampton. As part of this module, the students reflect on the outcomes of the project not just in terms of the pedagogy of the setting but also in terms of their own personal and professional growth.

I was struck recently by the potential impact of doing action research on the students' confidence as professionals. One student explained that her confidence as a pedagogical leader grew massively by carrying out an action research project. She saw that she was able to make meaningful changes that were properly considered by her colleagues.

The idea of pedagogical leadership – the idea that everyone can lead pedagogical change – came to life for the student through the action research. It helped her to see what it looked like in practice and how it could be developed further not just in her own practice, but in supporting others with theirs. Critical reflection is key, but the action research provided something practical, something tangible, to hang the critical reflection onto.

Conclusion

At LEYF, action research is an integral part of the commitment to fostering pedagogical leadership across the organisation. It is used at every level of the organisation as a tool to support critical reflection. It is a process that also helps professionals to consider, implement and evaluate change.

Action research ranges from looking across multiple nurseries at the impact of a bike lending scheme to an individual ECE professional investigating and developing their passion for doing woodwork with children. In all of the ways in which it is implemented the approach to action research is centred on collaboration and the magic that can happen when colleagues are all willing to learn from one another.

The experience of using action research to advance pedagogical leadership in an ECE organisation depends on the organisational culture. To ensure that it becomes embedded in the culture and drives pedagogical leadership, three key ingredients are essential: (1) dialogues that help the ideas to flow, (2) talent fluency, individuals' passions and interests are recognised, nurtured and celebrated and (3) formal and informal coaching designed to encourage everyone to be brave enough to step up and speak up.

References

Adelman, C. (1993). Kurt Lewin and the origins of action research. *Educational Action Research*, *1*(1), 7–24.

Cherrington, S., & Thornton, K. (2013). Continuing professional development in early childhood education in New Zealand. *Early Years*, *33*(2), 119–132.

Davis, G. (2012). A documentary analysis of the use of leadership and change theory in changing practice in early years settings. *Early Years*, *32*(3), 266–276.

Guglielmo, F., & Palsule, S. (2014) *The Social Leader: Redefining Leadership for the Complex Social Age*. Brookline, MA: Bibliomotion.

Henderson, L. (2017). 'Someone had to have faith in them as professionals': An evaluation of an action research project to develop educational leadership across the early years. *Educational Action Research*, *25*(3), 387–401.

Kline, N. (1999) *Time to Think: Listening to Ignite the Human Mind*. London: Hachette UK.

Moran, M. J. (2007). Collaborative action research and project work: Promising practices for developing collaborative inquiry among early childhood preservice teachers. *Teaching and Teacher Education*, *23*(4), 418–431.

Pascal, C., & Bertram, T. (2002) Accounting early for lifelong learning. In L. Abbot & H. Moylett (eds.), *Early Education Transformed*, pp. 109–120. London: Routledge.

Schein, E. H., & Schein, P. A. (2018) *Humble Leadership: The Power of Relationships, Openness and Trust*. Oakland, CA: Berrett-Koehler Publishers.

Schon, D. (1984) *The Reflective Practitioner: How Professionals Think in Action*. New York: Basic Books.

Stringer, E. T. (1999) *Action Research*. 2nd ed. London: Sage.

Storø, J. (2013). *Practical social pedagogy: Theories, values and tools for working with children and young people*. Bristol: Policy Press.

Taylor, L. A. (2017). How teachers become teacher researchers: Narrative as a tool for teacher identity construction. *Teaching and Teacher Education*, *61*, 16–25.

12

Interpretations of Pedagogical Leadership among Community-based Early Childhood Education Leaders in Azerbaijan

Ulviyya Mikailova and Gwendolyn Burchell

Introduction

Azerbaijan is currently making a shift from centralised control to decentralised leadership; and the sector of early childhood education (ECE) demonstrates this shift more noticeably than others. Growing recognition of the importance of ECE services and equality of access to the ECE services for all children forced the Azerbaijani government to open the ECE sector to a wider range of service providers. Legislative change and a drive to increase coverage of inclusive ECE has enabled new approaches in community leadership to emerge.

However, in reality, leading community-based ECE service provision is a complex social and pedagogical endeavour. While being prepared for providing education and care to young children through limited training, and being monitored time to time for the quality of this education and care, the reality is they must play multiple leadership roles as an entrepreneur running a small-scale social enterprise, a service manager, a pedagogical leader responsible for quality education and the development and well-being of young children. They face demands from parents, communities, local ECE authorities and project managers which requires them to maintain open communication with all interested parties in the context of their work. Furthermore, being female leaders in an environment dominated by male leadership provides an additional layer of complexity and challenge.

In this multidimensional social and pedagogical process, centre leaders must learn to develop and validate their pedagogical leadership through service provision, while interacting and building partnerships across the local and national context. They have to ensure implementation of a national ECE curriculum in remote rural areas where traditional parenting practices can sometimes contradict the principles of child-centred education. They are expected to follow curricular principles of child-centredness, respecting the child and his/her rights, providing opportunities for children to make a choice, listening for the child's voice, recognising parents as the primary educators of a child, as well as acting on other important concepts introduced in the curriculum.

This chapter explores the complexity of pedagogical leadership in community-based ECE practice in Azerbaijan. We investigate how the ECE leaders perceive, interpret, develop, communicate and perform pedagogical leadership and how this compares with international conceptualisations of pedagogical leadership.

Setting the Context: Early Childhood Education in Azerbaijan

The Republic of Azerbaijan is a country in the South Caucasus region with a population of 10.067 million. Azerbaijan ranked 87 out of 189 countries and territories in the 2018 UNDP Human Development Index, which the UNDP categorises as high in human development (Human Development Report, 2019).

The Ministry of Education (MoE) is the central body overseeing the education system, while local authorities are responsible for the provision of ECE services. Expenditure on education is 11.7 per cent of the total government expenditure according to the Law on National Budget for 2020.[1] ECE in Azerbaijan is provided to children from one to five/six years of age. It is provided in nurseries (to children of less than three years of age) and in kindergartens (for children aged three to five years).

While ECE in Azerbaijan is not compulsory, the regulatory framework in Azerbaijan promotes ECE. The Preschool Education Law (2017) emphasises the importance of preschool education and provides free access to public preschool education. Moreover, preschool preparation in the form of a School Readiness Program (SRP) provided either at primary schools or via ECE centres is highly encouraged for five to six-year-old children.

It is estimated that there are around 1.1 million children between zero and six years old in Azerbaijan, representing about 11 per cent of the total population (State Statistics Committee, 2020).[2] In all, 128,800 young children attend preschool institutions across Azerbaijan while only 29,200 children in rural areas can benefit from the ECE services due to lack of provision (SSC, 2020).

Despite continuous efforts to improve ECE service provision, Azerbaijan is significantly lagging in international standards. Access remains low with only 36 per cent of three to six-year olds enrolled in preschool education facilities, which makes Azerbaijan one of the countries in the Europe and Central Asia (ECA) region with the lowest access to preschool education (UNICEF, 2019).

Equity, access, inclusion and quality of early childhood education remain a challenge and a source of concern for the government. Unequal access to early education is particularly evident among children from rural and remote areas and children with disabilities.[3]

ECE in Azerbaijan has been traditionally provided by public ECE centres located mainly in urban and suburban areas with high-density populations. Private ECE services remain unaffordable or inaccessible for children from low income families, those living in remote rural areas and those with disabilities. Some projects piloting community-based ECE services were implemented by local non-governmental organisations since 2010, but did not significantly influence the overall national policy.

A shift in approaching the problem occurred in 2013 when Azerbaijan committed to the ambitious goal of ensuring 90 per cent of children (President Office, 2013) access ECE services. The government established a legal framework to promote the provision of ECE services including a series of national laws and regulations that promote preschool education, mandating a wider range of ECE service providers. Within this, community-based ECE centres were established in response to parents' needs. They offered a mix of paid and free-to-access services for the local community.

Since that time, two large ECE providers – Community-Based ECE Center (CBECE) founded by the Ministry of Education and 'Mektebim' founded by United Aid for Azerbaijan (UAFA, a not for profit organisation) – entered the field and have created fast growing country-wide networks of community-based ECE centres. Over 3,000 children aged 3–6 years old in 100 communities now have access to a community-based early learning programme in addition to existing kindergarten programmes[4] via CBECE and approximately 1,500 children had access to Mektebim prior to Covid-19.

Although ECE leadership is understood as a key issue for improving quality (Hujala, 2013), it has not been well explored in the Azerbaijani ECE context. A research paper on ECE leadership in Azerbaijan (Mikailova & Radsky, 2013) revealed the challenge of applying existing leadership typologies in emerging educational contexts in Azerbaijan. The research concluded that a more contextualised approach to leadership was necessary in order to support the development of educational leadership in Azerbaijan.

Investigating Pedagogical Leadership among Community ECE Leaders in Rural Azerbaijan

The research referenced in this chapter investigated the leadership experiences – and particularly interpretations and manifestations of pedagogical leadership – among nine community ECE leaders in remote rural areas of Azerbaijan. In-depth interviews with these leaders were conducted[5] to explore their perceptions of pedagogical leadership and quality early learning for young children; characteristics of effective leadership; the influence of pedagogical leaders on learning and development of children; their approach to the guidance of the national curriculum implementation; collaboration with parents; and their experiences of being a female leader in a national and regional context where male leadership dominates.

Due to Covid-19 and the six-week war between Azerbaijan and Armenia which imposed restrictions on inter-country movements, all the interviews were conducted remotely. These restrictions also affected those who could participate since we could only include those with internet connectivity. Furthermore, internet access was severely restricted for security purposes due to the war.

Both, CBECE and UAFA were asked to recommend four ECE leaders as research participants representing the two networks:

1. Community-based preschools implemented by CBECE, funded by EU and MoE.
2. 'Mektebim' – an inclusive enterprise approach to community-based preschool provision established by UAFA, in which the leader runs the preschool as a micro-enterprise.
3. In addition, one ECE leader was selected who still works for a community-based ECE centre established within a pilot project in 2010.

All the ECE leaders who were interviewed were female and were solely responsible for the leadership of their centres. Their two main functions were teaching the children and leading the centre, as one of the interviewed leaders said, 'Here I work . . . both as an entrepreneur and a teacher.'

The interviewed leaders shared a lot in common. Their age ranged from twenty-six to forty-four. They typically had just a few years of experience in ECE, though one participant had ten years of experience working in the sector.

Doing Pedagogical Leadership: What the ECE Leaders Reported

The themes presented in the following paragraphs are each illustrated with quotes from the leaders and, where appropriate, links are made to existing theoretical perspectives and research on pedagogical leadership:

1. Pedagogical leadership involves advocacy of child-centred pedagogies.
2. Pedagogical leadership involves a sense of social purpose, conceptualised in terms of community and self-actualisation.
3. Pedagogical leadership is a 'working model' among the community ECE leaders – an object of constant reflection and revision.
4. There are various influences on approaches to pedagogical leadership, which can be organised into internal influences and external influences.

Pedagogical Leadership Involves Advocacy of Child-Centred Pedagogies

In Azerbaijan, traditional teacher-centred education is hierarchical. The teacher asks questions to which there is a right or wrong answer that only the teacher knows. Azerbaijan wants to change this and has committed to adopting a child-centred pedagogical approach to ECE. Thus, all of the leaders interviewed had been given some training in child-centred methodologies. However, a key aspect of the pedagogical leadership they demonstrated was exploring what child-centred approaches would look like in practice:

> It is very important to teach a child a subject in a clear, more comprehensible way. As you know, children are addicted to entertainment, television, computers, telephones, and many technological devices. This is due to their desire to have fun. A leader should also present the topic in a more entertaining and different way to get the child's attention. If, as a leader, I am not open to innovation and continue to apply everything in the traditional way, then children will not adapt to the lesson and will still prefer games, television, phones. However, if the lesson

> is fun, different and interesting, children will want to learn more, have fun and be able to focus on the topic better. (ECE leader 1)

> In the beginning, the parent came and said that the child should learn poetry and know the alphabet. Why don't you teach these? Gradually we persuaded them that speech does not develop by memorizing poetry. (ECE leader 5)

> First of all, what I like most in the curriculum is 'individualism'. Everyone should be treated as an 'individual'. The most important thing is that I give the child some freedom. (ECE leader 6)

> Each child has a different character, and you, as a pedagogical leader, observe how the child should be treated. As you apply this method to each child individually, you will develop and become more experienced. Dealing with two children at home is not the same as dealing with 30 children in kindergarten. You know that every family is like a small state. Each of them has its own characteristics, way of life and form of upbringing. We have 30 children, 30 different families, different worlds, different characters, different characteristics. When dealing with them, you need to know which special method can make this activity easier and faster as the child develops. (ECE leader 9)

Pedagogical Leadership Involves a Sense of Social Purpose, Conceptualised in Terms of Community and Self-actualisation

The interviews suggested multiple factors which drive our research participants to act as leaders in general and as pedagogical leaders in particular.

The participants explained that they were motivated to undertake ECE leadership roles because they recognised a need for leadership at the community level:

> In general, every person should be a leader in his role in society and his family. If this is the case, I think kindergarten is the best place for my role. (ECE leader 8)

The participants believed that they make changes in the lives of children, justifying that the children being educated in the centres are very different from those who have not attended:

> This [centre] was very much needed in our rural areas…we are already seeing the results of our work. (ECE leader 5)

They described their work in terms of 'love', and that it was this love that enabled them to do the job despite the small amount that they earned from it:

I love my job. . . . When a person does what he loves, they can do it anyway. (ECE leader 3)

I have a very small amount as a salary. I do not believe anyone will work for this amount but I continue to work because I love my students so much. (ECE leader 2)

I can sit at home and do private tutoring for money, but I do not want to do it. I want to teach children something. What I taught will live after I die. Every child is a box of treasure. It must be opened and shown. (ECE leader 8)

As women leaders, the interviewees were aware that they had an opportunity for self-actualisation in the workplace that many rural women in Azerbaijan would rarely have access to. That is, these leaders were able to access opportunities in the public domain and develop a sense of their professional identity, which many other rural women in Azerbaijan are excluded from. For seven of the nine research participants, it was the first job of their career. Considering that there are few job opportunities in small rural communities, they see community-based ECE services as a way to build their social identity at the community level because their role extends beyond the group into the community in their area. This strengthens their self-confidence. Thus pedagogical leadership in this context is intertwined with processes and experiences of self-actualisation for women living in rural Azerbaijan: we could argue that it is as much about opportunities for women as it is about opportunities for children.

Pedagogical Leadership Is a 'Working Model' among the Community ECE Leaders – An Object of Constant Reflection and Revision

We were particularly interested in exploring pedagogical leadership among our research participants because this term had not yet been elaborated in a national approach to ECE. The research participants had not formally heard the term nor been introduced to it through official training. Without a centralised understanding of pedagogical leadership, and no formal training in it, participants had been constructing their own model of pedagogical leadership. This included a continuous process of providing services, reflecting on the services, interpreting what they do and making further changes in the way they teach and lead. Pedagogical leadership was therefore a 'working model'.

This resonates with Male and Palaiologou's (2015) understanding of 'leadership as praxis'; a state of being that unfolds independently of prior knowledge and understanding.

The participants recognised that they were constantly learning and developing through their day-to-day experiences and practices:

> Do you know how many nights I did not sleep in the beginning? (ECE leader 3.)

> Although at first, I felt inexperienced, now I see myself as an experienced pedagogical leader. (ECE leader 1)

> The more we work, the more we gain experience, and the more we gain experience, the more we develop the ability to make the right decisions in any situation. (ECE leader 9)

Using this praxeological lens, the participants began to describe themselves as pedagogical leaders:

> I think that a pedagogical leader is someone who inspires, stimulates, develops, supports people of his time, does not hesitate to teach them, and is not jealous of sharing the ability of knowledge. These leaders should share their love and excitement. (ECE leader 8)

There Are Various Influences on Approaches to Pedagogical Leadership, Which Can Be Organised into Internal and External Influences

In their research on pedagogical leadership Male and Palaiologou (2015) introduce a diagram which shows the interaction between pedagogy and social context and suggests that this can be split into internal and external axes of influences. They show how both sets of influences contribute to emerging leadership styles in ECE. We used these sets of axes to explore what we considered to be the key influences on how the rural women leaders we interviewed approach their leadership.

Internal Axes

The women interviewed contend with internal pressures that relate to gender, especially in a rural context. Leading an ECE centre gives them self-confidence in being a leader within the community, despite the gendered pressures on women (to be a good wife, stay home, cook, clean and look after the children). They act as a role model in their community, influencing others, including parents.

The participants saw themselves as leaders in relation to parents and children. They recognised the importance of parents as the primary educators of a child and stressed the importance of parental learning through parents' participation as assistants or volunteers in the provision. They needed to convince parents to be involved in ECE:

> Our parents think that upbringing is only a teacher's job . . . but a parent plays a key role. If the parent does the right thing, the teacher will play a supporting role. (ECE leader 7)
>
> I inform parents clearly as much as possible . . . what for example, his/her child learned today, he/she will learn other things tomorrow . . . what they will learn in a month. Then I talk about what will be learned next month. (ECE leader 3)
>
> I have gained the trust and confidence of parents. (ECE leader 9)
>
> Each child comes from a different home and is shaped differently. That's why we work with parents. (ECE leader 5)
>
> In the past, parents wanted their children to be the centre of attention, that is, my child should sit at the front desk, my child should not sit there, there were such things. Then this problem disappeared. I told them that we always arrange seats differently and often do not use them at all. (ECE leader 4)
>
> What matters most is communication, warmth, kindness to children, authenticity with parents and a love for the work. Of these, in my opinion, communication, authenticity and trust are most important. In the absence of any of these features, the parent will move away from you with the child. (ECE leader 2)

These quotes from the leaders all point towards their views on the importance of pedagogical leadership with parents and families. The leaders see an essential aspect of their role as the practical integration of parents into what they are doing in the settings, and the enhancement of parents' understanding of a child-centred pedagogy.

External Axes

The political and economic shift from communism to a market economy creates a need for educational reform that can shape children from the earliest ages to be creative thinkers. While the leaders may not be conscious of the input that their leadership is having on influencing this change in children, the fact that they have the space to function without bureaucratic control enables this change to evolve naturally during the formative years of these children.

> I think that first of all it has a great impact on the development of speech and their worldviews, they can work freely without their parents. . . . These children are also dreamers. For example, after I make something out of paper, I go home and the children try to make something with paper at home. (ECE leader 1)
>
> That is, upbringing is not something that depends only on the teacher. During this time, the environment and children also play a big role. Because children are also teachers. (ECE leader 9)
>
> I give children freedom. They are free within the rules. We have rules. For example, we don't bite, we don't push, we listen to the teacher, we share our toys, we pick them up after we play, and we don't argue. (ECE leader 7)
>
> At home, the child is instructed to stay calm, not to get dirty, not to annoy the teacher. I open the door and let the children out to play whatever they want. (ECE leader 6)

Through pedagogical leadership, the participants were shifting narratives not just about childhood but about individuality. They were celebrating the children not only as learners but also as teachers – as individuals actively constructing the world around them and expressing themselves in unique ways. This social dynamic links to the political context in which these shifts in ECE are happening, where there is a move away from centralised processes and systems towards a landscape of some diversity and community-based provision.

Conclusion

In summary, our key findings are that pedagogical leadership in community ECE provision in rural Azerbaijan currently centres on the advocacy and advancement of child-centred pedagogies. The pedagogical leadership of those we interviewed involved a strong sense of purpose that was conceptualised in terms of the community, as well as their own self-actualisation, particularly as women in a male-dominated leadership landscape. The pedagogical leadership voiced among the participants was a working model that they were learning 'on the job' through hands-on experiences and constant reflection. Finally we suggest that a way to think about the developing approaches to pedagogical leadership is through both internal and external influences. That is, there were internal individual drivers that were important to those leaders we spoke to, but also the wider sociocultural context, which is particularly relevant as ECE in Azerbaijan as it transitions away from centralised models of operating.

Notes

1. https://static.president.az/media/W1siZiIsIjIwMTkvMTIvMTYvOW93MG4xOWVtZl9RQU5VTl9ET1ZMRVRfQlVEQ0VTSS5wZGYiXV0?sha=f9f07f4e21813782
2. https://www.stat.gov.az/source/demoqraphy/ap/
3. https://www.unicef.org/azerbaijan/media/1406/file/Early_Childhood_EN_01092019.pdf
4. https://aztehsil.com/news/9125-cma-esasli-mektebeqeder-tehsil.html
5. The authors would like to thank Garib Huseynzada, ADA University Graduate Assistant, for his important contributions in gathering data (conducting interviews, transcribing and translating into English language) upon which the study is based.

References

Heikka, J., & Waniganayeke, M. (2011). Pedagogical leadership from distributed perspective within the context of Early Childhood Education. *International Journal of Leadership in Education. Theory and Practice*, 14(4), 499–512.

Hujala, E. (2013). Contextually defined leadership. In E. Hujala, M. Waniganayake, & J. Rodd (Eds.), *Researching Leadership in Early Childhood Education* (pp. 47–60). https://ilrfec.org/publication/researching-leadership-in-early-childhood-education/.

Male, T., & Palaiologou, I. (2015). Pedagogical leadership in the 21st century: Evidence from the field. *Education Management and Leadership*, 43(2), 214–231. https://journals.sagepub.com/doi/abs/10.1177/1741143213494889.

President Office. (2013). The State Strategy on Development of Education. https://president.az/az/articles/view/9779

State Statistics Committee. (2020). State Statistical Committee of the Republic of Azerbaijan. Children in Azerbaijan. Statistical Yearbook. https://www.stat.gov.az/source/demoqraphy/au/

The Preschool Education Law (2017). http://www.e-qanun.az/framework/35791 or another link is https://edu.gov.az/uploads/mektebeqeder/sened/mektebeqeder-tehsil-qanun.pdf

UNDP. (2019). *Human Development Report*. Azerbaijan. http://hdr.undp.org/sites/all/themes/hdr_theme/country-notes/AZE.pdf

UNICEF. (2019). Azerbaijan. https://www.unicef.org/azerbaijan/media/1406/file/Early_Childhood_EN_01092019.pdf

Pedagogical Leadership in Italian Early Childhood Education Settings

Managing Conflicts While Facilitating Participative Decision-making

Federico Farini

Introduction

This chapter discusses conflict management in contexts of pedagogical planning. Conflicts and their management represent a challenge for pedagogical leadership. Collegial models of management that favour participative decision-making processes are particularly exposed to the risk of conflicts. Pedagogical leaders have the difficult responsibility of managing conflicts that arise in pedagogical planning in ways that do not contradict principles of participative decision-making.

This is the case for the two Italian early childhood education (ECE) settings where the observation of pedagogical planning meetings was undertaken. Conflicts were observed in the organisation's review of learning activities and this chapter discusses the main forms of their management. The following section clarifies the chapter's theoretical approach to pedagogical planning and conflict management and what it means to study these processes as interactions. The third section introduces the methodology and the contexts of the research, while the fourth and the fifth sections are dedicated to the results of the research, illustrating the two main forms of conflict management emerging from the analysis of data: hierarchy-centred management and participation-centred management.

Pedagogical Planning as Interaction

Meetings dedicated to pedagogical planning are talk-saturated practices (Tracy & Dimock, 2004): that is, they are a form of interaction mainly dedicated to the coordination of actions. The coordination of actions leads to decision-making.

Pedagogical planning is a communication process that participants, including leaders, cannot control completely, because no participant can control how others understand communicative actions and the intentions underpinning them. However, pedagogical planning is not chaotic, because it is oriented by role performances and expectations. These can be observed in interaction through contextualisation cues, that is, elements of the interactions, sometimes minimal but nevertheless significant, that 'highlight, foreground or make salient' (Gumperz, 1992, p. 232) the expectations that structure interaction.

This chapter lends itself as an example of the analytical opportunities offered by a focus on interactions. In particular, the chapter illustrates how focusing on interaction allows the observation of contextualisation cues for the construction of an organisational culture in empirical social practice. The focus on interaction allows this chapter to explore the relationship between the organisational culture produced in empirical social practices and the organisational culture produced in institutionalised narratives.

Sociologists refer to the expectations that constitute the structures of communication as 'social structures'. These structures help participants to understand 'what' is communicated, and the understanding of the motives of communication, and 'who' communicates. The same communication uttered by different participants will be understood differently. A useful theory to understand the implications of expectations connected with 'who' communicates is *positioning* (Harré & van Langhenove, 1999). In each social context, including meetings of pedagogical planning, individuals are positioned in a network of expectations that supports understanding of communication as well as understanding of the motives of communication. Individuals can be positioned as social roles in a network of normative expectations that concern standardised performances or they can be positioned as persons, in networks of expectations that concern personal expressions.

Collegial Models of Management

From a sociological perspective, the expansion of collegial models of management emphasising the agency of the members of the organisation is an expression of the primacy that society assigns the individual (Beck & Beck-Gernsheim, 2002). Collegial models of management position participants as *roles*, expected to deliver *performances* and as *persons* who have recognised rights of personal expression. Leaders in collegial models of management are positioned as transformational and are expected to promote personalised expressions towards participative decision-making. Participative decision-making should impact positively on the organisation's capability to adapt to changing environments because it enhances reflexivity and reflection (Schippers et al., 2008; Allen et al., 2019; Farini & Scollan, 2019).

This is reflected in Yeung's vision of transformational leaders as *facilitators* (Yeung, 2004). Facilitation of active participation in decision-making enhances professional and personal development of the members of the organisation and nurtures a richer organisational culture. Yeung discusses empirical cues that allow us to recognise participative decision-making when observing organisational meetings: prompting, echoing, reaffirming, formulating personal expressions; proposing the gist of personal expressions to tease out their main points; probing personal expression via questions and the selection of speakers to extend the area of active participation. These are some of the actions that transform organisational interactions in opportunities for the exercise of *leadership that empowers* (Holmes et al., 2007; Pomerantz & Denvir, 2007).

About the Research

This chapter discusses decision-making processes in two ECE settings located in the region of Emilia-Romagna in Italy. Emilia-Romagna is home of the Reggio Approach, internationally renowned for its support for young children's agency and personalised participation in their own education (Rinaldi, 2006). A strong influence on many ECE settings in the Emilia-Romagna region is the concept of *pedagogia relazionale*, a pillar of the Reggio Approach. Pedagogia relazionale can be translated as *educating through relationships*. The epistemological foundation of pedagogia relazionale is that educating is only possible in relation with other people and in relation with the world (Spaggiari, 2004). Pedagogia relazionale emphasises working in a collegial manner, exchanging opinions and comparing points of view.

The two ECE settings participating in the research share a similar organisation, which is incidentally standard for State or Municipal ECE in Italy: three *sezioni omogenee* (age groups): three years old, four years old and five years old. Two *insegnanti* (teachers) work in each sezione. In each setting, a *coordinatrice* coordinates the activities. Nevertheless, the coordinatrice is not a setting manager but a local pedagogical leader who offers support in problem-solving, organises partnerships with families and interfaces with local authorities.

The management of the ECE settings involved in the research are committed to participative decision-making both ideologically and methodologically: enhancing the agency of children is indissolubly linked with enhancing the agency of practitioners towards collegial models of management.

The discussion of decision-making undertaken in this chapter is based on the analysis of audio recordings of eight pedagogical planning meetings.

Audio-recorded pedagogical meetings were transcribed using a simplified version of the transcription conventions of conversation analysis (Jefferson, 1978; Psathas & Anderson, 1990).

The discussion of data will use a selection of transcribed interactions, chosen because they are particularly meaningful examples of two main forms of conflict management. The discussion develops around the following questions:

- How are conflicts managed in pedagogical planning meetings?
- Are conflicts managed in line with the principle of collegiality?
- Are conflicts approached as an opportunity for personal expression?
- Is reflection enhanced by conflict management when personal expressions are supported?

The analysis of data through these questions leads to the identification of two main forms of conflict management. The first form (hierarchy-centred management of conflict, HCM) diverges from participative decision-making because it is characterised by a hierarchical management approach centred on roles performances, with little room for personal expressions. The second form of conflict management (participation-centred management of conflict, PCM), on the contrary, is compatible with participative decision-making and is instrumental to an organisational culture that values agency and personal expression.

Thus, a first outcome of analysis is that despite the organisational culture of both the ECE settings being founded on collegiality, HCM is not rare. Similar findings have been made in research focusing on the interactions in business meetings (Asmuss & Svennevig, 2009). However, a second outcome of the research is that participative decision-making within pedagogical leadership can be enhanced by taking a participative approach to conflict management (PCM) and embedding this as part of the organisational culture.

Hierarchy-centred Management of Conflict

The general characteristic of HCM is that the setting leaders, often the coordinator but sometimes senior teachers too, position others as subordinates, putting at the centre of communication role performances rather than personal expressions. Rather than the outcome of facilitated discussion, the management of conflict is decided by leaders who present decisions to others instead. In the corpus of data, when HCM frames conflict management, leaders or senior teachers access the role of *gatekeepers* of the interaction, restricting the area of participation for others. Gatekeeping limits the possibility of participation both with regard to acceptability of participation (role performances marginalise personal expressions) and the management of turn-taking. Gatekeepers may systematically prevent the inclusion of more participants in the discussion. The characteristic morphology of HCM consists of triplets of turns where a leader's assessment of performance triggers a teacher's justification which is then commented on by the leader. Triplets of leader-teacher-leader turn-taking generate interactive dyads that exclude participative decision-making.

HCM is characterised by interpersonal conflict; our data suggests that teachers tend to reject their positioning as subordinated. This is displayed by actions that suggest uneasiness about hierarchical relationships. HCM is not coherent with the stated culture of the organisations. The two excerpts presented here show HCM in action as well as its rejection from staff, with negative implications for the success of conflict management.

First, HCM is displayed through hierarchy-centred assessments of the teachers' role performances. In Extract 1, participants are T1, a senior teacher and two teachers working in the five-year-old sezione, T2 and T3. Although T1 works with young children, she is concerned about an activity that she had the opportunity to observe, albeit not for the whole duration.

Excerpt 1

1. T1: I think today was let's say complicated, it seems to me that there was not that engagement, I mean the children, and it seems to me as well that (T2) did not notice it and was not helping as I would have expected. To me, attention should be given not only on what is going on but also what is not, I mean let's say areas of disengagement. And it is difficult, for example for her (T3) as there is a focus on children's activity so

here's you (T2) who is not leading because it was not the division of work you should be actively monitoring and this comes even before getting involved with the activity in the sense of getting involved with the children who engage well. Maybe in terms of planning group it is important to share an understanding of the range of roles but the first is not a role really it is being quick in switching the focus, exiting a frame to enter another one. And I wonder is there a need, but this is for me too, a need to check understanding of activities so that if children are not engaging it could be a quick fix to work with them to construct a meaning of the activity but there is here the need to fully understand the rationale

2. T2: yes OK but actually there is a reason and it's a misunderstanding from your side because I was working close to children who we had taken back to the activities so they were part of the group who was not engaging and this is what you see as an activity rather than a children focus but this is because you did not see the whole process developing
3. T3: maybe more detailed discussion when planning the activities would actually help to foresee problems so that it is not running after children when problems happen and we are obviously not prepared as we plan for success rather than failure and we think the children would love it and we will engage them so when they don't and they sort of break up in small groups, mad splinters [laughs] then it's too late to get them all back
4. T2: it's difficult but I suppose it's not because I needed to know more about the activity's rationale it's just that stuff like that happens and it takes a process to sort it out without shouting and screaming and it was actually happening with the time it needs
5. T1: and this is why it is a problem, that process is not manageable so needs prevention and quick reaction on first sign of the first disengaging

In turn 1, T1 centres an extended narrative on role performances. The narration of non-optimal performances (*it seems to me as well that (T2) did not notice it and was not helping as I would have expected. To me, attention should be given not only on what is going on but also what is not*) is followed by the presentation to the teachers of more effective decision-making (*here's you (T2) who is not leading because it was not the division of work you should be actively monitoring and this comes even before getting involved with the activity in the sense of getting involved with the children who engage well*). T1 positions herself as a leader in the context of a hierarchical relationship.

This is displayed by comments that deliver a negative evaluation of performances rather than discussing problems collegially. Hierarchical positioning is both the condition and outcome of T1's narrative where she is the 'I' who decides actions that affect professional routines and identities for the 'us' group (*And I wonder is there a need [. . .] a need to check understanding*), although this is mitigated by self-inclusion in the subordinate 'us', who need more work to understand activities (*but this is for me too*).

In turn 2, a conflict arises as T2 rejects the subordinate positioning proposed by T1. Although mitigating it with a double disclaimer (*yes OK*) to avoid a direct rejection of T1's contribution, T2 defends her role performance and refuses to align to a narrative that positions her as someone in need of support. T1's hierarchical positioning escalates a conflict that diverts the focus of the interaction from pedagogical issues to be tackled cooperatively to the positioning of interactants vis-á-vis their professional identities. T2 rejects the mediation attempted by T3 in turn 3, because that still positions the two sezione teachers in a professional deficit. T2 emphasises her professional status and does that by soundly rejecting the validity of both T1 and T3 narrations (*I suppose it's not because I needed to know more about the activity's rationale it's just that stuff like that happens*). An opportunity for problem-solving is transformed into a confrontation centred around the right of positioning interlocutors. HCM finds an evident expression in turn 5: the conflict is deflagrated but T1 elects to manage it by ignoring it, imposing her interpretation of the situation (*this is why it is a problem, that process is not manageable so needs prevention and quick reaction on first sign of the first disengaging*). The interaction has now become a confrontation to defend the validity of previous contributions; this is the purpose of T1's comments. Turn 5 closes the exchange and the interaction moves to different topics. T1 accesses the role of gatekeeper to control participation in the interaction, creating unfavourable conditions for further discussion. Apparently T1 succeeds in imposing her interpretation of the observed events because that goes unchallenged the second time she presents it; however, the decision to ignore the conflict not only prevents the interaction from returning to the activity but also prevents collegiality in favour of HCM. Extract 1 shows a further negative consequence of HCM: the inability to co-construct a positioning that is acceptable for all participants fuels the development of interpersonal conflicts.

When HCM is made relevant as the framework of interaction, leaders claim superior epistemic rights associated with superior professional status: that is, with a hierarchy of roles. However, HCM contrasts with one of the ideological and methodological pillars of ECE practice in the region, *pedagogia relazionale*. This makes HMC unstable with two evident results: (1) leaders who enact HCM do not find cooperation from others to a point that they systematically have to rush the interaction to an end and (2) teachers who are re-positioned as subordinates systematically observe HCM as an aggression against their epistemic status and professional identity.

When leaders restrict teachers' spaces of personal expression and their responsibility in decision-making, HCM functions as a *listening filter* (Scollan & McNeill, 2019) that silences teachers' voices. In our corpus of data, teachers do not offer compliance to HCM but reluctant alignment, or even open rejection with the emergence of difficult interpersonal conflicts.

Participation-centred Management of Conflict

The second form of conflict management observed in the data is PCM. PCM is produced when the interaction is framed by participative decision-making; the structure of conflict management shifts from hierarchy to participation and expectations concern personal expressions rather than role performances.

Before turn 1, a discussion has developed about a problem: children are allowed to move between the room and the outdoor space during some activities; however, a few children have taken the role of gatekeepers trying to prevent others from going out, with ensuing conflicts being observed.

Excerpt 2

1. T4: so shouldn't we make clear some basic rules maybe we can use an activity and construct them with children because there is a general sharing of the expectation but an activity could work as let's say a symbolic seal. But I see the risk of getting children to do something they do not need to do
2. T3: we definitely should
3. T5: however, I see both sides of an argument here; the power of symbols but also the risk of imposing indirectly what we think is important and right whilst it is not strictly necessary

4. T2: I think we should be . . . we need to be careful not to use the activity like a Trojan horse to bring what we want in the children's world
5. T4: yes
6. Co: it's the teachers, the team, who have solid hands on this. Make your judgement if you see that's the problem, that fighting, fighting that could have be a one off really, if that fighting happens systematically that yes it could be a good idea to construct this sort of bills of rights with the children just ask them
7. T4: it's us and children [and must be true cooperation
8. Co: [yes I think it is
9. T4: yes
10. T5: OK
11. T3: yes
12. CO: so:
13. T6: so let's see if there is a need and if there is it is an opportunity to work with them and find how they feel about being together, really

In turn 1, T3 presents the idea of developing an activity to co-construct with children explicit rules of behaviour. In line with dialogic management of problems, T4 formulates her proposals in a way that promotes agentic participation, creating a favourable environment for personal expressions (turns 2–4). In turn 5, T4 aligns with T5 and T2's concerns displaying engagement in the discussion and appreciation of other participants' contributions. What marks a distinction between this situation of PCM and the previously discussed examples of HCM is the intervention of the coordinatrice (Co) in turn 6. Co positions all teachers as experts (*it's the teachers who have the solid hands on this*), supporting their epistemic authority. The management of different opinions (for instance the enthusiastic approval of T3 as opposed to the more nuanced view taken by T5 and T2) is part of a narration of collegial discussion on which the coordinatrice explicitly puts her trust. The leader accesses the role of *facilitator* of personal expression, promoting participation. This is the meaning of participation-centred management: management of disagreements does not rely on hierarchy but it relies on agentic participation. In the sequence of turns 6 to 9, Co and T4 develop an interweaving pattern of talk (Morgenthaler, 1990), which is characteristic of PCM. As shown by excerpt 2, PCM facilitates the discussion of pedagogical issues because the positioning of all participants as epistemic authorities in their professional field is not threatened by any interactional move. The couple of turns 10–11 displays a participative decision-making leading to turn 12 where Co does not access the role of 'chair' who summarises the outcome of the discussion claiming the high authority of a *primus inter* pares. Rather, Co facilitates teachers' active role in the definition of the solution, mirroring T4's original sensitivity towards the importance of the symbolic dimension. T6 celebrates the consensus reached in turn 13, accessing the role of chair which is another cue for the participating frame of the meeting.

PCM as illustrated by excerpt 2 diverges from HCM as displayed, for example, by excerpt 1. In excerpt 2, Co and T4 co-construct a solution, creating a narrative of decision-making as participated and shared, thus reinforcing the epistemic status of all participants: the latter point is crucial for the interpretation of Co's turn 12. When the interaction is structured by PCM and expectations concern personal expressions, conflict management can develop as an interweaving pattern of talk whereby participation is facilitated, because a positive value is placed on the possibility for all participants to contribute to decision-making.

Discussion and Conclusion

Participative decision-making and PCM are intertwined: they are forms of communication that are structured by expectations of personal expressions, where participants are positioned as epistemic authorities who have recognised rights to author and co-author knowledge. The analysis of interaction allows us to examine the intersection between the micro-dimension, that is the sequences of turn of talk, and the macro-dimension, that is the culture of the organisation. The expectations that structure interaction are made visible by contextualisation cues; in the excerpts discussed in sections 4 and 5, the management of turn-taking, the use of pronouns, the nature of questions are contextualisation cues for the positioning of participants.

Intersections between micro- and macro-dimensions do not necessarily entail coherence; the corpus of data produced in the research presented in this chapter offers instances where the micro-dimension of interaction contrasts with the macro-dimension of the organisational culture. This is the case with HCM in the contexts of the research, because with HCM the micro-dimension of interaction makes relevant expectations of role performance and hierarchical positioning that contrast with the participatory culture of the settings.

A genuine adhesion to the participative culture of the settings does not secure that in the reality of empirical social practices, day after day, leaders will necessarily position themselves as facilitator of participation rather than gatekeepers. Embracing the methodology and ethics of collegial management does not guarantee that leaders will not prioritise role performances against personal expression. The culture of the organisation can be strong and shared but cannot control the unpredictability and complexity of all interactions, where many contextual variables can play an important part, from professional exhaustion to interpersonal relationships, from stress to limited resources, from time constraints to problems in the partnership with families or local authorities.

While organisational culture cannot control interaction, organisational culture can nevertheless support reflection on conflict management when importance is recognised through training and time in the life of the organisation ring-fenced to allow collective reflection. Previous research in educational settings (Farini, 2009; Baraldi & Farini, 2011) suggests that reflection on activities can support organisational change when expectations concern equality in participation, empathy and personal expressions.

This chapter presents a limited range of conflict management scenarios. Both HCM and PCM should be understood as categories that include more nuanced and ambiguous forms of conflict management. The corpus of data offers examples of conflict management that oscillate between HCM and PCM. However, the scope of the chapter is to discuss how the culture of an organisation can be reinforced or challenged by the management of conflict, in a bid to promote reflection on the great influence that even the most ephemeral interaction can exert on the positioning of leaders and staff with implications for well-being and attitudes towards active participation and risk-taking. For this reason, clear-cut examples from the corpus of data have been selected.

It is possible to conclude the chapter by highlighting that, notwithstanding the symbolic power of pedagogia relazionale and the collegial organisational culture of the settings participating in the research, pedagogical leadership in meetings of pedagogical planning decision-making, particularly in situations of conflict, may depend on HCM where positioning concerns role performances rather than personal expression.

However, the corpus of data offers many instances, represented in the chapter by excerpt 2, where PCM facilitates participative decision-making that sustains non-hierarchical cooperative floor (Morgenthaler, 1990), thus favouring reflexivity (Schippers et al., 2008) and focusing the intelligence of the team on pedagogical planning rather than diverting it towards interpersonal conflict. The chapter suggests that the management of conflicts is central to pedagogical leadership. What matters is that conflicts arising in pedagogical planning are managed in a way that is participation-centred rather than hierarchy-centred, and that when the latter arises, there is sufficient time and space for reflection to explore what this might mean for the organisational culture.

References

Allen, S., Whalley, M., Lee, M., & A. Scollan (2019). *Developing Professional Practice in the Early Years*. Milton Keynes: Oxford University Press.

Asmuss, B., & Svennevig, J. (2009). Meeting talk. An introduction. *Journal of Business Communication, 46*(1), 3–22.

Beck, U., & Beck-Gernsheim, E. (2002). *Individualization: Institutionalized Individualism and Its Social and Political Consequences*. London: Sage.

Farini, F. (2009). Activities 2: Coordinating reflection'. In C. Baraldi (Ed.), *Dialogue in Intercultural Communities. From an Educational Point of View* (pp. 155–172). Amsterdam: John Benjamins.

Farini, F., & Baraldi, C. (2011). Dialogic mediation in international groups of adolescents. *Language and Dialogue, 1*(2), 207–232.

Farini, F., & Scollan, A. (2019). In, out and through digital worlds. Hybrid-transitions as a space for children's agency. *International Journal of Early Years Education, 28*(1), 36–49.

Gumperz, J. (1992). Contextualization and understanding. In A. Duranti & C. Goodwin (Eds.), *Rethinking Context: Language as an Interactive Phenomenon* (pp. 229–253). Cambridge: Cambridge University Press.

Harré, R., & Van Langenhove, L. (1999). *Positioning Theory. The Discursive Turn in Social Psychology*, In R. Harré & F. Moghaddam (Eds.), *The Self and Others: Positioning Individuals and Groups in Personal, Political and Cultural Contexts* (pp. 129–136). Westport, CT: Praeger Publishers.

Holmes, J. (2007). Monitoring organizational boundaries: Diverse discourse strategies used in gatekeeping. *Journal of Pragmatics, 39*, 1993–2016.

Jefferson, G. (1978). Sequential aspects of storytelling in conversation. In J. Schenkein (Ed.), *Studies in the Organization of Conversational Interaction* (pp. 219–248). Cambridge: Academic Press.

Morgenthaler, L. (1990). A study of group process: Who's got WHAT floor? *Journal of Pragmatics, 14*, 537–557.

Pomerantz, A., & Denvir, P. (2007). Enacting the institutional role of chairperson in upper management meetings: The interactional realization of provisional authority. In F. Cooren (Ed.), *Interacting and Organizing. Analyses of a Management Meeting* (pp. 31–52). London: Erlbaum.

Psathas, G., & Anderson, T. (1990). The practices of transcription in conversation analysis. *Semiotica, 78*(1/2), 75–99.

Rinaldi, C. (2006). *In Dialogue with Reggio Emilia: Listening, Researching and Learning*. London: Routledge.

Schippers, M. C., Den Hartog, D. N., Koopman, P. L., & Van Knippenberg, D. (2008). The role of transformational leadership in enhancing team reflexivity. *Human Relations, 61*, 1593–1616.

Scollan, A. & McNeill, E. (2019) Listening to children's voices in Irish social work through cultural and organisational filters. In F. Farini & A. Scollan (Eds.), *Children's Self-Determination in the Context of Early Childhood Education and Services: Discourses, Policies and Practices* (pp. 151–167). Amsterdam: Springer Nature.

Spaggiari, S. (2004). The path toward knowledge: The social, political and cultural context of the Reggio Municipal Infant Toddler Center and preschool experience. *Innovations, 11*, 2.

Tracy, K., & Dimock, A. (2004). Meetings: Discursive sides for building and fragmenting com-munity. In P. Kalbfleisch (Ed.), *Communication Yearbook 28* (pp. 127–164). Mahwah, NJ: Erlbaum.

Yeung, L. (2004). The paradox of control in participative decision-making: Gatekeeping dis-course in banks. *International Journal of the Sociology of Language, 166*, 83–104.

14

Advancing Pedagogical Leadership at National Level

Looking for a Policy Window

Sara Bonetti and Mona Sakr

Introduction

Discussions about the development of pedagogical leadership often focus on how individuals or particular organisations advance their own pedagogical leadership. While these investigations are fascinating, there is also a need to consider how pedagogical leadership can be facilitated on a wider scale. We need to think about the development of pedagogical leadership in regional, national and international contexts.

In this chapter, we consider ECE pedagogical leadership in the context of national policy. We begin by briefly framing pedagogical leadership through Meyerson's (2008) understanding of 'positive deviance' within organisations. We consider this understanding of pedagogical leadership in the contemporary policy context in England. We ask what policy realities currently stand in the way of large-scale advancement of pedagogical leadership across the ECE sector. To develop this discussion further, we introduce Kingdon's (2011) policy streams approach, which seeks to explain why policies shift and change when they do. We bring together our analysis of current national ECE policy with Kingdon's policy streams approach in order to consider whether there might be any 'policy windows' opening up and what would need to be aligned in order for the windows to open.

Based on these explorations and analyses, we argue that policy shifts to support pedagogical leadership in England will depend on (1) the framing of 'the ECE problem' in terms of quality rather than quantity, (2) the existence of viable policy solutions that address the perceived problem, are supported by collective and united voices in the sector and are backed by bodies of credible evidence and (3) support for individuals and organisations that can create a strong and united ECE voice for policy change (referred to by Kingdon as 'policy entrepreneurs').

Thinking about Pedagogical Leadership as 'Positive Deviance'

When pedagogical leadership flourishes, organisations ripple with continuous development and growth. Pedagogical leadership bubbles up from the passion, commitment and everyday actions of individuals working in organisations. We think about these particular individuals as catalysts – they are the people that can subtly agitate for change and help it to take root within a community. Meyerson (2008) describes this kind of subtle leadership as 'positive deviance'. This term describes those small improvements individuals make within organisations. Such individuals are 'tempered radicals', who, operating within organisations, work subtly and incrementally towards social change. Their small acts of self-expression and localised experimentation help to build up new norms and practices within the organisation. These individuals are prepared to try new things and go against the grain, but without radically or explicitly defying the status quo. They manage to fit into the organisational community while bringing about change from within.

While we recognise that pedagogical leadership is associated with the work of individuals, context is vital. Context sets the scene (or not) for individuals to bring about change through subtle and incremental means. For example, Meyerson's research found that positive deviance was more likely to flourish in certain conditions. Of particular importance was the condition of psychological safety. When members of an organisation feel psychologically safe, they are able to express themselves and make themselves heard without fear of judgement or derision. Within this, a particular kind of relationship with one's immediate manager was found to be important. If the manager minimised perceived power differences in their communication, staff were more open to the acts of self-expression and experimentation that comprise positive deviance. Similarly, the design and leadership in the organisation are essential to ensuring 'small wins' through positive deviance are shared. Managers need processes and systems in place that mean that incremental changes in one part of the organisation have the opportunity to influence practices in another part of the organisation.

However, how organisations function is shaped by wider levels of context. What helps ECE organisations to create conditions of psychological safety for example? What is it that supports the creation of the managerial relationships outlined earlier? What enables the development of ECE organisations that can not only support positive deviance but share it, so that it spreads throughout the organisation and creates a powerful culture of continuous learning and growth? Factors in the wider society, including much that is embedded in national policy, will impact on the potential of organisations in ECE to develop these capacities. All of the capacities outlined earlier require time. If everyone in an organisation feels stressed and under-valued, psychological safety is much harder to achieve. If staff have no space around their 'hours on the floor', opportunities to come together as a team for sessions of reflective practice might be harder to find. When there is little national support for leadership development in ECE, it is more likely that there is limited understanding of the skills, structures and processes through which small changes can be shared through organisations.

We argue that pedagogical leadership is therefore defined through interactions between the individual, the organisation and the wider policy landscape.

Supporting Pedagogical Leadership in the English National Context

Looking at the contemporary policy backdrop for pedagogical leadership in an English context, we see three key inhibitors at work: (1) economic fragmentation and under-investment, (2) de-professionalisation of the workforce and (3) clashes with a wider social discourse in which ECE is seen as 'just childcare'.

Economic Fragmentation and Under-investment

Within the ECE sector in England, private childcare on non-domestic premises provides 82 per cent of all childcare places on the early years (EY) register; this equates to 1.1 million places for young children (Ofsted, 2020). There is widespread recognition, however, that there is diversity and fragmentation among those private providers (Bonetti, 2020a, b). Private providers are varied in terms of size, the demographics of the communities that they serve, their financial characteristics, including profit and level of reserves, and their governance structures and practices.

Around one-third of private providers are unable to afford any professional training except compulsory training because they operate on a 'hand to mouth' basis (NDNA, 2018, 2019; Ceeda, 2019). A recent report – 'The Forgotten Sector' – published by the Early Years Alliance (2020) found that 25 per cent of providers thought that the Covid crisis would force them to close due to financial pressures. Local authorities distribute funding per pupil for a particular number of hours, but Ceeda (2019) found that this funding on average covers just four out of every five children accessing the funded places. Thus, there is a shortfall in funding rates of 18 per cent, which rises to 21 per cent if unpaid staff hours were properly costed. Given this shortfall, many providers try and subsidise funded places through full fees, but this is less possible in areas of disadvantage. As a result, providers working in disadvantaged areas – where such subsidisation is harder – are disproportionately affected financially.

As we explained in the previous section, pedagogical leadership requires time (and therefore resources) in order to flourish. It takes time to build up psychological safety among teams (Edmondson, 2018). It also takes time to develop coaching and management within an organisation, so that reflection and feedback can be most effective (Jones & Gorell, 2018). In a situation where many settings are financially precarious, there can be less time dedicated to pedagogical leadership practices.

De-professionalisation of the Workforce

The professionalism of the ECE workforce in England is a hugely contentious issue. There is a widespread recognition that quality ECE services are connected to the professionalism of the workforce – to the experience and qualifications that they bring to their work, as well as the in-service learning that can happen as part of the work (DfE, 2017; Melhuish & Gardiner, 2019). However, while there is support for this rhetoric, for example as part of the 2017 workforce strategy published by the Department for Education, the facts tell another story. The majority of those working in ECE are qualified to Level 3 and this is also the case among those working as managers in a setting. There is no official pay scale and recent research suggests that on average there are only very small salary increases when professionals extend qualifications beyond Level 3 (e.g. to undergraduate degree level) if ECE professionals stay within a private setting (Ceeda, 2019).

This has created a perception among the workforce that further upskilling beyond the minimum requirement provides no career benefit (Campbell-Barr & Bonetti, 2021). Previous initiatives that had pedagogical leadership built in – such as the early years professional status (EYPS), and to some extent the early years teacher status (which replaced EYPS in 2013) – have not been well supported by government. As those qualified to Level 6 and beyond are more expensive to employ, many private and voluntary settings are not in a position to recruit such individuals. We have seen numbers of those qualifying at this level dwindling over recent years (Ceeda, 2017, 2018, 2019; NDNA, 2018, 2019; Early Years Workforce Commission, 2021).

Clashes with a Wider Social Discourse in Which ECE Is Seen as 'Just Childcare'

It is only when ECE is seen by most people in society as a pedagogical endeavour – when it is thought about in terms of learning and development in the most holistic and uplifting sense – that we lay a groundwork for designing pedagogical leadership into ECE organisations. Current debates about the status of ECE and the purposes of ECE in wider society are important battlegrounds for the advancement of pedagogical leadership on a national level. It is much harder to develop a discourse of pedagogical leadership if it is not part of a wider thinking or understanding. Schein (2017) suggests that it is much harder to embed a practice (such as pedagogical leadership) into an organisation's culture if it clashes with what is valued in a wider cultural context. Thus, we need to consider whether ECE is perceived in wider society in terms of pedagogy and pedagogical leadership, or if – at the other end of the spectrum – it is seen as 'just childcare', there first and foremost to enable parents to go out to work. If the latter is true, weaving pedagogical leadership into the design of an ECE organisation becomes much harder.

Looking for a Policy Window: Kingdon's Policy Streams Approach

In John Kingdon's (2011) policy streams approach, policies develop through the flow of three 'streams': the problem stream, the policy stream and the politics stream. When the streams align, a policy window opens, which is a chance for significant policy change.

- The problem stream refers to the perception of a public problem that requires attention.
- The policy stream refers to the presence of constructive policy solutions that have been devised in advance and offer possible alternatives to the current policy landscape. These alternatives are seen as having credibility due to being backed by influential bodies or communities.
- The politics stream refers to what is going on in the political arena, including who is in power, the point of time in the election cycle and notable shifts in public opinion.

When these streams line up, a policy window opens and policy entrepreneurs (individuals or organisations with perseverance and influence) have the opportunity to push policy changes through:

> Policy windows mostly open occasionally, and might not stay open very long. Thus, actors who promote a specific solution, the policy entrepreneurs, must act rapidly before the opportunity passes by, or they will have to wait until the next chance comes along.
>
> (Guldbrandsson & Fossum, 2009, p. 435)

When we consider the policy context of pedagogical leadership in ECE, we can ask whether a policy window exists now or in the near future by analysing the three streams outlined in Kingdon's theory.

- *The problem stream.* Is there widespread recognition of a problem in ECE that needs to be fixed, and is the advancement of pedagogical leadership a recognisable solution to this problem?
- *The policy stream.* Are there constructive policy solutions on the table, supported by influential bodies, that would enhance pedagogical leadership in ECE?
- *The political stream.* Is the political landscape conducive to policy changes relating to pedagogical leadership in ECE at the moment? Is there a political appetite for changes to ECE that would help to grow pedagogical leadership?
- *Policy entrepreneurs.* Are there individuals or organisations in the arena who would be well positioned to push policies for pedagogical leadership 'over the line' should a policy window open?

To develop our analysis of advancing pedagogical leadership in the national policy context of England, we now consider these four elements of the policy streams approach in relation to the contemporary situation. We suggest what might need to change or manifest in each element in order for a policy window to open that could in turn advance pedagogical leadership across the sector.

The Problem Stream

For some, the current problem in ECE is the quantity of provision while for others, the emphasis is on the urgent need for more quality provision. Only the second framing of the problem creates a context in which it makes sense to push on a policy level for the advancement of pedagogical leadership in ECE.

The Covid-19 pandemic has sparked fears that the ECE sector will decrease in size and fewer children will have places as a result. Recent reports have highlighted the financial precariousness of the ECE sector, with 25 per cent of providers facing the risk of going under according to the Early Years Alliance (EYA, 2021). This has been cited as a problem because of the profound impact that this would have on the economy, and particularly women's contribution to the economy (Fawcett Society, 2021). While this highlights the quantity of ECE as problematic, it does not highlight quality ECE as an issue to be addressed. On the other hand, some public attention has been given to the quality of ECE, suggesting that current ECE provision is not effective enough to have a significant positive impact on the lives of children from the most disadvantaged backgrounds (Social Mobility Commission, 2016). Fundamental to this view is that quality ECE services are essential to the welfare of children and families, particularly those living in poverty, and that this matters to us as a society. The Covid-19 pandemic has raised awareness about this situation, building a narrative of the most disadvantaged children, including the very youngest, 'falling behind' in their education (e.g. Nursery World, 2021; The Guardian, 2021). The solution to this problem would involve a focus on ECE quality, and within this, pedagogical leadership would have a significant role to play. Thus, an understanding of the problem as one of quality is vital for making the case for policies that advance pedagogical leadership.

The Policy Stream

Various potential policies could be used to develop pedagogical leadership in the sector. Broadly these fall into three categories: (1) increased investment in ECE services so that organisations delivering ECE have more time to foster pedagogical leadership practices, (2) the development of national training and qualifications relating to pedagogical leadership and (3) greater emphasis on pedagogical leadership in national frameworks outlining quality ECE.

Increased investment in ECE services directly could happen along different lines, and some of these approaches have already been taken by previous governments but then dropped by subsequent governments (e.g. the Graduate Leader Fund, which offered money to settings to employ a graduate-level practitioner). Additional investment could be made by increasing the hourly rate for children accessing funded places. Alternatively, there could be top-up funding for settings when settings employ a graduate, if we all agree that graduates are able to bring more pedagogical leadership to the sector. It might mean top-ups for those working in areas of deprivation or increases in funding for children and families accessing provision who are below a particular income threshold.

Another route would be to develop national training programmes relating to pedagogical leadership. One option would be to resurrect the EYPS which was introduced in 2007 by the Children's Workforce Development Council (CWDC), the now defunct body which was established to ensure that those who work with children and families had the necessary skills. As a qualification, the EYPS could only be undertaken by graduates, and it required their work to be assessed in the context of an ECE provider, whether this was a placement or their current workplace. Fundamental to the creation of the EYPS was the value placed on building quality provision through the extension of pedagogical leadership, via individual graduates (McDowall Clark, 2012). Inherent to introducing the EYPS was the ambitious vision that by 2010 all Children's Centres *(a particular type of state-provided cross-sector provider for children's and families)* in England would have an Early Years Professional (EYP) on their team and that this would extend to all type of providers, including private, voluntary and independent setting (PVIs), by 2015. This vision would be funded by substantial government investment through the Graduate Leader Fund, which provided all settings with financial incentives to recruit graduates including EYPs.

However, in 2013, the EYPS was replaced by the Early Years Teachers Status (EYTS), which placed greater emphasis on teaching literacy and numeracy and less emphasis on the open-ended possibilities of pedagogical leadership for continuous quality improvement. The shift was argued on the basis that the EYPS was not having enough of an impact on early inequalities and a more direct approach to addressing educational disadvantage – focused on literacy and numeracy – was required.

The EYTS has been relatively untested since the Graduate Leader Fund was removed since many settings have struggled to afford to employ individuals with EYTS. Linked to this, numbers of individuals taking the qualification have decreased in the last four years, with only 595 individuals starting the training last year compared with initial number of 2,327 in 2013.

The rise and fall of the EYPS suggests two learning points. First, we need to carefully protect the vision of pedagogical leadership from a more narrow focus on instructional capacity, particularly relating to numeracy and literacy. We must build bodies of evidence that demonstrates that pedagogical leadership, as an expansive concept inextricably linked to organisational practices and relationships, makes the difference. Secondly, all qualifications need to be seen in the wider funding context for the sector. New training programmes that focus on pedagogical leadership can only be as successful as the capacity of the sector to employ those who complete the training. This is likely to require further government investment, with top-up funding to employ those with the qualification.

A third policy route for advancing pedagogical leadership would be to build it into quality frameworks – so that the early years foundation stage for example – highlighted the role of pedagogical leadership practices in quality provision and how this could be demonstrated in action. This could be effective in shaping the discourse in the sector and gearing it more towards pedagogical leadership but there would also need to be an investment in the professional learning to support such a shift. All of these policy shifts to advance pedagogical leadership in ECE depend on government investment, and therefore on the political appetite to develop the ECE vision for the future. This is considered in the following section.

The Politics Stream

We currently have a conservative government which has shown no significant interest in expanding or developing ECE provision. Having said this, part of the political response to the Covid-19 crisis has been a growing discourse around 'giving back' to those on the frontline. This includes those working in ECE, since ECE settings were asked to stay open during lockdown even when schools closed. Furthermore, as mentioned in 'the problem stream' analysis, there is public attention on growing inequities as a result of the pandemic and a focus on the negative consequences for disadvantaged children and families. What this means for pedagogical leadership in ECE is that there may be political appetite for investment in both the ECE workforce and the development of quality provision that support children living in poverty to succeed in line with peers. Politicians want to be seen to be supporting those who have been on the frontline during the pandemic (and ECE settings have gained public attention in this respect) and they want to be seen to be supporting those children and families that have been worst affected by the pandemic. They could achieve these political aims through funding geared at advancing pedagogical leadership practices in settings serving the most disadvantaged, for example, through top-up funding to employ graduates in these settings.

Policy Entrepreneurs

In Kingdon's policy streams approach, even when the three streams align and a policy window opens, it is essential that there is an individual or collective who can effectively advocate for the policy change to occur. In the English ECE sector, it is not clear who or what this policy entrepreneur would be. Various sector bodies seek to represent the sector but tend to be more closely aligned to particular types of provider. A potential cross-sector policy entrepreneur keen to draw attention to the importance of pedagogical leadership is the self-appointed Early Years Workforce Commission 2020--2021 (EYWC). In January 2021, EYWC published its first report 'A Workforce in Crisis: Saving Our Early Years', the phrase 'pedagogical leadership' is mentioned four times in the report, amidst specific recommendations with regards to the recruitment of graduates into the sector, and leadership development through training. The report recommends that:

> A targeted re-introduction of a Leadership Quality Fund should be considered so that higher qualified staff can work as pedagogical leaders in early years provision serving less advantaged communities, with enhanced pay and status, and there should be a place for the role of pedagogical leader in every setting.

In this extract, pedagogical leadership is positioned as key in addressing disadvantage among children and families by being at the centre of the development of quality ECE provision. It also suggests that pedagogical leadership, in more general terms, is important across the sector, regardless of the communities served or the type of provider. Thus, EYWC have put an emphasis on pedagogical leadership but it is not yet clear whether the EYWC will have the necessary clout to shift policy should a policy window open.

Conclusion

In this chapter, we have considered the English national context in which pedagogical leadership operates and how current policy realities inhibit the advancement of pedagogical leadership. Through Kingdon's policy streams approach, we have examined whether we can think about the current context as a 'policy window' and what would need to change or align in order to make this the case. Based on this analysis, we argue that generating a policy window for the advancement of pedagogical leadership will depend on (1) ensuring that the problem with regards to ECE is perceived in terms of quality rather than quantity, (2) having viable policy solutions on the table, based on credible and up-to-date evidence and (3) building up the clout of policy entrepreneurs – whether individuals or organisations – who can overcome division in the sector and present a strong and united voice. Although we have focused closely on ECE in England, we offer the chapter as part of an international dialogue about how to foster pedagogical leadership at a national scale. We hope that the framing of the analysis, via Kingdon's policy streams approach, may be helpful to those working in other countries and thinking about the potential for 'policy windows' in their national context.

References

Bonetti, S. (2020a) Early years workforce development in England: Key ingredients and missed opportunities. A report produced for the nuffield foundation. Accessed online 9 February 2021 from: https://epi.org.uk/wp-content/uploads/2020/01/Early_years_workforce_development_EPI.pdf

Bonetti, S. (2020b) Making the early years workforce more sustainable after Covid-19. Accessed online 9 February 2021 from: https://www.nuffieldfoundation.org/news/opinion/making-early-years-workforce-more-sustainable-after-covid-19

Campbell-Barr, V. and Bonetti, S. (2021) A systematic review of early years degrees and employment pathways. Published online: https://www.plymouth.ac.uk/uploads/production/document/path/18/18767/Final_Report_7.7.2020.pdf

Ceeda (2017) About early years 2017 survey. https://www.ceeda.co.uk/reports/

Ceeda (2018) About early years 2018 survey. https://www.ceeda.co.uk/reports/

Ceeda (2019) About early years: Annual report. Accessed online 9 February 2021 from: http://aboutearlyyears.co.uk/our-reports

Department for Education (2017) Early years workforce strategy. Accessed online 9 February 2021 from: https://www.gov.uk/government/publications/early-years-workforce-strategy

Early Years Alliance (2020) The forgotten sector: The financial impact of coronavirus on early years providers in England. Accessed online 9 February 2021 from: https://www.eyalliance.org.uk/sites/default/files/the_forgotten_sector_early_years_alliance_25june_2020.pdf

Early Years Workforce Commission (2021) A workforce in crisis: Saving our early years. Accessed online 9 February 2021 from: https://www.cache.org.uk/media/1863/a-workforce-in-crisis-saving-our-early-years.pdf

Edmondson, A. C. (2018) *The Fearless Organization: Creating Psychological Safety in the Workplace for Learning, Innovation, and Growth*. Hoboken, NJ: John Wiley & Sons.

Fawcett Society (2021) Businesses, parents, nurseries call for investment to stem Covid childcare crisis. Accessed online 9 February 2021 from: https://www.fawcettsociety.org.uk/news/businesses-parents-nurseries-call-for-investment-to-stem-covid-childcare-crisis

Guldbrandsson, K. and Fossum, B. (2009) An exploration of the theoretical concepts policy windows and policy entrepreneurs at the Swedish public health arena. *Health Promotion International*, 24(4), pp. 434–444.

Jones, G. and Gorell, R. (2018) *How to Create a Coaching Culture: A Practical Introduction* (2nd edition). London: Kogan Page.

Kingdon, J. (2011) *Agendas, Alternatives and Public Policies*. London: Longman.

McDowall Clark, R. (2012) 'I've never thought of myself as a leader but…': The early years professional and catalytic leadership. *European Early Childhood Education Research Journal*, 20(3), pp. 391–401.

Melhuish, E. and Gardiner, J. (2019) Structural factors and policy change as related to the quality of early childhood education and care for 3–4 year olds in the UK. *Frontiers*, 4, p. 35.

Meyerson, D. E. (2008) *Rocking the Boat: How to Effect Change without Making Trouble*. Boston, MA: Harvard Business School Publishing.

NDNA (2018) Workforce survey. Accessed online 9 February 2021 from: https://www.ndna.org.uk/NDNA/News/Reports_and_surveys/Workforce_survey/Workforce_survey_2018.aspx

NDNA (2019) Workforce survey. Accessed online 9 February 2021 from: https://www.ndna.org.uk/NDNA/News/Reports_and_surveys/Workforce_survey/nursery_workforce_survey_2019.aspx

Nursery World (2021) Disadvantaged children fall further behind due to Covid. https://www.nurseryworld.co.uk/news/article/disadvantaged-children-fall-further-behind-due-to-covid

Ofsted (2020) Main findings: Childcare providers and inspections as at 31 March 2020. Accessed online 9 February 2021 from: https://www.gov.uk/government/statistics/childcare-providers-and-inspections-as-at-31-march-2020/main-findings-childcare-providers-and-inspections-as-at-31-march-2020

Schein, E. H. (2017) *Organizational Culture and Leadership* (5th Edition). Hoboken, NJ: Wiley.

Social Mobility Commission (2016) State of the Nation. Accessed online 9 February 2021 from: https://publications.parliament.uk/pa/cm201719/cmselect/cmeduc/1006/100605.htm

The Guardian (2021) Disadvantaged pupils in England lag behind in Covid learning catch-up. https://www.theguardian.com/education/2021/oct/29/disadvantaged-pupils-in-england-lag-behind-in-covid-learning-catch-up

Conclusion

Sustaining the Vision of Pedagogical Leadership

June O'Sullivan and Mona Sakr

Introduction

In our concluding chapter, we make three recommendations to advance pedagogical leadership in early childhood education (ECE). These recommendations draw from the thinking shared by the contributors throughout this book. First, we argue that it is essential to maintain a rich understanding of what pedagogical leadership is and avoid adopting an overly narrow focus on instruction and instructional leadership. Secondly, we must prioritise pedagogical leadership on the understanding that it is a prerequisite for quality ECE. Finally, constructive discussions of pedagogical leadership depend on dynamic dialogues about pedagogy; we need to emphasise and enliven conversations about ECE pedagogies as part of everyday practice.

Pedagogy and Pedagogical Leadership, Not Instruction and Instructional Leadership

Despite the research that clearly demonstrates a correlation between pedagogical leadership and high-quality learning experiences for children, there is a lack of clarity on the definition of effective pedagogical leadership. There is also a lack of pedagogical agency in ECE, which hinders pedagogical leadership at all levels. The result is an inclination to translate pedagogy into the more simplistic notion of 'instruction' of children. We have seen education policy-makers conflate pedagogical leadership with instructional leadership and this must be resisted (Douglass, 2019).

Many of the chapters in this book (e.g. Palaiologou et al., Arnott and O'Sullivan) have explored the wider reaches of pedagogy. In these conceptualisations, pedagogy relates to everything that happens in ECE. It is not just how you instruct a child to complete a task; it is the values you bring to every single interaction that happens in and beyond an ECE setting. It is how you approach playing and learning with children. It is how you build relationships between adults in a setting. It is how you engage with siblings, parents, grandparents and the wider community. Pedagogical leadership needs to be aligned with pedagogy's broad scope and not just be about learning how children learn – though this is, of course, important. It is also about understanding how adults learn, how families live and engage with ECE and how communities are changed by high-quality ECE provision. Pedagogical leadership is also a form of social leadership in ECE – a means of challenging unfairness and social injustice. We – ECE professionals and researchers – need to initiate many more conversations about pedagogical leadership and ensure that our definitions of pedagogical leadership are not simply reduced to the language of 'instruction'. In doing the latter, we fail children and we particularly fail poor children, because instruction is just one element of the many layers that make up both pedagogies and pedagogical leadership for social change.

Pedagogical Leadership Is Essential, Not an Add-on

All of the contributors to this book present a common vision of pedagogical leadership as essential for quality ECE provision. They argue that for ECE to positively influence children's life chances pedagogical leadership must be robustly embedded into practice. This is the case even when working with the very youngest children, as argued by Cuttler in her chapter on pedagogical leadership with babies. In the argument that pitches care against education, we argue that care is a vital part of any effective pedagogical vision. However, as Grenier suggests, care is necessary but not sufficient to change the life chances of children from disadvantaged backgrounds. Pedagogical leaders need to demonstrate an understanding about the voice of the child and how we consider young children as active participants in their environment with rights and agency.

If we want ECE to make a social difference, we must invest in the widespread development of pedagogical leadership. We need, as suggested by Bonetti and Sakr, national policies and international initiatives that facilitate the advancement of pedagogical leadership whether through more training and qualifications or the required financial investment to enable the employment of more qualified individuals.

We need to learn more about the systems and processes that allow pedagogical leadership to flourish. This includes time for teams working in ECE to develop the practices that shape and embed pedagogical leadership. Corlett and Cuttler, as well as Leigh Mosty, have explored coaching, collaborative reflection and action research as key processes that could be woven into any setting to positively shape and grow pedagogical leadership.

Each contribution, whether looking at pedagogical interventions in practice, as discussed by Farini, or national policy contexts, as described by Halttunen et al., was clear that policies pushing for the continual increase in the amount of ECE provision are weakened if this expansion is not developed through a pedagogical leadership lens.

Pedagogical Leadership Is Distributed, Not Individual

We have seen diversity in thinking about the level and scale at which pedagogical leadership operates. Is 'pedagogical leader' a role that can be completed by a particular individual (e.g. O'Sullivan, Mikailova & Burchell, Perkins) or is pedagogical leadership a set of practices that can be distributed among a particular group of colleagues (e.g. Halttunen et al., Palaiologou et al.)? Is pedagogical leadership likely to build a theory of expertise that can be enacted, in small and big ways, by anyone in an organisation, regardless of level (e.g. Sakr, Leigh Mosty, Bonetti & Sakr, Cuttler & Corlett, Nicholson)? Or is pedagogical leadership a facet of the organisational culture (e.g. Farini, Arnott?).

We argue though that for pedagogical leadership to have the most transformative potential, our vision of pedagogical leadership needs to happen through a distributed approach so that everyone understands and carries out their role in leading the pedagogy. If pedagogical leadership is reduced to a set of tasks achieved by a particular individual carrying out a role marked 'pedagogical leader', it loses its power, as expressed by Halttunen et al. in this book. For continuous improvement to pedagogical work, everyone has a responsibility to propose new ideas, reflect on what works and to influence and support others.

Final Note

In the introduction to this book, we explained that we want to create and contribute to more conversations about pedagogical leadership with and between colleagues from across the ECE landscape. Conversations are valuable for encouraging reflective practice, making implicit knowledge explicit and enabling us to think aloud about our own practice and the theories that underpin it.

We hope that we have advanced the dialogue and opened the way for further discussions and debates about the importance of pedagogical leadership in ECE. We believe in the power of the learning community to become a mutually supportive and collaborative place where we can investigate our practice and where professionals, policy-makers and researchers can use conversations to facilitate learning and configure our praxeological ECE knowledge.

Conversations have the power to transform, and the more we talk about pedagogy and pedagogical leadership in ECE, the more we can ensure that it has a vital role in transforming ECE for the better for all children.

Index

action research   46–7, 121, 128, 129, 141–6, 150
  embedding sustainability   147–8
  growing confidence   152
activist professionalism   121
administrative duties   100–3
adult-child dynamics   22
advocacy   74, 159–60
affiliative style   84, 88
agency and control   27, 52, 53, 55, 59
anxiety   28, 52, 74
Armenia   158
arousal continuum   52, 53, 55
asset-based community development   13
Australian Children's Education and Care Quality Authority (ACECQA)   108
authoritative style   88, 89
autocratic style   80
autonomy   27, 127

Baby Room pedagogical leadership   4, 46, 65–7, 76
  caring and learning experiences   66–7
  growing   71–5
  vision of   67–71
Baby Room professionals   65, 66, 69, 70, 72–6
benevolent approach   19
bottom-up regulation   56, 59–60
brain   52, 54–6, 58–60
Bronfenbrenner five-element social-ecology model   37, 135
business model of leadership   36

career progression   119–20, 122, 125–7, 129
caring   11, 52, 56, 66–7, 70, 75, 76
catalytic pedagogical leadership   127
change management theory   6, 79, 80, 83, 86, 89, 90, 121
child-centred organisation   11

child-centred pedagogy   84–6, 156, 159–60, 164
children   163
  Black and Minority Ethnic (BAME)   19
  brain   36
  development   24, 36, 37, 40, 42, 43, 145
  from disadvantaged backgrounds   36, 39, 141, 187
  as learners   12, 17
  learning   3, 11, 12, 14, 15, 17, 21–5, 28, 29, 35, 39–41, 109, 111, 139
    (*see also* learning)
  life opportunities   6, 12
  outcomes   3, 18, 35, 37, 99
  transitions model   87–9
  well-being   35, 41, 106, 109, 145
Children's Centres   188
children's experiences   21–6, 29, 30, 40, 83
Children's Workforce Development Council (CWDC)   188
classroom/playgroup interactions   94
CLASS tool   3
coaching   6, 15, 16, 44, 72, 148, 151–2, 184
coaching leadership style   89
cognition
  development   68
  functions   54
  skills   36
Cognitive Behavioural Therapeutic approaches   59
collaborative reflection   120, 136
collegial models of leadership 167, 168–70
communication   7, 24, 40, 52, 59, 68, 69, 73, 109, 168
community-based ECE   155–8, 161
community collaborations   17–19
community leaders and leadership   7, 16–19, 74
community partnerships   16–17
confidence   35, 39, 42
conflict management   167, 170, 171, 174, 177

continuous improvement   41, 47, 109, 119, 122–4, 129
Covid crisis   145, 157, 158, 184, 187, 189
creative play   21
creativity   14, 44, 127–8
cultural capital   40
cultural-discursive architectures   111, 114
cultural integration   7
cultural values and traditions   28
curriculum   17, 19, 39, 79, 95–7, 106, 137, 155, 158

decision-making   21, 23, 107
democratic style   80, 81, 85, 101
dialogue   73
digital system   145
dissociative regulation   56, 60–2
distributed leadership   82, 109, 114, 197
dynamic pedagogies   25, 30

early childhood education (ECE)   1–5, 21, 22, 24, 30, 36, 47, 65, 66, 70, 74, 76, 90, 93–6, 99, 121, 129, 137, 157, 187, 188, 191, 195–8. *See also individual entries*
   action research in   142
   centres   105, 107, 109, 110, 134, 157
   contexts   79–80
   English sector   14–15, 183, 190
   high-quality   29, 141, 142
   organisations   120, 130, 183, 185
   pedagogic culture   25–7
   policies   138
   professionals   2, 48, 54, 55, 71, 75, 82, 84, 103, 119, 121, 142, 143, 146, 152, 184, 196
   staffs   39, 42, 45
   stakeholders   109
   training   15
   vision   134, 139–40
   in West   24
early childhood education (ECE) in Azerbaijan   7, 155–65
   context   156–8
   influences on pedagogical leadership approaches   162–4
   investigating pedagogical leadership   158–9
   leaders report   159–61
   pedagogical leadership as working model   161–2
early childhood education (ECE) students
   exploring leadership practices with   81–2
   and leadership   80–1
   observations and reflections   83–4
   and pedagogical leadership development   89–90
Early Childhood Graduate Practitioner Competencies (ECSDN)   80, 84
early childhood graduates   79
early childhood leaders and leadership   11, 22, 86, 100, 102, 157–9, 161–2. *See also* pedagogical leadership
early childhood programmes   51, 56
early learning programmes   59, 61
Early Years Alliance   184, 187
early years educators and education   12, 14, 15
Early Years Foundation Stage (EYFS)   17, 70, 75, 100
Early Years Professionals (EYPs)   188
early years professional status (EYPS)   120, 121, 185, 188, 189
early years (EY) sector   35
early years teacher (EYT)   120
Early Years Teachers Status (EYTS)   188, 189
Early Years Workforce Commission 2020-2021 (EYWC)   190
ECE directors (Ds) and deputy directors (DDs) in Australia, Finland and Norway   7, 105–15
   contexts   108–10
   data analysis   111–13
   deputy leadership   106
   pedagogical leadership   106–8
   practice theory   110–11
ECERS assessment tools   84
education(al)   39, 66, 96, 99, 100, 107
   leaders   109
   leadership   108, 158
   qualification   108–10, 113, 122
   reform   163
   theory   137
Effective Pre-School, Primary and Secondary Education project (EPPSE)   11, 13, 15

Emilia-Romagna   169
emotional development   70
emotional intelligence   80, 84
emotional state   53
empathic distress   52
empowering programmes   121
England   8, 35, 65, 66, 90, 181, 183, 191
English as an additional language (EAL)   17
English early years system   16
experiential learning   25

feminised values   81
Finnish Education Evaluation Centre (FINEEC)   109
Finnish National Agency for Education (EDUFI)   109
floor-based play   68
'The Forgotten Sector'   184
formal childcare   66
formal education   22, 40, 99
free play   40
funding   16, 18, 188

Graduate Leader Fund   188, 189
graduate-level practitioners   15
Greek Manpower Employment Organization   96
Green LEYF   7, 147–8
guided participation   28

hierarchy-centred management of conflict (HCM)   167, 170–4, 176, 177
higher education   43, 110
home culture   29
human ecology   21
hybrid model   96

Iceland   137
ideas, sharing of   148–50
independence   127–8
informal learning   22, 28
in-house continuing professional development (CPD)   119, 120, 122, 124–5, 129, 130
instructional leadership   5
intentional disconnection regulation. *See* dissociative regulation
internal distress   53

internal state   52, 53, 55, 56, 58
interpersonal care   2
interpersonal conflicts   171, 174, 177
invisible pedagogy   23, 24, 29
Italian early childhood education (ECE) settings   167–78
  collegial models of management   168–9
  hierarchy-centred management of conflict (HCM)   171–4
  participation-centred management of conflict (PCM)   174–6
  pedagogical planning as interaction   168
  research   169–70

Kingdon's policy streams approach   8, 181, 185–91
  policy entrepreneur   186, 190
  policy stream   185–9
  politics stream   185, 186, 189–90
  problem stream   185–7
knowledge
  generation   28
  status   28
  transmission   23, 24
Kotter's eight-stage model   83, 85

laissez-faire style   80
language skills   40, 69
leadership
  at community level   160–1, 164
  education programmes   110
  model   71
  roles   12, 22, 28, 79, 96, 100–3, 134, 135
  structures and functions   93
  styles   80, 83, 89, 93, 101, 102, 162
  theories   83, 86, 121
Leading Quality in Early Childhood   79
learning   26, 36, 40, 42–4, 47, 51, 67, 79, 83, 87, 94–5, 100, 107, 127, 133, 167
learning environment   24, 40, 42, 71, 73
Leuven scales   84
Lewin's three-step model   83, 88
LEYF Pedagogical Development Scale (LPDS)   40, 123, 145
line managers   108
London Early Years Foundation (LEYF)   4, 6, 7, 35, 71, 119, 121,

123–5, 127–30, 141, 147, 149,
        150, 152
    action research approach   142–5
    nurseries   122, 126
    organisation   148
    organisational approach   122
    pedagogical leader   41–3
    pedagogical leadership   43–7
    pedagogy   36–40, 145
    staff   40, 122, 145, 146

managerial and educational duties   100–2
managerial responsibilities   108
material-economic architectures   111, 114
mathematical confidence   46
meditation and prayer   61–2
mental health   52, 60
mind-wandering   61
mirror neurons   53
multiple intelligences theory   135

negotiation tactics   21
New Zealand   12
'No Child Left Behind' policy   138
non-cognitive skills   36
non-familial childcare   71, 74
Norway   7
novelty   52, 55
nurseries   39, 125, 152, 156
    full day-care   36
    managers   123
    workplace   36

Ofsted Early Years Inspection
        Handbook   65
organisational approach   119, 130, 143
organisational culture   3, 4, 111, 121,
        149, 153, 168–70, 176–8
organisational values   42, 140
Organisation for Economic Cooperation
        and Development (OECD)   2, 40,
        43, 94, 139
Ösp playschool   7
outdoor play   70

parallel pedagogy   45
parental relationship   67
parenting practices   156
parents   17, 28, 36, 39, 70, 73, 74, 87,
        88, 163

participation-centred management of
        conflict (PCM)   167, 170, 174–7
participative decision-making   167,
        169–71, 174–6
patterned repetitive somato-sensory
        activities   59–60
pedagogia relazionale   169, 174, 177
pedagogical approaches   5, 6, 37, 68, 73, 113
pedagogical conversations   44–5, 47
pedagogical leaders   4–6, 11, 17, 35,
        37–47, 51–6, 58–62, 69, 71–3, 79,
        80, 99, 107, 167
pedagogical leadership   1–8, 12, 17–19,
        27, 30, 35, 48, 79, 83–4, 86, 89, 90,
        105–10, 112–15, 119–20, 129–30,
        133–4, 136, 141, 146–8, 150, 152, 155,
        156, 195–8. *See also individual entries*
    advocacy of child-centred
        pedagogies   159–60
    with babies   6
    as catalytic leadership   120–1
    development in others   136
    in England, Greece and Sweden   6
    inspirations   13, 135
    internal and external influences   162–4
    at LEYF   43–7
    at local/national/international
        level   137
    as managing change   82–3
    model   37
    organisational approaches to
        develop   121–2
    sense of social purpose   160–1
    and teachers   123–4
    as working model   161–2
pedagogical leadership at national
        level   181–91
    de-professionalisation of
        workforce   184–5
    ECE in wider society   185
    economic fragmentation and under-
        investment   183–4
    Kingdon's policy streams
        approach   185–90
    as positive deviance   182–3
pedagogical leadership in England, Greece
        and Sweden   93–103
    context   95–7
    functions of leadership
        role   100–1

learning and teaching 94–5
  participants in understanding of pedagogy 97, 99–100
  qualitative study 97
  structures of leadership role 101–2
pedagogical planning 4, 7, 8, 22, 23, 167, 168, 170, 177
pedagogical practices 2, 23, 24, 35, 40, 68, 82, 94, 190
pedagogical praxis 93, 94, 102
pedagogic culture 21, 25–30
pedagogic discourse 21, 23
pedagogy 2, 5, 6, 18, 21–5, 43, 95, 99–100, 102, 103, 111, 195–6
pedagogy of care 66, 67, 75
peer cultures 22, 26
peer learning 15, 95
perceived lack of personal agency and control 52
personal expressions 168–70, 174–7
personal values 140
phonics approaches 18
physical care 5, 12
physical development 69, 73
physical skills 69
play pedagogy 24–5, 30, 40, 68
playrooms 25, 26, 29
poverty 39
power dynamics 28
preschools 26, 27, 36, 96–7, 101
  education 156, 157
  kindergartens 1, 156
private, voluntary and independent (PVI) 96, 100, 101, 188
private childcare 183–4
private education 19
private speech 68
process quality 3
professional development 11, 16, 74–5, 127, 129, 136, 142
professional inquiry 45, 46
professionalism 138, 139
professional knowledge 42, 43
psychological safety 182–4

quality assessment 109, 113

Reggio Approach 169
Reggio Emilia, Italy 7
relational neurobiology 56

relational regulation 56–8
resilience 56, 59
responsive approaches 24

scaffolding 39, 40
self-actualisation 159–61, 164
self-confidence 161
self-directive talk 68
self-hypnosis 61–2
service accreditation 109
shared leadership 136
situational leadership 82, 85
social identity 161
social pedagogy 36, 142
social play 29
social practices 168, 176
social structures 168
sociocultural theory 39
socio-political architectures 111, 114
Special Educational Needs or Disability (SEND) 17
spiral learning 39
state dependent functioning 52, 53, 56, 62
state dependent regression 55
state of calm 52, 56, 58
stress 51–3, 55–60, 62
stress-response system 52, 54–6, 58, 59
structural barriers 36, 39
symbolic play 68

tacit learning 28
talent fluency 148, 150
teacher-centred education 159
teacher-learner interactions 3
teachers 114, 122, 146
  and career progression 119–20, 122, 125–7, 129
  and continuous improvement 119, 122–4, 129
  developing specialised pedagogical leadership 120, 122, 127–9
  engagement 109
  role 171
teaching 42–3, 56, 75, 79, 94–6, 100, 107, 133
  quality 41
  techniques 43
tempered radicals 182
threat 52, 54–6, 59
top-down regulation 56, 58–9

traditional business models 80
traditional management hierarchies 81
training programmes 97, 129, 188, 189
transformational leaders and
    leadership 81, 169
transnational research 93, 94
trauma-responsive leaders 52, 56
trauma-responsive pedagogical
    leadership 6, 51–62
  conditions support regulation 56–62
  cortex 54–5
  creating environments to buffer stress
      and support children 62
  trauma-informed and 51–3
trauma-responsive practices 51–4, 62
trauma-sensitive environments 52

UK 35
unconscious bias 39
UNDP Human Development Index
    (2018) 156
unpredictability 52, 55

visible pedagogy 23
visionary leadership approach 84, 87
Vygotsky, L. 24, 28, 68

women leaders 161, 162
'A Workforce in Crisis: Saving Our Early
    Years' 190
working-class children 19, 46
workplace culture 125
Workplace Facebook 43

www.ingramcontent.com/pod-product-compliance
Lightning Source LLC
Chambersburg PA
CBHW062227300426
44115CB00012BA/2243